Co-operatives in India

History, Problems and Reforms

Co-operatives in India

History, Problems and Reforms

By

Babita Agrawal

Associate Professor and Head,
Department of Economics,
Arya Kanya Post-graduate College, Hapur

New Century Publications
New Delhi, India

NEW CENTURY PUBLICATIONS
4800/24, Bharat Ram Road,
Ansari Road, Daryaganj,
New Delhi – 110 002 (India)

Tel.: 011-2324 7798, 4358 7398, 6539 6605
Fax: 011-4101 7798
E-mail: indiatax@vsnl.com • info@newcenturypublications.com
www.newcenturypublications.com

Editorial office:
LG–7, Aakarshan Bhawan,
4754-57/23, Ansari Road, Daryaganj,
New Delhi – 110 002

Tel.: 011-4356 0919

First Published: **July 2012**

ISBN: **978-81-7708-317-0**

Published by New Century Publications and printed at Salasar Imaging Systems, New Delhi.

Designs: Patch Creative Unit, New Delhi.

PRINTED IN INDIA

About the Book

Co-operatives were first introduced in India under the Co-operative Credit Societies Act, 1904. As in many other countries, co-operatives started as a means of ensuring for the poorly-equipped citizens advantages which better placed persons were able to command by their own individual resources. After Independence in 1947, co-operatives, as instruments of economic development of the disadvantaged, particularly in the rural areas, received considerable emphasis during the successive Five Year Plans. The founders of planning in the country saw a village *panchayat*, a village co-operative and a village school, as the trinity of institutions on which a self-reliant and a just economic and social order was to be built. The non-exploitative character of co-operatives, voluntary nature of their membership, principle of one-man, one-vote, decentralised decision-making and self-imposed curbs on profits eminently qualified them as instruments of development combining the advantages of private ownership with public good.

Over the years, co-operative societies, apart from expansion in numbers and size, have assumed growing diversity of functions. Besides agricultural societies of all types (viz. credit, processing, marketing, farming, irrigation, consolidation), there are industrial co-operatives, labour societies, consumers' co-operatives in rural as well as in urban areas, housing societies, processing factories and urban banks.

This book provides a comprehensive account of the historical evolution of co-operatives in India, their problems, policy measures to strengthen them and their role in the changed scenario in the context of liberalization, privatization and globalization.

Author's Profile

Dr. Babita Agrawal is presently an Associate Professor and Head of the Department of Economics, Arya Kanya Post-graduate College, Hapur. She holds Ph.D. in Economics from Ch. Charan Singh University, Meerut and has teaching experience of more than 19 years of undergraduate classes including 9 years of post-graduate classes.

She is a member of the managing committee of Smt. Brahma Devi Saraswati Balika Vidya Mandir, Hapur and joint editor of *Economic Journal* published by Uttar Pradesh-Uttarakhand Economic Association, Varanasi. She received the Best Teacher Award for the year 2004 from Bharat Vikas Parishad, Hapur.

Contents

Preface

In India, as in many other countries, co-operation started as a means of ensuring for the poorly equipped citizens advantages which better placed persons were able to command by their own individual resources. The principle of mutual aid, which is the basis of co-operative organisation, and the practice of thrift and self-help which sustain it, generate a sturdy feeling of self-reliance which is of basic importance in a democratic way of life. By pooling their experience and knowledge and by helping one another, members of co-operative societies can not only find the solutions of individual problems but also become better citizens.

Role of Co-operatives

In an unregulated economy, the terms of contract are frequently weighted in favour of persons of large means. Those who have the command of scarce resources are left free to drive a bargain with those who need such resources but are ill-equipped to compete for their possession. In a relatively stagnant agricultural economy of small holders, undergoing a transition from barter to money economy and from local to national and international exchange, the possession of capital naturally confers a strategic advantage.

An increasing measure of responsibility for organising and financing rural economic development is being shouldered by co-operatives. Both the natural evolution of co-operative activity, and the impetus of the special need created in several parts of the country by agrarian legislation regulating the business of moneylenders, scaling down of debts, restricting rents and abolishing landlordism are responsible for the striking increase in the operations of co-operative credit societies.

Co-operation is in fact being transformed steadily yet surely, from a tolerated exception into a general rule. In industry, commerce, transport and retail distribution co-operatives are gaining experience and strength. Different State Governments sometimes emphasize different fields of co-operative activity in keeping with local conditions. There can be no doubt, however, that a new awareness of an opportunity to build up a form of business organisation more suited to the conditions and needs of the times than the joint stock company has come over the people of small means everywhere. The joint stock company is too cumbersome as an organization for the small producer, agricultural or industrial. What is needed and what the co-operative society has provided is a simpler form of organization more suited to the needs of the people to be served and therefore likely to be more acceptable.

Co-operation as an instrument of economic development of the disadvantaged, particularly in the rural areas has received considerable emphasis during the successive Five Year Plans. The founders of planning in the country saw a village Panchayat, a village co-operative and a village school, as the trinity of institutions on which a self-reliant and just economic and social order was to be built. The non-exploitative character of co-operatives, voluntary nature of their membership, the principle of one man one vote, decentralised decision making and self-imposed curbs on profits eminently qualified them as an instrument of development combining the advantages of private ownership with public good.

Having begun primarily in the field of credit as a defensive mechanism against the usurious money lenders, co-operatives have come to embrace a large gamut of activities to serve the interests of the producers and consumers. Credit, however, still continues to be the predominant activity.

Co-operatives are expected to play a major role in the distribution of inputs and services to the farmers on the one hand and in assisting marketing and processing of agricultural produce on the other.

In November, 1958, in its Resolution on Co-operative Policy, the National Development Council agreed that co-operatives should be organised on the basis of the village community as the primary unit, and that responsibility and initiative for social and economic development at the village level should be placed fully on the village co-operative and the village panchayat. The co-operative and the panchayat were to be regarded as the primary agencies for carrying out the community development programme which aims at the improvement of all aspects of rural life through the efforts of the people. The village agricultural plan was considered to be the foundation of the programme for co-operative development and was to be given the highest priority.

Types of Co-operatives

Even more striking than the expansion in numbers and size, is the growing diversity of functions assumed by co-operative societies. Besides agricultural societies of all types, viz. credit, processing, marketing, farming, irrigation, consolidation etc., there are industrial co-operatives, labour societies, consumers' co-operatives in rural as well as in urban areas, housing societies; processing factories; and urban banks.

When co-operation was first introduced under the Co-operative Credit Societies Act, 1904, it was confined to the organisation of the co-operative credit societies in urban and rural areas with a view to relieving indebtedness and promoting thrift. The Co-operative Societies Act, 1912, permitted the registration of co-operative societies for promoting non-credit activities as well as federations of primary societies into organisations at higher levels. Both in the field of credit and of non-credit activities the co-operative structure consists of primary societies at the base in villages or towns, central organisations at the district level and apex organisations at the State level. Following are the more popular forms of co-operation:

1. Multi-purpose Co-operative Societies.
2. Co-operative Credit Societies.
3. Co-operative Sale/Purchase Societies.

4. Co-operative Farming.
5. Industrial Co-operatives.
6. Co-operative Marketing.
7. Co-operative Processing.
8. Consumer Co-operatives.
9. Labour and Construction Co-operatives.

Co-operatives and Panchayats

Panchayats have an indispensable role to play in the rural areas. As representing the best interests of all sections of the community their status is unique. Many activities such as, framing programmes of production for the village, obtaining and utilising governmental assistance for the betterment of the village (e.g. construction of roads, tanks etc.), encouraging villagers to improve the standards of cultivation, organising voluntary labour for community works and generally assisting in the implementation of economic an social reform legislation passed by the States, will naturally fall within the purview of the panchayat.

For the working of individual programmes of economic development, where not only the general interest but also the specific responsibility and liability of a member have to be ensured, a more integrated and binding form of association is needed. Specific and practical tasks of reclaiming land, of providing resources for better cultivation, of marketing the produce of the villagers, both agriculturists and artisans, can be best performed through co-operatives. The co-operative agencies will naturally have to conform to the principles of business management, namely, of satisfactory service and economical working. That they are not profiteering associations and that they function for mutual service makes them desirable agents of democratic planning. It is, therefore, necessary that co-operative agencies in the village should have the closest possible relationship with the principal democratic body namely, the panchayat. Though in the discharge of their functions the two bodies have specific fields to operate, in a number of common functions by having mutual representation and by having common ad-hoc committees, it will be possible to build up a structure of democratic management of developmental plans through both the organisations, the panchayats and the co-operative societies.

Co-operatives and Economic Planning

In a regime of planned development, co-operation is an instrument, which while retaining some of the advantages of decentralisation and local initiative will yet serve willingly and readily the overall purposes and directives of the plan. The co-operative form of organization can no longer be treated as only a species within the private sector. It is an indispensable instrument of planned economic action in a democracy.

Economic development along democratic lines offers a vast field for the application of co-operation in its infinitely varying forms. Small units can obtain the advantages of scale and organisation mainly by coming together. The character of economic development in India with its emphasis on social change, therefore, provides a great deal of scope for the organisation of co-operative activity. The building up of a co-operative sector as part of the scheme of planned development is, thus, one of the central aims of national policy.

In areas which offer special opportunities for its development, the co-operative form of organisation has advantages which neither the system of private enterprise nor that of State ownership can match. In particular, it offers a means of achieving results valuable to the community by drawing equally upon incentives which are social and incentives which are individual. Where it succeeds, co-operation brings large gains to the community, but the human factors involved in it are complex and in some ways it is much more difficult for the co-operative form of organisation to succeed than it is for a completely socialised enterprise or for an individual entrepreneur. It is, therefore, necessary to take effective measures to enable co-operation to succeed, whenever possible, and especially in fields which are assigned to it in the scheme of national development.

Because of historical circumstances in India, agricultural credit accounts for the greater part of development in the field of co-operation. The provision of adequate credit on reasonable terms is undoubtedly a most important part of co-operation.

Co-operatives, like village panchayats, are institutional agencies for achieving social cohesion. In a country whose economic structure has its roots in the village, co-operation is something more than a series of activities organised on co-operative lines; basically, its purpose is to evolve a system of co-operative community organisation which touches upon all aspects of life. Within the village community there are sections of the populations who need special assistance. Co-operation should therefore mean an obligation towards all families in the village community and the development of land and other resources and of social services in the common interest of the village as a whole. This is the underlying approach in setting co-operative village management as the main direction of reorganisation in the rural economy.

Land Reforms and Co-operative Institutions

There is a close connection between the success of land reform and the success of co-operation which is not always appreciated. For co-operation to succeed fully it is essential that the reorganisation of the agrarian structure should be carried out speedily so as to eliminate features which reduce the productive capacity of the community and permit exploitation. Thus, land reform programmes should do much to stimulate the growth of the co-operative movement. In the nature of things, as a result of land reform the number of small cultivators increases, those with large holdings or considerable surpluses disappear and the new owners need a great deal of credit. Also, as the national extension net work is established and the rural people are ready and willing to participate in development programmes on an increasing scale, their requirements for credit and finance greatly increase. Co-operative institutions are the medium through which many activities in the village are to be reorganised and financed. It is therefore essential that in devising the land reform programme care should be taken to ensure that while its objectives are secured, co-operative credit institutions are not placed under handicaps which might affect their financial soundness.

Problems and Challenges Faced by the Co-operatives

Co-operatives in India came into being as a result of the Government taking cognizance of the agricultural conditions that prevailed during the latter part of the 19th century and the absence of institutional arrangements for finance to agriculturists, which had resulted in mounting distress and discontent. Small, local, locally worked institutions, co-operative in form, which would satisfy the postulates of proximity, security and facility for providing credit, were seen as the answer to this situation. However, subsequent events during both pre- and post-Independence period have led to a vast growth of co-operatives covering various sectors of the Indian economy.

Though India can claim to have the world's largest and most diverse co-operative movement, barring some exceptions co-operatives in India, in general, are fraught with a number of problems and challenges. Apart from certain inherent weaknesses, they are constrained by the overwhelming role of the government as well as prescriptive and restrictive legislation and have been unable to retain an autonomous and democratic character.

The problems and challenges that co-operatives face today are numerous. These encompass the functional aspects of co-operatives namely Membership, Governance and Operations which could be considered as internal to the organization. These problems are further compounded by two important external factors, namely politicization of co-operatives and the control/interference by governments. Following can be listed as major problems of various types of co-operatives.

1. Ensuring Active Membership.
2. Lack of Recognition of Co-operatives as Economic Institutions.
3. Structure of Co-operatives.
4. Board and Management Interface and Accountability.
5. Professionalization and Accountability.
6. Lack of Capital.
7. Linkages and Competitiveness.
8. Accessibility to Finance/Credit by Members.
9. Sickness in the Co-operative Sector.
10. Aligning Governance with Objectives.
11. Politicization of Co-operatives and Interference by Government.

Co-operatives are often criticised for being dominated by vested interests. The solutions sought so far have been in the nature of limiting the number of terms of office etc. While these measures are useful as far as they go, they still do not impinge on the basic question of commitment of an office bearer to the objectives of the society. An office bearer of a marketing society, who does not market his own produce through his marketing co-operative, is hardly likely to have any stake in the performance of that society.

Likewise, an office bearer of a credit co-operative bank, who is himself a defaulter in payment of dues is hardly likely to pursue recovery discipline in his society. It will be necessary to take a close look at the bye-laws of various types of co-operatives and to suitably revise these, wherever necessary to ensure that such commitments are built into the bye-laws as to eliminate mere office seekers from the management of the society. In fact, dairy co-operatives of the Anand Pattern have a specific clause built into the bye-laws about the supply of milk to the co-operative for a certain minimum number of days in a year as an essential qualification for office. A similar provision needs to be built in the bye-laws of other type of co-operatives also.

Measures to Strengthen Co-operatives

The success of co-operatives ultimately depends upon their ability to perform their functions—whether they relate to production, finance, marketing, distribution or construction—efficiently and to the satisfaction of the members and the community. The loyalties of the members can be retained not on the basis of monopoly, agreements or under duress but on the strength of the goodwill secured by rendering service. Some of the measures taken in recent years to improve the functioning of co-operatives are as under:

1. Improvement of personnel.
2. Co-operative education and training.
3. Co-operative education and training activities in the North-Eastern Region.
4. Assistance to National Co-operative Development Corporation (NCDC) for Co-operative Development.
5. Co-operative spinning mills.
6. Co-operative storage and cold storage.
7. Integrated Co-operative Development Projects (ICDP).
8. Co-operatives in underdeveloped states.
9. Strengthening of National Level Co-operative Federations.
10. Revitalization of co-operatives.
11. Market Intervention Scheme (MIS).

The recent changes introduced by the Government in several fields provide an opportunity for co- operatives to play a much larger role in several areas such as marketing of agricultural produce, creation of marketing infrastructure, establishment of agro-processing units etc.

The global economy, and in particular the Indian economy, is passing through transformation. The positive dimension of globalization includes liberal economic policies, reduction of state intervention, and easy access to monetary capital and consequently new opportunities for economic participation. This is already evidenced in India in the form of increased economic growth and state withdrawal from many economic and social domains. On the other hand, there is apparently a misplaced perception developing in India that co-operatives may not be able to deliver in the context of the globalized market conditions and the changes that are taking place as a result.

Under the circumstances, there is a need for resurgence of co-operatives as important players. Co-operatives have tremendous opportunities because (a) they have a special identity, (b) they have both social and economic objectives, (c) they are value- and community-based, (d) they are people-oriented and (e) they have a network of linkages through the co-operative movement.

Constitution (One Hundred and Eleventh Amendment) Bill, 2009

Since most farmers in India belong to the category of small and marginal farmers, the strengthening of co-operatives is seen as a measure to empower them. An amendment to the Constitution, for the purpose of empowering co-operatives through voluntary formation, autonomous functioning, democratic control and professional management, has been mooted. After the approval of the Government, the Constitution (One Hundred and Sixth Amendment) Bill, 2006 was introduced in the Lok Sabha on May 22, 2006. The Lok Sabha referred this Bill to the Standing Committee on Agriculture for its examination and report. The Standing Committee's Report was submitted in Lok Sabha on August 20, 2007. This report was considered by the Government and it was decided to move official amendments to the Bill. Accordingly, official amendments to the Bill were moved in the Lok Sabha. However, the Bill could not be discussed in the Lok Sabha for passing. The Bill lapsed on dissolution of 14th Lok Sabha on May 18, 2009.

It was decided to reintroduce the Bill for amendment to the Constitution. Accordingly, the Constitution (One Hundred and

Eleventh Amendment) Bill was introduced in the Lok Sabha on September 30, 2009. The Bill was referred to Standing Committee of Parliament on Agriculture which considered the Bill and submitted its report to the Lok Sabha on September 3, 2010. The suggestions made by the Standing Committee were considered by the Government and it was decided with the approval of the Cabinet to move official amendments to the Constitution (One Hundred and Eleventh Amendment) Bill, 2009. Accordingly, notices were sent for moving the official amendments. The process is under way.

Co-operatives and Globalization

Co-operatives in India have mostly played the role of an agent of the government. Co-operatives are seen to be the institutions that carry the State programmes to people, and in turn get State support.

Globalization and liberalization of economic policies creates new spaces in two forms. First, the governments are withdrawing from different domains hitherto solely or generally occupied by them creating vacant spaces, be it in manufacturing or service sector. Secondly, additional opportunities are continuously being created in newer areas, under the new economic environment. Many of these domains are not regarded as being commercially attractive. However, they are very important for people and communities and there is definitely a demand for these services. As such, the challenge would be to make them commercially viable and profitable. Traditional areas of social sector such as education, health, transportation, water supply, forest management, electricity are some of the areas where co-operative solutions could be superior to either public or private approaches to utility management. In fact privatization efforts in India are already on in this area. Co-operatives have been working in all these areas and have the potential to prove their strength and hence they could be effective alternatives to privatization.

Further co-operatives could play a major role in newer

areas such as precision farming, sun farming, water harvesting, micro finance. Other potential areas are information technology, communications, tourism and hospitality etc., the demand for which is ever growing and which could provide alternative means of livelihood for co-operative members. Outsourcing of services would also be the practice as firms grow in size and specialization. Such outsourcing would expectedly lead to savings in transaction costs. Entering such services through the co-operative route could prove an attractive alternative employment generating avenue.

Globalization would also result in restructuring leading to displacements occurring due to exit policies, labour re-engineering, closure of less competitive units, adoption of new technologies and consequent down sizing, mergers, acquisitions etc. including displacement from the agricultural sector. Displaced specialists could form co-operatives for providing essential specialized services, which institutions would be increasingly outsourcing. There has been a sharp reduction in the population dependent on agriculture and landless labourers have increased in number. The alarming rate of unemployment among youth continues. Collective endeavours through co-operatives of such marginalized sections of the people can work, as many services would still be required by existing concerns which may not wish to have such service providers on their pay roll.

Cartels or pre-determined market sharing by private enterprises can jeopardize free and fair trade. Co-operatives could provide the role of the constructive competitors. This could be either through a stand-alone co-operative or by entering strategic partnership with the private sector in the form of co-operative-private sector collaborations etc. Co-operatives by their very presence would help to maintain the balance in terms of price and quality. For this reason co-operatives need to enter all those areas where full domination by the private corporate might eventually spell bad news to the consumers.

Agriculture will continue to be very important in terms of percentage share of dependent population. The logic of agriculture would be applicable to almost the entire rural population. Self-help initiatives by farmers in the area of cultivation, marketing, accessing agricultural inputs, finding jobs for the landless labourers, displaced rural artisans etc., would continue to be a major role for the co-operative sector. None else is equipped to handle this.

Co-operatives are the best channels to keep the spirit of collectivism and democracy afloat. The presence of a large network of social organizations, like co-operatives, would aid in the generation and utilization of social capital and more the social capital, greater would be the possibility of development. Therefore, co-operatives have a futuristic role of fostering collectivism and preserving the social capital base of the country.

It is thus clear that co-operatives have a significant role to play in the future settings of the Indian economy. In fact they have a more important role to play in the future compared to their agency role of the past. It is only the presence of a strong and wide network of co-operatives that can make the process of globalization less painful and global integration smooth. It is the co-operatives again who are equipped to work as pressure groups to voice views of the people in the market.

The 1990s witnessed a paradigm shift towards market-oriented economic policies and a careful dismantling of obstacles in its wake. This has helped the smaller, emerging economies gain access to world markets, emergent technologies and collaborations. This has also given them a window to the developed world and helped them understand the significant role of globalisation as an instrument, which could be utilised not just to achieve economic efficiency, but also eradicate poverty.

Co-operatives are one of primarily, autonomous, economic institutions of user members united voluntarily to meet their common economic, social, cultural needs and aspirations through a jointly-owned and democratically-controlled enterprise. They are self-reliant and self-sustaining institutions functioning in a free, fair and transparent way in keeping with the principles and values of the co-operative movement. To arrest the practice of concentration of power in a few hands to the detriment of the larger member community, education for awareness building should be an integral part of a co-operative.

Co-operatives in India being a State subject have been and continue to be variously governed through multiple individual State Acts. The Acts endow governments with draconian powers which have in many cases militated against the very concept of a co-operative. Supersession of elected boards of co-operatives and appointment of special officers for long periods without elections are examples of the interference of state governments in co-operative functioning.

In terms of the decent work paradigm, co-operatives could lead the way by demonstrating what is really meant by freedom, equity, security and human dignity. Thus, co-operatives by being true to their basic principles provide locally-based answers to globalization. Therefore, contrary to the belief that globalization impedes the growth of co-operatives, they are the vital agencies to face the challenges posed by globalization.

The growth of co-operatives sector has not been uniform in all parts of the country. The primary reasons for this situation are control of co-operatives by dominant vested-interest groups, poor management, dependence of co-operatives on higher tiers and government for financial assistance and limited range of business activities. The function of thrift has not been given due importance by co-operatives leading to resource crunch and ultimately to their inability to serve the poor.

One of the major issues concerning the co-operative sector is the professionalisation of management. If the co-operatives have to compete in a more open economic regime, the State

Governments will have to professionalise the management of co-operatives and especially the co-operative processing units, This is crucial for overall co-operative development vis-à-vis other sectors. For achieving this, it will be necessary to convince the State Governments of the need for granting functional autonomy to co-operatives.

From the Eighth Five Year Plan (1992-97) onwards, co-operatives have found no mention in the Five Year Plans drawn up by the Planning Commission. It is important that due recognition is given to co-operatives as a third sector of the economy and its development, particularly in terms of its marginalized and weaker segments.

Hapur **Babita Agrawal**
May 2012

Part I
Co-operatives in India: History, Problems and Reforms

1

Philosophy and Forms of Co-operatives

Co-operatives have an important role to play in banking, input supply, marketing, agro-processing and other agri-businesses to protect farmers from the vagaries of existing imperfections in the supply of inputs, production, value addition and marketing. Co-operatives should function as economic enterprises and not as an extended arm of the state. They require an entrepreneurial approach, competitive edge through suitable enterprise focus and strategic alliances with private and public sector units.

With economic liberalisation and market competitiveness, co-operatives would require much larger capital and other financial resources. Changes in the legal framework and regulatory system would help gain greater access to capital/financial resources. The management of the co-operatives needs to be made professionally competent, with clear demarcation of functions of the elected members and the managers.

1.1 Philosophy of Co-operatives

In India, as in many other countries, co-operation started as a means of ensuring for the poorly equipped citizens advantages which better placed persons were able to command by their own individual resources. The principle of mutual aid, which is the basis of co-operative organisation, and the practice of thrift and self-help which sustain it, generate a sturdy feeling of self-reliance which is of basic importance in a democratic way of life. By pooling their experience and knowledge and by helping one another, members of co-operative societies can not only find the solutions of individual problems but also become better citizens.

In an unregulated economy, the terms of contract are frequently weighted in favour of persons of large means. Those who have the command of scarce resources are left free to drive a bargain with those who need such resources but are ill-equipped to compete for their possession. In a relatively stagnant agricultural economy of small holders, undergoing a transition from barter to money economy and from local to national and international exchange, the possession of capital naturally confers a strategic advantage.

An increasing measure of responsibility for organising and financing rural economic development is being shouldered by co-operatives. Both the natural evolution of co-operative activity, and the impetus of the special need created in several parts of the country by agrarian legislation regulating the business of moneylenders, scaling down of debts, restricting rents and abolishing landlordism are responsible for the striking increase in the operations of co-operative credit societies. Co-operation is in fact being transformed steadily yet surely, from a tolerated exception into a general rule. In industry, commerce, transport and retail distribution co-operatives are gaining experience and strength. Different State Governments sometimes emphasize different fields of co-operative activity in keeping with local conditions. There can be no doubt, however, that a new awareness of an opportunity to build up a form of business organisation more suited to the conditions and needs of the times than the joint stock company has come over the people of small means everywhere. The joint stock company is too cumbersome as an organization for the small producer, agricultural or industrial. What is needed and what the co-operative society has provided is a simpler form of organization more suited to the needs of the people to be served and therefore likely to be more acceptable.

Co-operation as an instrument of economic development of the disadvantaged, particularly in the rural areas has received considerable emphasis during the successive Five Year Plans. The founders of planning in the country saw a village Panchayat, a village co-operative and a village school, as the trinity of institutions on which a self-reliant and just economic and social order was to be built. The non-exploitative character of co-operatives, voluntary nature of their membership, the principle of one man one vote, decentralised decision making and self-imposed curbs on profits eminently qualified them as an instrument of development combining the advantages of private ownership with public good.

Having begun primarily in the field of credit as a defensive mechanism against the usurious money lenders, co-operatives have come to embrace a large gamut of activities to serve the interests of the producers and consumers. Credit, however, still continues to be the predominant activity.

Co-operatives are expected to play a major role in the distribution of inputs and services to the farmers on the one hand and in assisting marketing and processing of agricultural produce on the other.

In November, 1958, in its Resolution on Co-operative Policy, the National Development Council agreed that co-operatives should be organised on the basis of the village community as the primary unit, and that responsibility and initiative for social and economic development at the village level should be placed fully on the village co-operative and the village panchayat. The co-operative and the panchayat were to be regarded as the primary agencies for carrying out the community development programme which aims at the improvement of all aspects of rural life through the efforts of the people. The village agricultural plan was considered to be the foundation of the programme for co-operative development and was to be given the highest priority.

1.2 Types of Co-operatives

Even more striking than the expansion in numbers and size, is the growing diversity of functions assumed by co-operative societies. Besides agricultural societies of all types, viz. credit, processing, marketing, farming, irrigation, consolidation etc., there are industrial co-operatives, labour societies, consumers' co-operatives in rural as well as in urban areas, housing societies; processing factories; and urban banks.

When co-operation was first introduced under the Co-operative Credit Societies Act, 1904, it was confined to the organisation of the co-operative credit societies in urban and rural areas with a view to relieving indebtedness and promoting thrift. The Co-operative Societies Act, 1912, permitted the registration of co-operative societies for promoting non-credit activities as well as federations of primary societies into organisations at higher levels. Both in the field of credit and of non-credit activities the co-operative structure consists of primary societies at the base in villages or towns, central organisations at the district level and apex organisations at the State level.

1.2.1 Multi-purpose Co-operative Societies: The States as a whole are conscious of the importance of developing co-operative societies as a means of re-organisation of rural life. Among co-operative bodies working in rural areas, the multi-purpose society has quite rightly come to occupy an important place. It has come to be realised that division of the needs, activity and assets of a villager into mutually exclusive parts such as credit, production, sale etc. is somewhat artificial. Attempts should be made to have in each village a co-operative organisation which will cater for the multiple needs of its members. In some parts of the country efforts are now being made to transform many of the credit societies, which historically have been the most important co-operative organisations, into multi-purpose societies, the emphasis now being placed on the concentrated and all-sided development of rural areas would suggest the desirability of encouraging such transformation.

1.2.2 Co-operative Credit Societies: Recently there has been a noticeable increase of money incomes in the agricultural sector of the economy. While, therefore, on the one hand, larger sums will come to be disbursed in rural areas, it is of the utmost importance to see that monies so spent do not go outside the system of organised credit. In other words, rural savings and monies generally in the hands of the rural population have to be kept flowing into credit organisations. A co-operative society is calculated to do this much better than almost any other organisation. In the co-operative form of organization the provision of resources such as credit goes with the practice of thrift. It can also function as an authorised agent for savings, promoting savings schemes sponsored by the State or Central Governments. The establishment of credit societies in villages is thus a sine qua non of the organisation of credit in the context of planned investment in the developmental schemes.

Development of co-operatives has been envisaged as a significant strategy to build strength in the people with limited means. The co-operative movement aims at saving the rural poor, small farmers, marginal farmers, agricultural labourers and small artisans from exploitation by money lenders. Today, India has a wide network of primary agricultural credit societies (PACS) at village level. At district and state level, co-operative federations have also been set up in almost all states.

One of the basic weaknesses of the co-operative credit system is the non-viability of a large number of primary agricultural credit societies, During recent, years, programmes of rationalisation of the co-operative credit structure, at the primary level, have been under way.

1.2.3 Co-operative Sale/Purchase Societies: The purchase of the agriculturist's requirements and the sale of his produce are key activities in the business of farming and their importance is likely to be even more crucial in a socially regulated economy. Due to his inability to secure a fair deal at these two stages the average agriculturist is denied the full fruits of his industry. The organisation of co-operative sale and purchase societies and of other marketing organisations is vital both for its direct and indirect benefits. With credit and marketing co-operatively organised all over the country, the stage will be set for a much more ambitious and constructive programme of rural development.

1.2.4 Co-operative Farming: In most parts of the country for ensuring economic cultivation an increase in the unit of cultivation is necessary. Here again, co-operative farming has direct relevance. Without undermining the sense of proprietorship and the incentive to industry that it gives, co-operative farms can produce all the advantages that a larger unit possesses.

The role of co-operative farming in .the reconstruction of the rural economy has been stressed time and again. With the growth of population and the need to secure rapid increase in agricultural production and rural employment, it is essential to intensify efforts to develop co-operative farming throughout the country.

In the general pattern of organisation of co-operative farming, stress is laid on the principle that co-operative farming is a voluntary movement and there should be no question of compelling any cultivator to join a co-operative farming society. Membership in co-operative farming societies should be confined to those who are prepared to work on the farm or in ancillary activities and, ordinarily, absentee landholders should not be admitted as members.

Members joining a co-operative farming society are expected to pool their lands for a minimal period of five years, withdrawals during this period being permitted in exceptional circumstances. Co-operative farming societies are expected to give a reasonable return on account of land contributed by members in addition to income in lieu of work done by them.

1.2.5 Industrial Co-operatives: In the rural areas, the needs of employment will not all be met by farming only. There are in the villages several classes of artisans who under the pressure of competition from organised industry are finding it difficult to maintain their traditional employments. While the formation of agricultural co-operatives is by now a familiar experience, industrial co-operatives are still in their infancy. Their activity is so directly in touch with the moving events of a competitive market that the uncertainties of their business often loom larger than their basic importance. Moreover, co-operative financing and marketing agencies have yet very limited experience of doing business with industrial co-operatives. As a result of these factors, the future of industrial co-operatives is yet not well-established as appears to be the case with agricultural co-operatives.

Industrial co-operatives have had a large measure of success in the handloom industry, in coir and in certain village industries. However, their expansion as a general movement has been impeded on account of various practical difficulties.

1.2.6 Co-operative Marketing: Compared to co-operative credit, 'the development of co-operative marketing of agricultural produce is of recent origin. Following the recommendations of All India Rural Credit Survey Report, an integrated programme of co-operative marketing was taken up in the Second Five Year Plan (1956-61) and followed up in the Third Five Year Plan (1961-66). As a result, co-operative marketing structure has been built up at various levels.

In addition to their role in the sale of agricultural produce on terms favourable to the producer, marketing societies are intended to serve as distributors of articles required by cultivators for agricultural production. They are also essential for linking up the grant of agricultural credit with marketing. Statistics concerning the activities of marketing societies are inadequate in several respects. Their principal problems are to secure sufficient finance for current operations, to improve management and to ensure continued support from their members. Price stabilisation policies will greatly facilitate the growth of co-operative marketing and the expansion of credit.

1.2.7 Co-operative Processing: Development of co-operative processing is essential not only for increasing rural incomes and facilitating credit for production but also for building up a co-operative rural economy. Where co-operative processing units have been successfully established, they have proved invaluable as instruments of development in several allied fields. Co-operative processing is, however, a recent development. Comparatively greater progress has been achieved in sugar and cotton ginning and pressing than in other processing industries.

The major weaknesses noticed in the working of the co-operative processing units, particularly rice mills and fruit and vegetable processing units, have been the under-utilisation of capacity and deficiencies in technical and financial management. The co-operative processing units would be required to focus their attention on removing these weaknesses so that they emerge as useful organisation for providing better return to the producers for the raw materials supplied to them, particularly by the oilseeds growers.

1.2.8 Consumer Co-operatives: A large number of consumer stores came into existence for the distribution of controlled commodities during and after the Second World War.

In the rural areas, retailing of consumer articles is conceived essentially as the responsibility of primary agricultural credit societies supported by marketing co-operatives. In this field, the expansion in business has been significant. The progress, however, has been largely accounted for by distribution of foodgrains and other controlled articles. Moreover the progress has been extremely uneven and has been confined to a few States.

1.2.9 Labour and Construction Co-operatives: The importance of organising labour co-operatives for carrying out irrigation and other projects in rural areas has been stressed frequently since the First Five Year Plan (1951-56). In several States, notably in Punjab, Mumbai, Andhra Pradesh and Rajasthan, efforts have been made to set up labour co-operatives, labour contract societies, etc. for taking up works involving mainly unskilled and semi-skilled labour with a view gradually to diminishing the role of contractors.

The aim should be to build up labour co-operative organisations and voluntary organisations as important instruments for undertaking development and providing employment through works carried out mainly on behalf of Government Departments, Panchayat Samitis and Panchayats. Once such organisations come into existence, new possibilities for enlarging their scope and extending their benefits to the community in many directions will emerge.

In short, co-operatives have, over the years, significantly diversified their activities to include credit, banking, input distribution, agro-processing, storage and warehousing. In dairying and oil processing activities, co-operative sub sector has emerged as an important countervailing factor to the private traders, for the benefit of both producers and consumers. Co-operatives have also contributed significantly in the sphere of consumer protection. Given adequate freedom of action in their management, co-operatives can emerge strong and efficient.

1.3 Co-operatives and Panchayats

Panchayats have an indispensable role to play in the rural areas. As representing the best interests of all sections of the community their status is unique. Many activities such as, framing programmes of production for the village, obtaining and utilising governmental assistance for the betterment of the village (e.g. construction of roads, tanks etc.), encouraging villagers to improve the standards of cultivation, organising voluntary labour for community works and generally assisting in the implementation of economic an social reform legislation passed by the States, will naturally fall within the purview of the panchayat.

For the working of individual programmes of economic development, where not only the general interest but also the specific responsibility and liability of a member have to be ensured, a more integrated and binding form of association is needed. Specific and practical tasks of reclaiming land, of providing resources for better cultivation, of marketing the produce of the villagers, both agriculturists and artisans, can be best performed through co-operatives. The co-operative agencies will naturally have to conform to the principles of business management, namely, of satisfactory service and economical working. That they are not profiteering associations and that they function for mutual service makes them desirable agents of democratic planning. It is, therefore, necessary that co-operative agencies in the village should have the closest possible relationship with the principal democratic body namely, the panchayat. Though in the discharge of their functions the two bodies have specific fields to operate, in a number of common functions by having mutual representation and by having common ad-hoc committees, it will be possible to build up a structure of democratic management of developmental plans through both the organisations, the panchayats and the co-operative societies.

1.4 Co-operatives and Economic Planning

In a regime of planned development, co-operation is an instrument, which while retaining some of the advantages of decentralisation and local initiative will yet serve willingly and readily the overall purposes and directives of the plan. The co-operative form of organization can no longer be treated as only a species within the private sector. It is an indispensable instrument of planned economic action in a democracy.

Economic development along democratic lines offers a vast field for the application of co-operation in its infinitely varying forms. Small units can obtain the advantages of scale and organisation mainly by coming together. The character of economic development in India with its emphasis on social change, therefore, provides a great deal of scope for the organisation of co-operative activity. The building up of a co-operative sector as part of the scheme of planned development is, thus, one of the central aims of national policy.

In areas which offer special opportunities for its

development, the co-operative form of organisation has advantages which neither the system of private enterprise nor that of State ownership can match. In particular, it offers a means of achieving results valuable to the community by drawing equally upon incentives which are social and incentives which are individual. Where it succeeds, co-operation brings large gains to the community, but the human factors involved in it are complex and in some ways it is much more difficult for the co-operative form of organisation to succeed than it is for a completely socialised enterprise or for an individual entrepreneur. It is, therefore, necessary to take effective measures to enable co-operation to succeed, whenever possible, and especially in fields which are assigned to it in the scheme of national development.

Because of historical circumstances in India, agricultural credit accounts for the greater part of development in the field of co-operation. The provision of adequate credit on reasonable terms is undoubtedly a most important part of co-operation.

Co-operatives, like village panchayats, are institutional agencies for achieving social cohesion. In a country whose economic structure has its roots in the village, co-operation is something more than a series of activities organised on co-operative lines; basically, its purpose is to evolve a system of co-operative community organisation which touches upon all aspects of life. Within the village community there are sections of the populations who need special assistance. Co-operation should therefore mean an obligation towards all families in the village community and the development of land and other resources and of social services in the common interest of the village as a whole. This is the underlying approach in setting co-operative village management as the main direction of reorganisation in the rural economy.

1.5 Land Reforms and Co-operative Institutions

There is a close connection between the success of land

reform and the success of co-operation which is not always appreciated. For co-operation to succeed fully it is essential that the reorganisation of the agrarian structure should be carried out speedily so as to eliminate features which reduce the productive capacity of the community and permit exploitation. Thus, land reform programmes should do much to stimulate the growth of the co-operative movement. In the nature of things, as a result of land reform the number of small cultivators increases, those with large holdings or considerable surpluses disappear and the new owners need a great deal of credit. Also, as the national extension net work is established and the rural people are ready and willing to participate in development programmes on an increasing scale, their requirements for credit and finance greatly increase. Co-operative institutions are the medium through which many activities in the village are to be reorganised and financed. It is therefore essential that in devising the land reform programme care should be taken to ensure that while its objectives are secured, co-operative credit institutions are not placed under handicaps which might affect their financial soundness.

2

Co-operative Movement during Pre-Independence Period

The history of co-operatives in India is more than a hundred years old. The first piece of co-operative legislation was the Co-operative Credit Societies Act of 1904, which was amended in 1912 to permit the formation of societies for purposes other than credit. As a result, societies for a variety of purposes began to be organized. This process of diversification was, however, slow in its pace. When individualism was the order of the day, co-operation represented a defensive act of association on the part of individual citizens. However, with the adoption of the principle of social regulation, the co-operative societies, which from their commencement in India have been socially sponsored and supported, came to occupy a more positive role.

The agricultural conditions and absence of institutional arrangements to provide finance to agriculturists during the latter part of the 19th century led to mounting distress and discontent. The Famine Commission of 1880 and 20 years later, the Famine Commission 1901 both highlighted the deep indebtedness of the Indian farmer, resulting in many cases in his land passing into the possession of the money lending classes. The Deccan Riots and the prevailing environment of discontent resulted in the government taking various initiatives but the legislative measures did not substantially improve the situation.

In 1901, the Famine Commission recommended the establishment of Rural Agricultural Banks through the establishment of Mutual Credit Associations, and such steps as were taken by the Government of North Western Provinces and Oudh. The underlying idea of a number of persons combining together was the voluntary creation of a new and valuable security. A strong association competent to offer guarantees and advantages of lending to groups instead of individuals were major advantages.

2.1 Co-operative Credit Societies Act, 1904

Taking cognizance of these developments and to provide a legal basis for co-operative societies, the Edward Law Committee was appointed by the Government to examine and recommend a course of action. Based on the recommendations of this Committee, the Co-operative Credit Societies Act was enacted on March 25, 1904. The Act was restricted to credit co-operatives. By 1911, there were 5,300 societies in existence with a membership of over 3 lakh.

The 1904 Act provided for constitution of societies, eligibility for membership, registration, liabilities on members, disposal of profits, shares and interests of members, privileges of societies, claims against members, audit, inspection and enquiry, dissolution, exemption from taxation and rule making power. All other operational and managerial issues were left to the local governments, namely to formulate suitable rules and model bye-laws of the co-operative societies. The institution of the Registrar, visualized as a special official mechanism to be manned by officers with special training and appropriate attitudinal traits to prompt and catalyze co-operative development was the result of the Act of 1904.

2.2 Co-operative Societies Act, 1912

With the developments in terms of growth in the number of co-operatives, far exceeding anticipation, the Co-operative Societies Act of 1912 became a necessity and co-operatives could be organized under this Act for providing non-credit services to their members. The Act also provided for Federations of co-operatives.

With this enactment, in the credit sector, urban co-operative banks converted themselves into Central Co-operative Banks with primary co-operatives and individuals as their members. Similarly, non-credit activities were also co-operatively organized such as purchase and sales unions, marketing societies, and in the non-agricultural sector, co-operatives of handloom weavers and other artisans.

After the 1912 Act, the first Co-operative Housing Society, the Madras Co-operative Union in 1914, the Bombay Central Co-operative Institute in 1918 and similar institutions in Bengal, Bihar, Orissa, Punjab etc. came up. Other than consumer co-operatives and weavers co-operatives, other non-agricultural credit co-operatives generally performed well and grew in strength and operations during this period.

The agricultural credit scenario was a matter of concern and various committees looked into the problems of co-operative banks in various provinces. The Royal Commission on Agriculture in 1928 also reviewed the co-operative sector and among others recommended the setting up of land mortgage banks.

In both agricultural and non-agricultural non-credit sectors, societies were organized, but most faced difficulties in operation as a result of opposition by private marketing agencies and also the inexperience of their office bearers. This focused attention on strengthening of co-operative institutes and unions for education and training. A prominent development of this time was the setting up of the All India Association of Co-operative Institutes in 1929.

2.3 Maclagen Committee on Co-operation (1914)

The First World War adversely affected the growth of co-operatives. Although member deposits in co-operatives increased sharply, the War affected the exports and prices of cash crops adversely, resulting in increased overdues of loans of primary agricultural societies. To take stock of the situation, a Committee on Co-operation under Sir Edward Maclagen was appointed by the Government in October 1914, to study the state of co-operatives and make recommendations for the future. The Committee's recommendations basically related to credit co-operatives. It recommended building up a strong three-tier structure in every province with primaries at the base, the Central Co-operative Banks at the middle-tier and the Provincial Co-operative Bank at the apex, basically to provide short-term and medium-term finance. Considerable emphasis was laid on ensuring the co-operative character of these institutions and training and member education, including training of the Registrar and his staff.

The Committee recommended as follows:

1. Numbering not less than 10, individuals combine together as they are unable to obtain credit individually.
2. Real security consists not of material assets of members, but their ability and desire to use credit productively and to repay loans out of profits made. Productive use of credit and moral pressure on co-members to duly repay would ensure loan security.
3. Societies to be co-operative and business like, small in size.
4. One vote per member, transparency of business transactions, development of thrift and obtaining maximum capital from savings.
5. Period of the loan be fixed based on purpose of loan and the circumstances of the borrower.
6. Rates of interest to be initially substantial, although lower than that on credit from moneylenders.
7. Efforts increase deposits both from members and non-members.
8. Maximum borrowing limit of the society be annually fixed.
9. Obtaining share capital in instalments excellent means of inculcating thrift and providing capital.
10. Interest rates not to be reduced until reserve funds have reached substantial figure.
11. Frequent audit by higher co-operative institutions with Government Audit once in 2 or 3 years, with cost being

met by the societies.

12. Registrar should ensure supervision and control of primary societies without assuming detailed direction.
13. To meet their deposits due, Banks must equilibrate their finances with care, providing for retention of adequate fluid resources.
14. Need for Registrars staff to be increased and agriculture and industry in the provinces to be coordinated under one head; appointment of a Development Commissioner and a Co-operative Adviser also recommended.
15. For coordination and control, a strong apex or provincial bank needed.

Under the Government of India Act, 1919, Co-operation as a subject was transferred to the provinces. The Bombay Co-operative Societies Act of 1925, the first provincial Act to be passed, among others, introduced the principle of one-man one-vote.

2.4 Royal Commission on Agriculture (1928)

The Royal Commission on Agriculture, appointed to make recommendations for improvement of agriculture and promotion of welfare and prosperity of the rural population, submitted its report in April 1928. Main recommendations of the Commission were as under:

1. Main activities of the co-operative movement must continue to be directed to expansion of the rural credit system; defects pointed out by the Committee on Co-operation 1914-1915 still persisted and although the number of societies has increased there was no qualitative improvement.
2. Need for member education stressed.
3. Role of the Registrar to be not merely a registering officer, but to provide supervision, assistance, counsel and control.
4. To ensure continuity, Registrar not to be transferred for a minimum period of 5 years.
5. More Government contribution in backward tracts and for

certain activities such as irrigation, consolidation of land holdings etc.

6. Importance should be attached to every phase of activity; the term rural reconstruction expressed more accurately the nature of activities within the movement.
7. Establishment of land mortgage banks with guarantee of interest on its debentures by Government under the Co-operative Act to meet the requirements of the cultivator other than small needs.
8. Central Organization for control of debenture issue and measures for financial disciplines.
9. Single purpose co-operatives by and large favoured; need for extension of co-operative principles in fields other than co-operative credit; co-operative input and sale societies also identified as areas for development.

The setting up of the Reserve Bank of India (RBI) in 1934 was a major development in the thrust for agricultural credit. The Reserve Bank of India Act, 1934 itself required the RBI to set up an Agricultural Credit Department. As co-operatives were to be channels for rural development, with the establishment of popularly elected governments in 1935, programmes were drawn up in which rural indebtedness received priority. The Mehta Committee appointed in 1937 specifically recommended reorganization of Co-operative Credit Societies as multi-purpose co-operatives.

The Second World War boosted the prices of agricultural commodities leading to increased returns to farmers and consequently reduction in over-dues to the co-operatives. To counter shortages of essential commodities for domestic consumption as well as raw materials, the Government resorted to procurement of commodities from producers and rationing, for which it decided to utilize the co-operatives. This provided a momentum to the growth of multi-purpose co-operatives.

The period between 1939 and 1945 provided a further stimulus to the growth of the Urban Co-operative Credit structure. Many societies had started banking functions and had grown in size and operations over a period of time, with substantial diversification of activities.

2.5 Multi-Unit Co-operative Societies Act, 1942

With the emergence of co-operatives having a membership from more than one state such as the Central Government sponsored salary earners credit societies, a need was felt for an enabling co-operative law for such multi-unit or multi-state co-operatives. Accordingly, the Multi-Unit Co-operative Societies Act was passed in 1942, which delegated the power of the Central Registrar of Co-operatives to the State Registrars for all practical purposes.

2.6 Co-operative Planning Committee (1945)

Following the recommendations of the 14th Conference of Registrars of Co-operative Societies held in 1944, the Co-operative Planning Committee (Chairman: R.G. Saraiya) was constituted in January 1945 to draw up a plan of co-operative development in the country. It submitted its report in November 1945. The Committee felt that supply of credit touches only one aspect of the life of the cultivator and the activities of primary co-operative societies should be so extended as to cover the whole of his life. The main recommendations of the Committee were as under:

1. Multi-purpose society should serve as a Centre for general economic improvement. Apart from financing crop production, it should act as an agent for sale of produce to the nearest co-operative marketing organization; supply farmers with their production needs and dairy consumption requirements; serve as milk collecting station for the nearest dairy and provision of veterinary services, maintain agriculture machinery to be jointly used by members and encourage subsidiary occupations by its members.
2. Membership of such societies should be a minimum of 50

and confined to an area of operation, which would ensure adequate business as well as efficient supervision and control.

3. Except in cases where unlimited liability has been successful, the society should be one of limited liability.
4. Linking of agricultural credit with marketing. Credit societies should give loans on the condition that the borrowing member would sell the marketable surplus through his primary society to the nearest marketing society of the area.

The Committee also dealt in detail with co-operatives in the areas of animal husbandry and fisheries, agricultural marketing and processing, agricultural credit, labour and civil construction, consumers, urban credit, housing societies, women and co-operation, co-operative administration and education training and research.

3

Post-Independence Developments in the Co-operative Sector

After India attained Independence in 1947, co-operative development received a boost, with co-operatives accorded a vital role in the various plans formulated by the Planning Commission.

3.1 All India Rural Credit Survey Committee, 1951

A major watershed initiative soon after Independence was the appointment of the All India Rural Credit Survey Committee, (Chairman: A.D. Gorwala) in 1951. The Committee submitted its report in 1954. It observed that large parts of the country were not covered by co-operatives and in such areas where it had been covered, a large segment of the agricultural population remained outside its membership. Even where membership did exist, the bulk of the credit requirement (75.2 percent) was met from other sources.

The Committee recommended introduction of an integrated system of rural credit, partnership of the government in the share capital of the co-operatives and also appointment of government nominees on their boards, thus participating in their management. The creation of the State Bank of India was also a major recommendation of the Committee.

The Government and the elected representatives accepted the basic approach and the major recommendations of the Committee. The Union Government acquired a major interest in the Imperial Bank of India which was converted into the State Bank of India. A National Co-operative Development and Warehousing Board was set up. The Reserve Bank of India Act was amended to enable it to play an active role in building up of co-operative credit institutions.

The All India Co-operative Congress, held in Patna in 1956, accepted the principle of state participation and government representation on the board of directors of co-operatives. It resolved that the number of such nominees should not exceed one-third of the total number of directors or three, whichever is less, and made applicable even to co-operatives having government share capital in excess of 50 percent of total share capital. This recommendation was accepted by the Central Government.

In 1953, the Government of India and the Reserve Bank of India jointly constituted a Central Committee for Co-operative Training to establish necessary training facilities for co-operative personnel. The All India Co-operative Union and the State Co-operative Unions were entrusted with training of members and office bearers of co-operative organizations.

The main recommendations of the Committee were as under:

1. Large parts of the country were not covered by co-operatives. Even in areas where membership existed, bulk of credit requirement (75.2 percent) was met from other sources.
2. Non-economic causes for the failure of the co-operative movement were basically structural and functional and included low educational levels and lack of training.
3. Location of both power and finance continues to be largely urban and hence more responsive to urban than rural interest.
4. Integrated scheme of rural credit based on State partnership, including financial partnership in co-operatives and training with a rural bias.
5. Caution against state interference in day-to-day working of

co-operatives. While societies at the rural base level should become fully co-operative by process of replacing share capital, partnerships at higher levels should be retained till base level societies develop sufficient strength.

6. Setting up of a National Agricultural Credit Long-term Operations Fund and National Agricultural Credit Stabilization Fund to be reviewed at the end of 5 years, responsibility for which would be with the Reserve Bank of India.
7. Creation of the State Bank of India.
8. Establishment of a Central Land Mortgage Bank in each State with more than 51 percent of State share capital.
9. Apex Co-operative Marketing Federations.
10. Licenses to be issued on a priority basis to co-operative processing plants.
11. State plans for rationalizing and strengthening Central Co-operative Banks.
12. District Marketing Societies on territorial or commodity basis with at least 51 percent State Government share capital and suitable technical staff.
13. Establishment of primary land mortgage banks and primary marketing societies located at important mandis or at taluka centres after due consideration of the conditions of each area.

Meanwhile, Industrial Policy Resolution, 1956 emphasized the need for State assistance to enterprises organized on a co-operative basis for industrial and agricultural purposes, and "to build up a large and growing co-operative sector".

3.2. Committee on Co-operative Law, 1957

This Committee (Chairman: S.T. Raja) was set up in 1956 to evolve a simple law for co-operatives. The Committee submitted its Report in May 1957 and recommended a Model Bill for consideration of the States. Main recommendations of the Committee were as under:

1. Increasing decentralization of powers of Registrar.
2. Registration of societies to conform to economic interests of members, social justice and sound business practices.
3. Unlimited liability in the case of societies.
4. Amalgamation to be in accordance with wishes and interests of members.
5. Membership not to be open to firms, partnerships and companies.
6. Nominal or associate members to have no voting powers or share in profits of the societies.
7. One-man, one-vote and no proxy.
8. Ceiling on individual shareholding (₹ 5,000).
9. Powers of the General Body were specifically laid down in the Model Bill.
10. Any transfer of assets/property by members without previous consent of the society to be void, notwithstanding any law in force.
11. State partnership, preferably to be direct.
12. Contributions to reserve fund out of profits to be not less than 25 percent.
13. All states should set up Co-operative Tribunals.

Many State Governments amended their Acts, as a result of the recommendations of the Model Bill.

From the mid-1960s onwards agro-processing co-operatives, particularly in the sugar and spinning sector, grew in number and contribution, driven primarily by the Government's policy of encouraging large-scale industries in the co-operative sector and term loan assistance from financial institutions.

After the Indo-China war in 1962, both the Consumer Co-operative Structure and the Public Distribution System (PDS) were strengthened. The Government as a matter of policy decided to give preference to consumer or other co-operatives in the allotment of fair price shops and certain States allotted new fair price shops only to co-operatives.

With the growth of public deposits in Urban Co-operative Credit Societies, it was felt necessary to insure these under the Deposit Insurance Scheme of Reserve Bank of India. Selective provisions of the RBI Act, 1934 and later Banking Regulation Act, 1949 were made applicable to Co-operative Banks w.e.f. March 1, 1966 to regulate their banking business and facilitate insurance coverage of deposits. Thus, they became an integral part of the banking system of the country.

Agricultural Refinance Corporation was set up in 1962 by the Government of India to provide long-term loans to co-operatives, through Central Land Mortgage Banks.

In 1963, the National Co-operative Development Corporation (NCDC) was established as a statutory corporation by an Act of Parliament. The establishment of the NCDC gave a great boost to the growth of co-operative marketing and processing societies.

Several other significant organizational developments also took place during this period such as the setting up of various National Co-operative Federations and re-organization of the National Co-operative Union of India (NCUI). In 1967, the Vaikunth Mehta National Institute of Co-operative Management was set up in Pune. Growth of consumer co-operatives was also an important development of this period. Simultaneously, the growth of Land Development Banks also accelerated and rural co-operatives for dairy, poultry, fishery and labour were set up.

The National Bank for Agriculture and Rural Development (NABARD) Act was passed in 1981 and NABARD was set up to provide re-finance support to co-operative banks and to supplement the resources of commercial banks and regional rural banks (RRBs) to enhance credit flow to the agriculture and rural sector.

3.3. Report of Sir Malcom Darling, 1957

After studying the functioning of co-operatives in India, Sir Malcom Darling was not in favour of the new large-sized society pattern, mainly due to its large area of operation. Main recommendations were as follows:

1. Area of operation of a society should not normally exceed a distance of 2 miles from its headquarter village.
2. Societies undertaking banking should not be allowed to undertake trading, since banking and trading did not go together.
3. Small societies should not be amalgamated without the full and free consent of a large majority of their members.
4. The old name Thrift and Credit Society should be restored and scrupulously insisted upon at the time of registering a rural credit society at the primary level.

3.4 National Development Council (NDC) Resolution, 1958

Another important development, at this time, which affected the co-operative sector, was the NDC Resolution (1958). The Resolution on Co-operative Policy stressed that co-operatives should be organized on the basis of the village community as the primary unit and that there should be close coordination between the village co-operative and the Panchayat. The Resolution also recommended that the restrictive features of existing co-operative legislation should be removed.

Highlights of the Resolution were as under:

1. Co-operatives to be organized on a village basis with primary responsibility on Panchayat.
2. Various programmes for increasing agricultural production to be carried out through co-operatives.
3. Village societies to be federated through unions and also become members of marketing societies.
4. National savings movement to utilize co-operatives as

primary agencies in rural areas.

5. Development of marketing societies, on the basis of careful surveys of marketable surplus in different areas was emphasized.
6. Emphasis on training of co-operative personnel.

3.5 Working Group on Co-operative Policy, 1958

This Group was appointed by the Government of India to consider the administrative and organizational arrangements needed for the implementation of 1958 Resolution of the National Development Council (NDC). The Group recommended as follows:

1. Village co-operative should be organized on the basis of village community as the primary unit and include within itself all the families living in the village, whether they are cultivators, agricultural labourers, artisans or other groups such as fishermen etc. It should provide to them not only credit, but also agricultural requisites and consumer goods.
2. It would be more advisable not to combine the credit function, which was of primary importance to all the people in the village, with such other functions in which only a few people might be interested or which might involve long-term investment or financial risks. Thus, a village might have, in addition to village multi-purpose society, one or more co-operatives for specific tasks and specific interests.
3. The Group recommended two patterns of organizations: (a) organization of credit societies each of which would ordinarily have the village as the area of operation and in any case not cover a population of more than 1,000 and (b) organization of credit unions for a group of villages to undertake credit activities.

These recommendations were communicated by the Government of India to the State Governments in May 1959 for co-operative revitalization.

3.6 Working Group on Co-operative Farming, 1959

This Working Group (Chairman: S. Nijalingappa) was set up to examine and suggest measures for promoting joint farming co-operative societies. Main recommendations of the Group were as under:

1. Flexibility in organization, voluntary membership and more than one society in a village, if required.
2. Decision-making power to vest with General Body. If required, sub-committees for different subjects, where membership is large.
3. Model by-laws prescribed.
4. Government to participate initially in share capital, which may be retired over a 10 year period through creation of share redemption fund or members contribution.
5. Assistance under various Government schemes, as well as extension services should be made available.
6. Education and training for ensuring success of society.

3.7 Committee on Co-operative Credit, 1960

This Committee (Chairman: V.L. Mehta) was appointed in September 1959 which submitted its report in May 1960. Its main recommendations were as under:

1. Co-operatives should strengthen themselves financially and otherwise and extend their range of credit and distribution operations.
2. Government contribution to share capital should be on a matching basis.
3. Specified subsidy for a period not more than 5 years.
4. Loans to tenant cultivators.
5. Share capital of government to be conditional on minimum contribution being raised by members over a specified period.

6. Nominees of the Government should not have veto rights and Government should not interfere in the day-to-day working of the co-operative.
7. At the village level, only one institutional agency for supply of credit, viz. the co-operative.
8. Arrangements for linking credit with marketing should be strengthened. Co-operative marketing societies should be permitted to make outright purchases from the producers.
9. State to provide initial assistance for co-operatives, but not to interfere in internal management.
10. Special concessions to be given to scheduled castes and scheduled tribes.

3.8 Working Group on Panchayats and Co-operatives, 1961

This Working Group (Chairman: S.D. Mishra) was set up to suggest measures for co-operatives and panchayats to perform their respective roles in coordination. The Group submitted its Report in October 1961. The Group recommended as follows:

1. Provide accommodation and also land to co-operatives for godowns etc. and processing licenses to co-operatives preferentially.
2. Panchayat to deposit its funds with the village co-operative.
3. All commercial agricultural functions to be run by the co-operative.
4. Close coordination for drawing up village agricultural production plans and credit requirements.
5. All economic and technical matters to be co-ordinated at Zila Parishad/Panchayat level.
6. Work programmes of panchayats to be executed through labour co-operatives or community effort.

3.9 Study Team on Co-operative Training, 1961

This Study Team (Chairman: S.D. Mishra) submitted its report in 1961 and recommended as follows:

1. District and State Co-operative Unions to be strengthened to undertake co-operative training and education.
2. Schools to teach co-operation as also universities, rural institutes and teacher training institutes.
3. Member education to be peripatetic and based on the problems of the co-operatives.
4. Specialized courses for institutional and departmental personnel should be organized including courses in banking, industrial co-operation, consumers co-operation etc.
5. Field studies and research programmes to be undertaken through universities, co-operative unions, rural economic division of RBI and the National Board of Co-operative Training.
6. Co-operative institute for advanced study and research to be set up.

3.10 Committee on Consumers Co-operatives, 1961

Set up by the National Co-operative Development and Warehousing Board, the Committee (Chairman: P. Natesan) submitted its report in 1961. Main recommendations of the Committee were as under:

1. Setting up of consumer stores in larger towns and cities, service co-operatives to function as consumer stores at village level, with special attention to viability.
2. As a rule, avoidance of trading activities along with banking.
3. Initial government share capital to be retired within a period of 10-15 years.
4. Trading against cash.
5. Creation of Price Fluctuation Fund.

6. Rebates to members to be credited to share accounts.
7. Incentives to managers through commission on sales.
8. Audit fee to be linked to profit instead of turnover.
9. Sales tax exemption on sales to affiliated primaries.
10. Government requirements to be met preferentially through consumer co-operatives.

3.11 Committee on Co-operative Processing, 1961

Appointed by the National Co-operative Development and Warehousing Board, the Committee (Chairman: R.G. Saraiya) submitted its report in 1961. It recommended as follows:

1. Linking of credit with processing.
2. Preferential licensing policy.
3. Members to be producers.
4. Membership to be opened to Primary Credit Societies in area of operation to facilitate recovery of crop loans.
5. Credit Guarantee Scheme of Government of India to be extended to co-operative processing units.
6. Preferential treatment in case of taxation.

3.12 Committee on Taccavi Loans and Co-operative Credit, 1962

The National Development Council (NDC) in 1958 had recommended making taccavi loans and other facilities through co-operatives to encourage increase in their membership. Progress was, however, not appreciable and Government of India appointed this Committee in July 1961 to examine the whole question of implementation of the policy. Main recommendations of the Committee were as under:

1. Panchayats would prepare production plans which would be implemented through co-operatives.
2. Co-operatives would be associated in preparation of plans.
3. Co-operatives would be the institutional agency for credit to agriculturists, except in certain cases involving financial

risks or delayed returns where Government would continue direct finance.

4. Government funds should supplement the resources of co-operatives and Government budget provisions should continue.
5. Co-operative dues be given priority over taccavi loans.
6. Co-operatives adopt system of credit based on repaying capacity and adequate security.
7. Distress taccavi loans be granted by financially strong co-operatives, which would function purely on agency basis.
8. Co-operative banking structure be rationalized.
9. Land mortgage banking should be a federal one with central land mortgage bank at state level and primary land mortgage banks at lower level.
10. Co-operatives to continue to charge economic lending rate on short- and medium-term loans.

3.13 Committee on Co-operative Administration, 1963

Set up in 1963, the Committee (Chairman: Vaikunthlal Mehta) was asked to make recommendations regarding staffing at various levels, criteria for determining staff strength, training of staff and procedures for recruitment. The Committee recommended as under:

1. IAS officers to be inducted as Registrars, taking account of suitability and with sufficient orientation of the co-operative department.
2. Technical experts to be taken on loan from concerned departments.
3. Divisional Offices of co-operatives to have the same jurisdiction as Revenue Department.
4. Co-operative enterprises of all kinds to be under administrative control of the Registrar.
5. Audit to remain the statutory duty of the Registrar and separate Audit Wing under a Chief Auditor to be set up.

6. President of the Board of Directors should be entitled to record his views on the work of the government official in his confidential report.
7. Promotion of federal bodies and consideration of transfer to them of statutory powers of the Registrar.

3.14 Second Working Group on Industrial Co-operatives, 1963

This Working Group (Chairman: B.P. Patel) submitted its report in May 1963. The Group recommended as follows:

1. Banks to be selected and developed for industrial loans.
2. Federations of industrial co-operatives to be set up at important market centres on a single or multi industry basis.
3. At least one State Level Industrial Co-operative Federation.
4. State Acts to be suitably amended for needs of industrial co-operatives.
5. New District Industrial Co-operative Banks where considerable concentration of small industrial units exists.
6. List of areas in which SBI expected to operate to be drawn up.

3.15 Mirdha Committee on Co-operatives, 1965

The Committee was asked to (a) lay down standards to determine genuineness of co-operative societies, (b) suggest measures to weed out non-genuine societies, (c) review existing co-operative laws and practices to eliminate vested interest and (d) suggest measures to overcome factors inhibiting self-reliance and self-regulation in the co-operative movement. Main recommendations of the Committee were as under:

1. The Registrar in consultation with apex institutions should lay down detailed conditions for ensuring minimum

performance level such as minimum membership, minimum share capital before registration, promoters to be from different families, scrutiny before registration and careful watch after.

2. Targets to be dependant on financial resources and administrative preparedness.
3. All members to be admitted except moneylenders in credit societies and traders in marketing societies. Similarly, contractors, transporters etc. not to be admitted to labour co-operatives, transport co-operatives respectively.
4. Open membership and provision for appeal against refusal to admit a member.
5. Sanction of loans to managing committee members or their relatives to be put up to general body for information.
6. General Body to decide on number of terms a person may hold office in the Management Committee and number of societies.
7. Elections to be held at least with a gap of 2 years to enable committee members to work.
8. Government nomination not to exceed one-third of committee members or three whichever is less and only government servants should be nominated.
9. Audit should be entrusted to a government agency independent of the Registrar.
10. Federal co-operatives to take responsibility for supervision.
11. Co-operative institutions to be allowed to raise deposits and a system of ensuring or guaranteeing deposits be evolved to build up public confidence.

3.16 All India Rural Credit Review Committee, 1969

The Committee (Chairman: Venkatappaiah) submitted its report in July 1969 and made the following recommendations:

1. Agricultural Credit Corporations to be set up in States.

2. Appropriate staffing and upgradation through training.
3. Special grants by State Government to co-operative banks for employment of staff and to write off irrecoverable debts in certain cases.
4. Supersession of management and appointment of Administrative Officer in special cases.
5. Reactivation of dormant societies or their liquidation.
6. Data verification of land records to ensure reliability of credit finance.
7. Scales of finance to be fixed up and credit to consist of two components, viz. cash and kind.
8. Supersession of management where society affairs are unsatisfactory.
9. State Acts and Rules to incorporate provisions for defaulters to be disqualified from continuing on Board of Directors.
10. Financing of defaulters to be barred, those unable to repay on account of crop failure to be provided with conversion facilities or in certain cases to be granted extensions.
11. Special care to be taken for financing small cultivators.
12. RBI Act to be amended to provide for the constitution of Agricultural Credit Board, which would function through separate Standing Committees and may also deal with non-agricultural aspects of rural credit and all relevant aspects of co-operative credit.
13. Grant of pledge loans by marketing societies to members to be continued subject to certain safeguards.
14. Training should emphasize practical aspects of working.

3.17 Banking Commission, 1972

This Commission (Chairman: R.G. Saraiya) was set up in 1969 to review the working of co-operative banks and recommend coordinated development of commercial and co-operative banks. The Commission submitted its report in 1972 and made the following recommendations:

1. Primary credit societies to be strengthened to enable them to function as Rural Banks.
2. Rural Co-operative Banks to have Associate Members who can avail facilities of the Bank, but will not have voting rights.
3. Flexibility to co-operative banks as in the case of commercial banks.
4. Diversification of farming essential; hence primary units to be functionally equipped to provide credit for all productive purposes to farmers.
5. Real as well as financial assets should be accepted as security.
6. Guarantee for financing small and marginal farmers under the schemes of the Credit Guarantee Corporation.
7. Removal of impediments to take action against defaulters.
8. Deposit Insurance Scheme should be extended to co-operative banks.
9. Establishment of National Co-operative Bank not favoured.
10. Strong case for combining Agricultural Refinance Corporation and Agricultural Finance Corporation.
11. Establishment of Urban Co-operative Banks be encouraged.

Committee on Integration of Co-operative Credit Institutions, 1976

This Committee (Chairman: R.K. Hazari) was set up in 1975 to study the feasibility of integrating the long-term and short-term structure of co-operative movement. The Committee submitted its report in 1976 and made the following recommendations.

1. Need for proper linkage between production and investment credit to intensify modernization of agriculture

and rectify imbalances in the credit structure.

2. Commercial and co-operative credit can jointly play an important role in agricultural finance.
3. Compartmentalised approach means the farmer has to approach different agencies for his needs. Public sector agencies are a specialized class of borrowers.
4. A 3-tier structure at the State, District and Primary level was suggested. A District Co-operative Development Bank (DCDB) at the district level and State Co-operative Development Bank (SCDB) at the State level through transfer of staff, assets, and liabilities of the DCCB.
5. Gradual decentralization of sanctioning powers.
6. System of farmers' passbooks to be introduced.
7. Group guarantees, where hypothecation not possible.

3.19 Committee on Urban Co-operative Banks, 1978

This Committee (Chairman: Madhava Das) was set up in 1978. Its main recommendations were as under:

1. There is a need to stop the practice of primary credit societies commencing banking business without first obtaining licence from RBI.
2. Primary credit societies should not be allowed to use the word *bank, banker* and *banking* as a part of their name to enable the public to distinguish between such societies and banking institutions coming under the purview of Banking Regulation Act, 1949.
3. Corresponding legislative amendments required to give effect to these recommendations.
4. Existing primary credit societies may be allowed a maximum period of 4 years from the date of coming into force of the amended provisions of the Banking Regulation Act, 1949. During the intervening period, till such amendments are carried out in the statute, the societies should either reach the level of prescribed

viability standards to qualify for the licence or take suitable steps to go out of the purview of Banking Regulation Act, 1949.

3.20 Committee to Review Arrangements for Institutional Credit for Agriculture and Rural Development (CRAFICARD), 1981

CRAFICARD (Chairman: B. Sivaraman) was set up to examine the feasibility of integrating the long-term and medium-term credit structure and review the 2-tier versus 3-tier credit system. It submitted its report in January 1981 and made the following recommendations:

1. No single pattern feasible for the entire country.
2. Farmers Service Societies to be developed.
3. Reorganisation drive for societies, which would be single contact point for all types of credit including other rural producers such as artisans, craftsmen, agricultural labour etc.
4. Separate categories of membership for weaker sections and others.
5. Exemptions to defaulters to be completely stopped.
6. Publishing list of defaulters to act as a deterrent for default.
7. Training to be emphasized and planned.
8. RRBs to be given preferential licensing in rural areas.
9. A 2-tier structure may exist in the smaller states and UTs, while a 3-tier structure may be the general pattern for the larger states.
10. Differential rates of interest to be permitted for small and large farmers.

3.21 Multi-State Co-operative Societies (MSCS) Act, 1984

With the objective of introducing a comprehensive central legislation to facilitate the organization and functioning of genuine multi-state societies and to bring uniformity in their administration and management, the MSCS Act of 1984 was enacted. The earlier Multi-Unit Co-operative Societies Act of 1942 was repealed.

3.22 Committee on Democratization and Professionalization of Co-operative Management, 1985

The Committee (Chairman: Ardhanareeswaran) examined various State Co-operative Acts and made the following observations:

1. Existing Co-operative Societies Act contain provisions which militate against the democratic character and the autonomy of co-operatives.
2. Over the years, the Registrar has acquired undue powers in respect of management decisions of the co-operatives, which should be curtailed.
3. Role of the Registrar should be made more positive and he should be looked upon as a development agent.
4. Federal co-operative societies should play a more active part in the developmental functions relating to promotion, organization, proper functioning and growth of the affiliated co-operative societies.

3.23 Committee on Structure and Role of National Co-operative Societies, 1987

This Committee (Chairman: B. Venkatappiah) was set up to assess the performance of National Level Co-operative Federations and examine various parameters of their functioning. The Committee was also required to indicate the directions in which re-organization and re-orientation of federations was required in the context of emerging needs and the role of co-operatives in overall development, particularly in rural areas. It made the following recommendations:

1. A co-operative federation is answerable to its constituent

units and can justify its existence only in terms of the services it renders to those units.

2. NAFED should play a more important role as a leader of the co-operative marketing structure rather than as agent of government price support operations.
3. Federations in the credit sector should develop their research and consultancy wings and undertake micro level studies on simplification of loaning procedures, streamlining accounting methods, funds flow to weaker sections etc.
4. District federations of labour co-operatives should be organized in all districts with 15-20 primary societies.
5. National Federation of Industrial Co-operatives be divested of its co-operative character together with its formal status as a federation.
6. Responsibility of benefiting weaker sections devolves on the entire federal structure.
7. Inter-sectoral coordination through a *single window system* and linking of marketing of agricultural produce with distribution of consumer goods may be attempted.
8. Members of National Federations should be limited to state level federation. Lower level co-operatives may be admitted as members on a wholly transitory basis where there are no state federations.
9. Only experts to be nominated on the Board of co-operatives and nominated members should not have the right to vote in election.
10. New co-operative national federations should be organized only for facilitating operations of its constituents, spokesmanship, promotional and consultancy work. Business functions should be taken up only to the extent entrusted by its units.

3.24 Agricultural Credit Review Committee, 1989

This Committee (Chairman: A.M. Khusro) was required to examine the problems of agricultural and rural credit, take stock of structural and operational deficiencies, constraints and quantitative and qualitative gaps. It made the following recommendations:

1. Prompt elections.
2. Changes in co-operative law against protracted supersession.
3. Completion of reorganization of primary societies based on viability norms, wherever the exercise has not been done.
4. A programme of development for all such primary agricultural credit societies (PACS), which have not reached the loaning business of ₹ 10 lakh, to be taken up for increasing its loan business, enlarging its package of profitable non-credit activities, augmentation of resources (deposits) and reduction in overdues.
5. Improvement in quality of staff and accountability.
6. Staff to be selected by societies.

3.25 Committee on Model Co-operatives Act (MCA), 1991

Appointed by the Planning Commission, Government of India in 1990, this Committee (Chairman: Choudhary Brahm Parkash) was asked to make a broad review of the status of co-operative movement. It submitted its report in 1991, suggesting future directions and drafted a Model Co-operatives Act (MCA). Main recommendations of the Committee were as under:

1. State policy on co-operatives and the principles of co-operation are stated in the beginning of MCA as a guide to its remaining provisions and to facilitate the government to conform to the basic ideology of co-operation.
2. Procedure for Registration of a new co-operative be

simplified and all artificial restrictions by way of area of operation, economic viability etc. removed.

3. MCA gives no rule-making power to the government. The law itself lays down the broad parameters necessarily to be observed by co-operatives and leaves all other matters relating to constitution, management and business of the society to be conducted in accordance with its bye-laws.
4. MCA gives no power to the Registrar or the Government to issue orders for any of the following in a co-operative: (a) supersession of the Board of Director, (b) compulsory amalgamation or division of societies, (c) compulsory amendment of the bye-laws, (d) veto/rescind/annul the resolution, (e) issue directives.
5. Co-operative Federations/Unions are to assume greater responsibility towards the member co-operatives and in particular to ensure regular conduct of elections to the Board of Management and timely conduct of annual audit of accounts.
6. Role of the Registrar under MCA is confined to the registration and liquidation of co-operatives, conduct of inquiry and in case of default to conduct elections, audit and to convene meeting of general body.
7. MCA prohibits co-operatives from accepting funds from the Government by way of equity.
8. To ensure the character of co-operative as a member user organization, special obligations have been imposed on members.
9. Board of Directors is made accountable for timely conduct of elections, regular convening of meetings of the managing committee and the general body and for participation therein and for the timely conduct of the audit of the books of accounts.
10. MCA prohibits officers of the Government to work in a co-operative.

11. MCA provides for the Constitution of Co-operative Tribunal for settlement of disputes including appeals on matters relating to constitution, management and business of a co-operative and to take cognizance of any offence under the Act.

3.26 High Level Committee on Formation of Co-operative Business as Companies, 1999

This Committee (Chairman: Y.K. Alagh) was asked to draft a legislative framework to enable formation of co-operative business as companies and to convert existing co-operative business into companies under a regulatory framework similar to that of private limited companies. The Committee submitted its Report to the Department of Company Affairs, Government of India on March 15, 2000 with the following recommendations:

1. Conversion of inter-State co-operatives to producer companies would be purely voluntary.
2. Member equity may not be publicly traded, but may only be transferred, with the approval of the Producer Company's Board of Directors. Producer companies would not be vulnerable to takeover by multinationals or other companies.
3. Conversion option by inter-State co-operative society to producer company can be exercised only if two-thirds of the Members of the concerned society vote in favour of a resolution to that effect.
4. The new form of company would be designated as *producer company* to indicate that only certain categories of persons can participate in the ownership of such companies. The members of the producer company have necessarily to be *primary producers*, that is persons engaged in an activity connected with, or relatable to, primary produce.

5. The objects of a producer company have been defined to include, among other things, production, processing, manufacture and sale of primary produces as well as allied matter.
6. Provision for converted producer company to go back to the original fold of co-operative.

3.27 Multi-State Co-operative Societies Act, 2002

The Multi-State Co-operative Societies (MSCS) Act, enacted in 1984, was modified in 2002, in keeping with the spirit of the Model Co-operatives Act. Unlike the State Laws, which remained as a parallel legislation to co-exist with the earlier laws, the MSCS Act, 2002 replaced the earlier Act of 1984.

3.28 National Co-operative Policy (NCP), 2002

In 2002, the Government of India enunciated NCP with the objective to facilitate an all round development of co-operatives in the country. NCP promises to provide co-operatives with the necessary support, encouragement and assistance, to ensure their functioning as autonomous, self-reliant and democratically managed institutions, accountable to their members, and making a significant contribution to the national economy.

Based on the recommendations made at a Conference of State Ministers for Co-operation, the Government of India in 2002 constituted a Ministerial Task Force to formulate a plan of action for implementation of NCP. The Task Force suggested that a single law instead of parallel laws should be introduced in the States. It also recommended, among others, that in order to depoliticize co-operatives, Members of Parliament or Members of Legislative Assemblies should not be allowed to hold office of any co-operative society.

3.29 Task Force on Revival of Rural Co-operative Credit Institutions, 2005: See Section 4.10 of Chapter 4 of this book.

3.30 High Powered Committee on Co-operatives, 2009

The year 2004 was the centennial year of the Indian co-operative movement. The world order, in which co-operatives along with other business organizations are required to function, has indeed changed since the first co-operative law in India was enacted in 1904. New paradigms and changing contours and structures of the business landscape have their own inexorable logic.

Following the recommendations of the Conference of State Co-operative Ministers in December 2004, this High Powered Committee on Co-operatives (Chairman: Shivajirao G. Patil) was constituted by the Government of India for preparing a road map for co-operatives over the coming years.

The Terms of Reference of the Committee were as follows:

1. To review the achievements of the co-operatives during the last one hundred years.
2. To identify the challenges being faced by the co-operative sector and to suggest measures to address them to enable the movement to keep pace with the changing socio-economic environment.
3. To suggest an appropriate policy and legislative framework and changes required in the co-operative legislation in the country with a view to ensure the democratic, autonomous and professional functioning of co-operatives and amendments to the Multi-State Co-operative Societies Act, 2002.
4. Any other incidental or consequential issue as deemed necessary by the Committee for its consideration.

The Committee envisioned co-operatives as primarily, autonomous, economic institutions of user members. It saw them as self-reliant and self-sustaining institutions functioning in a free, fair and transparent manner in keeping with the principles and values of the co-operative movement.

Summary Recommendations of the Committee are given below:

1. Considering the importance of a progressive and enabling legislation, which provides a level playing field for co-operatives with other corporate entities, the law enacted in each State should be amended to truly reflect the letter and spirit of the Model Co-operatives Act proposed by the Choudhary Brahm Parkash Committee Report. Even in States where a parallel law has been enacted, considering its poor utility and problems faced, a single enabling law be enacted, which is member-centric and based on co-operative principles, replacing the existing State Acts. The laws enacted with the Model Co-operatives Act as the basis should also consider the following:

- With a view to enhance member participation in co-operatives and enable them to do away with non-user members, the Acts must provide for a definition of *active member*, right to vote and contest only to active members and an enabling provision for speedy exit of non-user members.
- In order to improve the effectiveness of Boards particularly their trusteeship role and fiduciary responsibilities, ensure accountability and professionalization of the organization, the laws should provide for clearly defined roles and responsibilities of the co-operative's board vis-à-vis that of paid executives/managers and a fair but enforceable provision for fiduciary responsibility as provided in the Companies Act.
- With a view to build in professionalism, the Acts should provide for cooption of experts/subject matter specialists.

- Considering the need to remove all such loopholes in the law, which have contributed to the politicization of co-operatives, it is necessary that the laws also provide for rotational retirement of Board members and restriction on contribution to political and religious organizations.
- Keeping in view the need of co-operatives, which have already received equity contribution from the government, the laws should also provide for repatriation of government equity and where co-operatives are unable to return the government equity, they may enter into an MoU with the co-operative agreeing to such conditions that the government may stipulate.
- In order to enhance competitiveness, the laws should enable co-operatives to decide their organizational structure and staffing including recruitment policies, service conditions and remuneration.

2. State Governments should put in place a policy framework for facilitating the functioning of co-operatives with free and fair means, in no less equal terms with any other organization engaged in economic activities.
3. States should refrain from deputing officers to occupy key positions in co-operatives except on an explicit request from a co-operative and ensure that the officers if deputed to hold key positions are given a minimum tenure of three years.
4. Utility of various tiers of the co-operative structure be examined in each case and actions be taken for de-layering wherever the structures are not found to be cost effective.
5. Co-operatives should undertake member awareness and education programmes on a continuing basis in order to sensitize members regarding their rights, responsibilities/obligations in respect of the organization to which they belong and make special efforts to facilitate women and youth participation in co-operatives.

6. A scheme of Central Government and State Government budgetary provision for soft loans to farmers for share capital participation should be considered seriously.
7. Retained earnings in co-operatives are the most important form of collective capital. However, if a substantial portion of retained earnings is taken away in the form of income tax, the rate of accretion to the reserves becomes much slower, affecting the health of the co-operative and its growth. Full income tax exemption is, therefore, recommended for all co-operative societies. This will be a major incentive for the co-operatives to strengthen their capital base.
8. The share of co-operative banks in rural credit has been steadily declining and is around 18 percent. Co-operative banks presently depend for their activities on their own funds which are very limited and refinance from NABARD. Since adequate refinance through NABARD cannot be relied upon and many of the co-operative banks are weak and unable to raise funds from the market, there is a strong need for an alternative organizational set up to mobilize funds and to bridge the systematic gap in the co-operative credit and banking structure.
9. Co-operatives in various countries have adopted different strategies to augment their equity. The system of tapping share capital from non-members through different classes of shares or special purpose vehicles is also prevalent. Depending upon the business of the co-operative, financial instruments need to be developed for raising capital.

3.31 Summing Up

Co-operatives in India came into being as a result of the Government taking cognizance of the agricultural conditions that prevailed during the latter part of the 19th century and the absence of institutional arrangements for finance to agriculturists, which had resulted in mounting distress and discontent. Small, locally-worked institutions, co-operative in form, which could ensure security and facility for providing credit, were seen as the answer to this situation. However, subsequent events during both pre- and post-Independence period have led to a vast growth of co-operatives covering various sectors of the Indian economy.

Given the vast network of co-operatives in the country and their diverse problems, the task of strengthening and streamlining their functioning is indeed daunting. The situation is further complicated by the fact that co-operatives is a State subject under the Constitution of India and State co-operative laws and their implementation differs vastly. Changes in political authority at State level have, over the years at different times, resulted in wholesale supersession of co-operative institutions in many States vitiating their continued functioning as democratically elected co-operative institutions.

In the ultimate analysis, it cannot be ignored that while the co-operative route is a dignified way of growth for all, it is particularly so for the marginalized segments of the country, offering the small man as it does the chance to enter a world of bigness.

Although presently the globalized production systems are very different, the basic issues remain the same—markets that serve only sectarian interest, large masses remaining impoverished, capital gaining advantage over labour and a State which seems to be increasingly supportive of a free market. In the Indian context, it is pertinent to mention that a large segment of the population continues to depend on agriculture and agriculture-related sectors of the economy. As such co-operatives are all the more relevant in the current context.

The preoccupation of the government with the co-operative sector and its potential for bringing about development, right up to the 1990s, resulted in an increase in the number of co-operatives and their contribution, making the Indian co-operative movement one of the largest movements of its kind in the world. Though India can claim to have the world's largest and most diverse co-operative movement, barring some exceptions, co-operatives in general are fraught with a number of problems and challenges. Apart from certain inherent weaknesses, they are constrained by the overwhelming role of the government as well as prescriptive and restrictive legislations and have been unable to retain an autonomous and democratic character. Co-operation is a state subject under the Constitution of India and state-wise variations exist in terms of policies and practices, impacting upon the growth of co-operatives.

4

Agricultural Credit and Rural Co-operatives

Rural indebtedness is noted as a major reason for the spurt in farmer suicides during recent times across a number of states. In most, if not all, such cases, the economic status of the suicide victim was very poor, being small and marginal farmers. After the Green Revolution, agricultural activities have become cash-based individual enterprises requiring high investment in modern inputs and wage labour. This is evident from the list of states with high incidence of farmer suicides, which are not necessarily backward or predominantly agrarian or with low income. Increased liberalization and globalisation have in fact led to a shift in cropping pattern from staple crops to cash crops like oilseeds and cotton, requiring high investment in modern inputs and wage labour, and increasing credit needs but when the prices decline farmers have no means to supplement their incomes.

4.1 Credit and Agricultural Development

Being the backbone of the Indian economy, agriculture has all along been treated as a priority sector for the allocation of institutional credit. The low growth rate of agriculture in the past few years has further strengthened the channels of credit flow to this sector.

Agricultural production in India depends upon millions of small farmers. It is the intensity of their effort and the efficiency of their technique that will help in raising yields per acre. Because of inadequate financial resources and absence of timely credit facilities at reasonable rates, many of the farmers, even though otherwise willing, are unable to go in for improved seeds and manures or to introduce better methods or techniques. It is, therefore, of the utmost importance that the financial requirements of the farmers are adequately met.

Provision of sufficient and timely credit at fair rates of interest has, therefore, to be considered as an integral part of agricultural development. Assistance rendered by way of credit has, however, to be related to specific items of productive work or of essential costs of cultivation. Following guidelines from the RBI, commercial banks are increasingly devoting attention to agricultural sector to meet its credit needs.

Agricultural growth is crucial for alleviating rural poverty. Access to institutional credit to more farmers and appropriate quantity and quality of agricultural credit are crucial for realising the full potential of agriculture as a profitable activity.

The Government has taken many policy initiatives for strengthening farm credit delivery system for providing credit at affordable rates of interest to support the resource requirements of the agricultural sector. The emphasis of these initiatives has been on providing timely and adequate credit support to farmers with particular focus on small and marginal farmers and weaker sections of society to enable them to adopt modern technology and improved agricultural practices for increasing agricultural production and productivity. The policy essentially lays emphasis on augmenting credit flow at the ground level through credit planning, adoption of region specific strategies and rationalization of lending policies and procedures and bringing down the rate of interest on farm loan.

4.2 Credit Needs of the Indian Farmers

Need for agricultural credit arises because modern farm technology is costly and the personal resources of the farmers are inadequate. Provision of agricultural credit, as an input, is essential for widespread use of improved agricultural methods.

Credit requirements of the farmers may be classified (a) on the basis of purpose, and (b) on the basis of time. They need credit for productive as well as for unproductive purposes.

Productive purposes include all such activities which help in the improvement of agricultural productivity such as purchase of inputs and permanent improvements in land. Unproductive credit needs include celebration of marriages and other social and religious functions and litigation.

Finance required for productive purposes can be divided broadly into the following categories:

- Short-term (for periods up to 15 months).
- Medium-term (from 15 months up to 5 years).
- Long-term (above 5 years).

Short-term loans are required for purchasing seeds, manures and fertilizers or for meeting labour charges etc. These are expected to be repaid after the harvest.

Medium-term loans are granted for purposes such as sinking of wells, purchase of bullocks, pumping plants and other improved implements etc.

Loans repayable over a longer period (*i.e.* above 5 years) are classified as long-term loans. These are utilised for payment of old debts, purchase of the heavier machines, making permanent improvements and increasing the size of the holding.

4.3 Sources of Credit for the Farmers

Sources of agricultural credit are grouped into two categories: (a) institutional sources and (b) non-institutional sources. Institutional sources include co-operative societies, commercial banks and other government agencies. Non-institutional sources comprise moneylenders, landlords, relatives etc.

Till Independence in 1947, money lenders and the landlords were the principal sources of rural credit. Over the years, the operations of moneylenders have declined in view of debt relief legislations, the system of licensing moneylenders and restrictions on the use and transfer of land as security. Similarly, the abolition of all privileged tenures, both in zamindari and ryotwari areas, has discouraged investment by the landlords and larger cultivators.

4.3.1 Institutional Arrangements: Agricultural credit is disbursed through a Multi-agency network comprising of commercial banks, regional rural banks and co-operatives. With their vast network (covering almost all the villages in the country), wider coverage and outreach extending to the remotest part of country, the co-operative credit institutions, both in short and long-term structure are the main institutional mechanism for dispensation of agricultural credit.

4.3.2 Moneylenders: It is true that the institutional sources of credit have weakened the hold of moneylenders on the rural masses. However, the benefits of institutional credit have not percolated to all sections of rural population. Landless workers and marginal farmers have not benefited adequately due to their ignorance of new sources of credit and also on account of their weak repaying capacity. These underprivileged rural sections still depend on the moneylenders and suffer their exploitative practices.

Historically, moneylenders have played a significant role in meeting the credit needs of the rural producers. With stringent laws against money lending and the phenomenal growth of the formal credit delivery system, it was thought that money lenders would soon be out of business. Instead they have been in the business of lending in several disguises.

There are two types of moneylenders in rural areas: (a) agriculturist moneylenders who carry on the business of money lending along with farming, and (b) professional moneylenders whose only occupation is money lending. Although the relative importance of moneylenders has declined over the years, they are still an important source of credit for the rural people, particularly the small farmers and the artisans.

Moneylenders are popular because, unlike government agencies, they give credit for every purpose. They are easily approachable by the credit seekers and there are not many formalities in transacting a loan. However, the malpractices adopted by the moneylenders to exploit the needy farmers cannot be overlooked. These malpractices pertain to charging of high rate of interest and adopting unfair means in the maintenance of accounts.

Agricultural growth is crucial for alleviating rural poverty. Access to institutional credit to more farmers and appropriate quantity and quality of agricultural credit are crucial for realising the full potential of agriculture as a profitable activity.

Provision of sufficient and timely credit at fair rates of interest has, therefore, to be considered as an integral part of agricultural development. Assistance rendered by way of credit has, however, to be related to specific items of productive work or of essential costs of cultivation.

4.4 Co-operative Credit Societies

These societies form an integral part of the rural credit system in India. They are the main source of institutional credit to the farmers. These societies are chiefly responsible for breaking the monopoly of moneylenders in providing credit to the agriculturists. There are around 1 lakh such societies in the country at present. In spite of their suitability and useful role in building up a just socio-economic rural life, co-operative societies suffer from various weaknesses. The heavy overdues of co-operative societies are a cause for concern. The rising overdues have reduced the borrowing and lending activities of these societies. Moreover, these societies have paid inadequate attention to the needs of landless workers and rural artisans. Influential people in the villages have been the main beneficiaries of co-operative credit. Of late, there has been a tendency on the part of political leadership to write-off loans of the farmers. The RBI has repeatedly expressed concern in this regard because non-repayment of loans by the existing borrowers can adversely affect recycling of funds and the credit chances of the prospective borrowers.

4.5 Co-operative Banks

Co-operative banks in India are more than 100 years old. These banks came into existence with the enactment of the Agricultural Credit Co-operative Societies Act in 1904. Co-operative banks form an integral part of the banking system in India. These banks operate mainly for the benefit of rural areas, particularly the agricultural sector. Co-operative banks mobilise deposits and supply agricultural and rural credit with a wider outreach. They are the main source of institutional credit to the farmers. Co-operative banks are chiefly responsible for breaking the monopoly of moneylenders in providing credit to agriculturists. They have also been an important instrument for various development schemes, particularly subsidy-based programmes for the poor. Co-operative banks operate for non-agricultural sector also but their role is small.

Though much smaller as compared to scheduled commercial banks, co-operative banks constitute an important segment of the Indian banking system. They have an extensive branch network and reach out to people in remote areas. They have traditionally played an important role in creating banking habits among the lower and middle-income groups and in strengthening the rural credit delivery system.

Unfortunately, financial reforms have not impacted the functioning of co-operative banks. This was brought out clearly in the following observation of the Reserve Bank of India, "Since the introduction of reforms, there has been very little perceptible improvement in either stability or efficiency of co-operative banks. In particular, the asset quality and profitability of scheduled Urban Co-operative Banks (UCBs) showed some deterioration in the reform period. Positive impact of reforms, as has been witnessed in the case of commercial banking sector, may take longer to get manifested for co-operative banks given the late start of the reform process in this sector." [1]

The financial reforms process initiated in 1991 has tried to achieve regulatory convergence among various financial intermediaries in view of their systemic importance. Therefore, the basic objectives and instruments of reforms for co-operative banks have been the same as for State Co-operative Banks (SCBs). However, given the special characteristics of co-operative banks, they have been extended certain dispensations in terms of pace and sequencing of reforms.

4.5.1 Classification of Co-operative Banks: The co-operative banking structure in India comprises urban co-operative banks and rural co-operative credit institutions.

A. Urban Co-operative Banks (UCBs): UCBs consist of a single tier, *viz.* primary co-operative banks, commonly referred to as urban co-operative banks.

B. Rural Co-operatives: Based on the nature of their lending operations, rural credit co-operatives have traditionally been bifurcated into two parallel wings: short-term and long-term.

4.6 Rural Co-operatives

4.6.1 Short-term Rural Co-operatives: The short-term provide crop and other working capital loans to farmers and rural artisans primarily for short-term purposes. These credit institutions have a three-tier federal structure. (a) At the apex of the system is a State Co-operative Bank (SCB) in each State. (b) At the middle (or district) level, there are Central Co-operative Banks (CCBs) also known as district co-operative banks. (c) At the lowest (or village) level are the Primary Agricultural Credit Societies (PACS). The smaller States and Union Territories (UTs) have a two-tier structure with SCBs directly meeting the credit requirements of PACS.

A. State Co-operative Bank (SCB): SCB is the highest agency of the three-tier co-operative credit structure in a state. It serves as a link between RBI and the CCBs and PACS. The RBI provides credit to lower level co-operatives through the SCB. This function of the RBI has now been taken over by NABARD. The SCB also acts as a *balancing centre* for CCBs in the sense that surplus funds of some CCBs are made available to other needy CCBs. The SCB exercises general control and supervision over CCBs and PACS.

B. Central Co-operative Banks (CCBs): These banks act as a link between the SCB and the PACS. The main task of CCBs is to lend money to affiliated village primary societies. The CCBs are expected to attract deposits from the general public.

C. Primary Agricultural Credit Societies (PACS): These societies form the basic unit of the co-operative credit system in India. These voluntary societies based on the principle of one man one vote have posed challenge to the exploitative practices of the village moneylenders. The farmers and other small-time borrowers come in direct contact with these societies. The success of the co-operative credit movement depends largely on the strength of these village level societies. There were 94,647 PACS in the country as on March 31, 2010.

As a result of the expansion of the activities of PACS, the role of moneylenders in providing credit to agriculturists has decreased over the years. A major objective of PACS is to serve the needs of weaker sections of the society. For this purpose, the people with limited means, particularly scheduled castes and scheduled tribes, are encouraged to become members of these societies. Government has promoted multi-purpose societies in tribal areas for the benefit of people living there.

4.6.2 Long-term Rural Co-operatives: The long-term provide typically medium and long-term loans for making investments in agriculture, rural industries and, in the recent period, housing. Generally, these co-operatives have two tiers, *viz.*

A. State Co-operative Agriculture and Rural Development Banks (SCARDBs): These banks operate at the State level.

B. Primary Co-operative Agriculture and Rural Development Banks (PCARDBs): These banks operate at the *taluka/tehsil* level.

4.7 Rural Co-operatives: History and Recent Policy Measures

Rural credit co-operatives in India were originally envisaged as a mechanism for pooling the resources of people with small means and providing them with access to different financial services. Democratic in features, the movement was also an effective instrument for development of degraded waste lands, increasing productivity, providing food security, generating employment opportunities in rural areas and ensuring social and economic justice to the poor and vulnerable.

The history of the co-operative credit movement in India can be traced back to 1904 when the Co-operative Societies Act was passed. In 1919, *co-operation* became a provincial subject. The Co-operative Planning Committee, 1945 found that a large number of co-operatives were "saddled with the problem of frozen assets because of heavy overdues in repayment."

The co-operative banks in India play an important role in catering to the banking needs of the rural population. Soon after Independence in 1947, the inadequacy of rural credit engaged the attention of the Government of India and the RBI. The agricultural credit system as it has emerged over the years is the result of both evolution and intervention, and symbolises the nation's response to the dissatisfaction with the discredited colonial credit delivery system.

The Reserve Bank of India Act, 1934 has specific provisions relating to agricultural credit. Section 54 of the RBI Act specifically authorised the creation of an Agricultural Credit Department within the RBI to deal not only with the rural credit but also with the long-term finance including refinance. Section 17 of the Act empowered it to provide agricultural credit through state co-operative banks or any other banks engaged in the business of agricultural credit.

The foundation for building a broader credit infrastructure for rural credit was laid down by the All India Rural Credit Survey (1954). The Committee of Direction that conducted the survey recommended the creation of National Agricultural Credit Fund, which was subsequently created by the RBI. The Agricultural Refinance Corporation (ARC) set up by the RBI in 1963 provided funds by way of refinance, but credit co-operatives still did not function too well. Decentralised credit planning through the Lead Bank Scheme was also introduced to spearhead the credit allocation for, *inter alia*, agricultural lending. In order to emphasise the developmental and promotional role assigned to the ARC in addition to refinancing, the ARC was renamed as the Agricultural Refinance and Development Corporation (ARDC) in 1975.

Despite all these efforts, the flow of credit to the agricultural sector failed to exhibit any appreciable improvement as the co-operatives lacked resources to meet the expected demand. To solve these problems, the Regional Rural Banks (RRBs) were set up in 1975. In order to strengthen the institutional credit for agriculture and rural development, National Bank for Agriculture and Rural Development (NABARD) was set up on July 12, 1982. On its establishment, NABARD took over the entire functions of the ARDC, the refinancing functions of the RBI in relation to co-operatives and Regional Rural Banks (RRBs).

The rural credit co-operative system has served as an important instrument of credit delivery in rural and agricultural areas. The separate structure of rural co-operative sector for long-term and short-term loans has enabled these institutions to develop as specialised institutions for rural credit delivery. At the same time, their federal structure has helped in providing support structure for the guidance and critical financing for the lower structure. These institutions had wide outreach with as many as 94,647 primary agricultural co-operative societies (PACS), the grass root organisation of the rural co-operative banking structure, operating in the country at end-March 2010.

The rural co-operative credit institutions, however, are beset with many problems which include the following.

1. Low resource base.
2. High dependence on refinancing agencies.
3. Lack of diversification.
4. Huge accumulated losses.
5. Persistent NPAs.
6. Low recovery levels.
7. Various other types of organisational weaknesses.

NABARD and the RBI, therefore, have been taking several supervisory and developmental measures in consultation with the Government of India for the revival of weak institutions and orderly growth of this important segment of the financial sector.

4.8 Primary Agricultural Credit Societies (PACS)

Primary agricultural credit societies (PACS) are the foundation of the co-operative credit system on which the superstructure of the short-term co-operative credit system rests. It is the PACS which directly interface with individual farmers, provide short-term and medium-term credit, supply agricultural inputs, distribute consumer articles and arrange for marketing of produce of its members through a co-operative marketing society.

PACS continue to rely heavily on external support and have not yet been able to become self-reliant in respect of resources through deposit mobilisation and internal accruals, affecting their growth and expansion of business activities.

PACS need to function as viable units responsive to the needs, aspirations and convenience of its members, particularly those belonging to the more vulnerable sections of the society. They must function effectively as well-managed and multi-purpose institutions mobilising the savings of the rural people and providing a package of services including credit, supply of agricultural inputs and implements, consumer goods, marketing services and technical guidance with focus on weaker sections.

Some of the critical challenges facing primary level co-operative credit institutions, apart from improving resource mobilisation, are the following.

1. Increasing diversification in business portfolio.
2. Improving volume of business.
3. Arresting decline in membership by the borrowers.
4. Reducing cost of management.
5. Correcting imbalances in loans outstanding.
6. Improving skills of the staff and imparting professionalisation.
7. Strengthening management information system (MIS).
8. Reducing involvement in non/less profitable business.

4.9 Problems of Rural Co-operatives

Rural co-operatives form an integral part of the rural credit system in India. They are the main source of institutional credit to the farmers. These societies are chiefly responsible for breaking the monopoly of moneylenders in providing credit to the agriculturists. There are around 94,647 lakh such societies in the country at present.

Despite the phenomenal outreach and volume of operations, the financial health of a very large proportion of rural credit co-operatives has deteriorated significantly. The institutions are beset with problems like low resource base, high dependence on external sources of funding, excessive governmental control, dual control, huge accumulated losses, imbalances, poor business diversification, low recovery etc. These institutions do not, therefore, inspire confidence among their existing and potential members, depositors, borrowers and lenders. Thus, there is a need to find ways for strengthening the co-operative movement and making it a well-managed and vibrant medium to serve the credit needs of rural India, especially the small and marginal farmers.

Moreover, these societies have paid inadequate attention to the needs of landless workers and rural artisans. Influential people in the villages have been the main beneficiaries of co-operative credit. Of late, there has been a tendency on the part of political leadership to write-off loans of the farmers. The RBI has repeatedly expressed concern in this regard because non-repayment of loans by the existing borrowers can adversely affect recycling of funds and the credit chances of the prospective borrowers. A national approach on this issue is required so that co-operative credit system may fulfil the task assigned to it.

It is part of a historic policy infirmity which allowed co-operatives to be treated as *refinance windows* instead of incentivising them into becoming genuine thrift and credit institutions.

The rural co-operative credit institutions are beset with many problems which include the following:

1. Low resource base.
2. High dependence on refinancing agencies.
3. Lack of diversification.
4. Huge accumulated losses.
5. Persistent non-performing assets (NPAs).
6. Low recovery levels.
7. Various other types of organisational weaknesses.

NABARD and the RBI, therefore, have been taking several supervisory and developmental measures in consultation with the Government of India for the revival of weak institutions and orderly growth of this important segment of the financial sector.

4.10 Task Force on Revival of Rural Co-operative Credit Institutions, 2005

The Government of India had constituted this Task Force (Chairman: A. Vaidyanathan) in August 2004 to propose an action plan for reviving the rural co-operative banking institutions and suggest an appropriate regulatory framework for these institutions. The Task Force in its Report submitted to the Central Government on February 15, 2005 made several recommendations to strengthen the rural co-operative credit structure in the country.

The major recommendations of the Task Force were as under:

1. Co-operative Credit Structure (CCS) is impaired in governance, managerial and financial fronts and hence needs to be revived and restructured.
2. Financial restructuring should be contingent on commitment to and implementation of legal and institutional reforms by the State Governments.
3. Financial assistance should be made available for (a) wiping out accumulated losses, (b) covering invoked but unpaid guarantees given by the State Governments, (c) increasing the capital to a specified minimum level, (d) retiring Government share capital and (e) technical assistance.
4. Availability of financial assistance from the Government of India should be strictly subject to legal and institutional reforms in the co-operative sector to ensure that the co-operatives become truly democratic and member-driven. These reforms should include: (a) ensuring full voting membership rights on all users of financial services including depositors, (b) removing state intervention in administrative and financial matters in co-operatives, (c) removing provision for Government equity and participation in the Boards of Co-operatives, (d) withdrawing restrictive orders on financial matters and (e) permitting co-operatives the freedom to take loans from any financial institution and not necessarily from only the upper tier and similarly place their deposits with any financial institution of their choice.
5. The Task Force also recommended certain major amendments to the provisions of the Banking Regulation

Act, 1949 enabling removal of dual control and bringing the co-operatives under the regulatory control of the RBI. These included: (a) all co-operative banks should be on par with the commercial banks as far as regulatory norms are concerned (b) RBI should prescribe *fit and proper* criteria for election to the Boards of Co-operative Banks, (c) RBI should prescribe certain criteria for professionals to be on the Boards of Co-operative Banks, (d) CEOs of the co-operative banks should be appointed by the respective banks themselves and (e) co-operatives, other than co-operative banks as approved by the RBI, should not accept non-voting member deposits. Such co-operatives should also not use words such as *bank*, *banking*, *banker* or any other derivative of the word *bank* in their registered name.

6. Total financial assistance was estimated tentatively at ₹ 14,839 crore. The Task Force, however, recommended a special audit to ascertain the exact requirement of assistance. The financial assistance should be shared by the Government of India, State Governments and the CCS, based on the origin of losses within a flexible matrix.
7. NABARD should be designated as the nodal *implementing and pass through agency* to co-ordinate and monitor the progress of the programme representing the Government of India. NABARD should prepare model MoUs, model balance sheet proforma for PACS and CCBs.

4.11 NABARD and the Co-operative Sector

National Bank for Agriculture and Rural Development (NABARD) provides refinance to state co-operative agriculture and rural development banks (SCARDBs), state co-operative banks (SCBs), regional rural banks (RRBs) and other financial institutions approved by the RBI. The ultimate beneficiaries of refinance from NABARD could be individuals, partnership concerns, companies, State-owned corporations or co-operative societies.

4.11.1 Credit Extended by NABARD: NABARD

provides short-term credit facilities to SCBs in respect of eligible CCBs for the following purposes:

1. Financing seasonal agricultural operations.
2. Marketing of crops.
3. Pisciculture activities.
4. Production and marketing activities of primary weavers/other industrial co-operative societies.
5. Labour contract/forest labour co-operative societies.
6. Individual rural artisans through PCS.
7. Procurement, stocking and distribution of chemical fertilisers.
8. Approved agricultural, allied and other marketing activities.

Besides short-term credit limits are also sanctioned to SCBs on behalf of apex/regional weavers/other industrial societies for financing procurement and marketing and trading-in-yarn.

Short-term limits are also provided to RRBs for financing seasonal agricultural operations, marketing of crops and pisciculture activities.

Medium-term facilities are also provided to SCBs and RRBs for converting short-term into medium-term loans and for approved agricultural investments.

Long-term loans are provided to the State Governments for contributing to the share capital of co-operative credit institutions.

In pursuance of the announcement made by the Finance Minister in June 2004 for enhancing the credit flow to the agriculture sector, NABARD advised SCBs, CCBs and RRBs on the measures to be taken under various schemes to give relief to farmers. It was apprehended that the implementation of these measures coupled with providing conversion/rescheduled loans to farmers may result in a liquidity problem for co-operative banks and RRBs, impairing their ability to provide fresh loans and achieve the desired growth rate during the year. In order to mitigate this,

NABARD introduced a liquidity support scheme during 2004-05 for these institutions. SCBs were sanctioned a liquidity support of ₹ 1,770 crore during 2004-05. NABARD also sanctioned long-term loans to 9 State Governments amounting to ₹ 39 crore as contribution to the share capital of co-operative credit institutions.

4.12 Advisory Committee on the Flow of Credit to Agriculture and Related Activities from the Banking System (Chairman: V.S. Vyas), 2004

As indicated in its mid-term review of November 2003, the RBI constituted this Advisory Committee which submitted its interim report in April 2004 and the final report in June 2004. It made the following recommendations:

1. A review of mandatory lending to agriculture by commercial banks to enlarge direct lending programmes.
2. Public and private sector banks should increase their direct agricultural lending to 12 percent of net bank credit in the next two years and to 13.5 percent two years thereafter, within the overall limit of 18.0 percent of total agricultural lending.
3. Banks should increase their disbursements to small and marginal farmers under Special Agricultural Credit Plan (SACP) to 40 percent by March 2007.
4. SACP to be restricted to direct lending and extended to private sector banks.
5. Reduction in cost of agricultural credit by enhancing the cost effectiveness of agricultural loans.
6. NPA norms for agricultural credit to be aligned with crop seasons. Loans for allied activities to be classified as NPA after 180 days of default. Credit flow to small borrowers to be improved through reduction in cost of borrowing, revolving credit packages, procedural simplification, involvement of Panchayati Raj institutions and micro finance.
7. SAA to be modified to remove rigidities. SAA to be

mandatory only for Government sponsored programmes and the format of village surveys to be changed in view of current realities.

Based on the recommendations contained in the interim report of the Vyas Committee, the RBI, in its Annual Policy Statement for 2004-05, announced a number of measures to improve credit delivery to agriculture. These included, (a) treating loans to storage units designed to store agricultural products, irrespective of location, as indirect credit to agriculture, (b) treating investment by banks in securitised assets representing lending to agriculture as direct (indirect) lending to agriculture and (c) waiver of margin/security requirement for agricultural loans up to ₹ 50,000 and in case of agri-business and agri-clinics for loans up to ₹ 5 lakh. In addition, RBI also aligned repayment dates with harvesting of crops by treating loans granted for short duration crops as NPA, if the instalment of the principal or interest thereon remains unpaid for two crop seasons beyond the due date. Loans granted for long duration crops are treated as an NPA, only if the instalment of the principal or interest thereon remains unpaid for one crop season beyond the due date.

As recommended by the Advisory Committee, RBI announced that micro finance institutions would not be permitted to accept public deposits, unless they comply with the extant regulatory framework. The recommendation relating to service area approach (SAA) was accepted and an announcement to this effect was made in the RBI's mid-term review of Annual Policy Statement for 2004-05.

In connection with the implementation of the recommendations of the Vyas Committee, the *Economic Survey, 2005-06* observed, "Continuing its endeavour to enhance the flow of credit to agriculture by removing delivery bottlenecks, the RBI, together with NABARD, implemented most of the recommendations of the Advisory Committee on Flow of Credit to Agriculture and Related Activities from the Banking System (Chairman: V.S. Vyas). Out of 99 recommendations made by the Committee, 33 were accepted and implemented by October 2005. These related to the following matters.

1. Procedural modifications and rationalisation of systems and procedures.
2. Tie-ups with related farm machinery manufacturers by banks.
3. Use of a flexible revolving credit limit to small borrowers of production or investment loans for meeting temporary shortfalls in family cash flows.
4. Co-opting joint liability group (JLG) and self-help group (SHG) approaches in addressing issues relating to financing oral lessees.
5. Addressing delays/refusal in opening savings bank accounts of SHGs.
6. Improving staffing in the rural areas to promote retail lending to agriculture.
7. Use of individual volunteers, farmers' clubs or NGOs/SHGs as direct selling agents.
8. Building synergy between good working primary agricultural credit societies and commercial banks.
9. Use of IT in rural branches.
10. Working out appropriate incentive structure for prompt repayment.
11. Making the rates of interest on small loans reasonable.
12. Improving the efficiency of credit delivery to small borrowers and association with contract farming.

Furthermore, some of the recommendations, *viz.*, stepping up credit for marketing and introduction of negotiable warehousing receipt system, support of State Governments for collecting dues, reduction of stamp duty on agricultural loans, legal amendments to Agricultural Produce Marketing Committee (APMC) Act by the State Governments, amendment to NABARD Act for operational autonomy, which were referred to the Government of India for examination, have been accepted." [2]

4.13 Expert Group on Investment Credit in Agriculture (Chairman: Y.S.P. Thorat), 2005

With a view to increasing the flow of credit to agriculture, the RBI set up this Expert Group to formulate a strategy for increasing investment credit in agriculture. The Group in its Report submitted in June 2005 identified several factors which constrain growth in investment in agriculture. These included the following.

1. Meagre growth in minor irrigation and farm mechanization.
2. Declining public sector investment.
3. Limited credit absorptive capacity.
4. Lack of effective mechanism for technology transfer and poor extension services.
5. Inadequate extension services.
6. Limited infrastructure for agro processing, storage, warehousing, value addition and marketing.
7. Restrictions on purchases outside the *mandis*.
8. Weather aberrations and output price fluctuations.
9. Inadequate risk mitigation mechanism.
10. Non-availability of land records.

The Group emphasised the need to accelerate investment in agriculture in order to achieve the desired level of growth. It also highlighted the need for investments to be appropriately structured, timed and well implemented in order to attain maximum effectiveness.

Major recommendations of the Group are set out below.

1. In view of various changes in the Indian rural canvas over the past few years, there is need for a shift in the thrust areas for investment credit to agriculture. Apart from the traditional investments such as land development and irrigation, increased focus needs to be accorded to the entire supply chain management of agriculture products, reform of agriculture markets and public management in agricultural infrastructure.
2. State Governments need to lay emphasis on legal

provisions/computerisation of land records, legal support for recovery, reforms in agricultural marketing, improving credit absorptive capacity through supporting infrastructure, strengthening infrastructure, improving extension network and developing marketing links.

3. NABARD should take special steps to facilitate capacity building of credit institutions in appraisal skill, particularly in North Eastern States, and design appropriate products for financing rural infrastructure projects outside the RIDF by mobilising resources from the market or banks at competitive rates of interest.
4. Water management policies and investment in water conservation be designed jointly by the State Governments and banks for improving productivity in agriculture.
5. The State Governments and NABARD should make investments in participatory community projects and in soil treatment to make wasteland and fallow land cultivable.
6. With a view to strengthening the institutional credit mechanism, short-term credit be integrated with term credit and efforts be made to reach the 'unreached' areas, promote supplementary credit delivery channels, outsource monitoring services, provide loan support for diversified agriculture, review HR policies, share the pool of technical expertise and make use of the model bankable projects prepared by NABARD.
7. The RBI along with banks could adopt agency models for credit delivery.
8. Government of India/State Governments and organisations engaged in agricultural research and development (R&D) to reorient R&D activities.
9. To mitigate the risk in financing of agriculture, the Group suggested several measures. These included:

- developing suitable financial products and commodity exchanges;
- allowing banks to operate on behalf of farmers and

participate in commodity futures;
- establishing a risk fund for fragile agriculture;
- designing special risk mitigation packages for low asset-based borrowers;
- using warehousing receipts with price hedging instruments;
- adopting technology for dissemination of market intelligence;
- sharing borrower information; and
- financing value chain by banks/through RIDF.

4.14 Working Group on Warehouse Receipts and Commodity Futures, 2005

In pursuance of the announcement made in the Mid-term Review of Annual Policy Statement for the year 2004-05, the RBI constituted this Working Group (Chairman: Prashant Saran) with a view to examining the role of banks in providing loans against warehouse receipts and evolving a framework for participation of banks in the commodity futures market. The Working Group in its Report submitted in April 2005 recommended that banks may be permitted to offer futures-based products to farmers in order to enable them to hedge against price risk.

The Working Group was entrusted with the task of evolving broad guidelines, criteria, limits, risk management system as also a legal framework for facilitating participation of banks in commodity (derivative) market and use of warehouse receipts in financing of agriculture. The major recommendations of the Group are set out below.

1. As banks at present are not allowed to deal in goods, the Central Government may issue a Notification under clause (o) of sub-section (1) of Section 6 of the Banking Regulation Act, 1949 permitting banks to deal in the business of agricultural commodities, including derivatives.
2. Considering the experience that banks already have in

dealing with agricultural commodities, it would be prudent at the current stage to permit banks to deal with derivatives in agricultural commodities only.

3. A system needs to be evolved by which warehouse receipts become freely transferable between holders as it would reduce transaction costs and increase usage.
4. An umbrella structure, which may act as a Closed User Group (CUG) for everyone engaged in the agricultural commodities business, be created. The umbrella structure is envisaged as an electronic platform that would offer straight through processing for everyone connected with commodities. There can be more than one CUG which would be subject to regulation and supervision by a regulatory authority such as Forward Markets Commission (FMC).
5. Proprietary positions in agricultural commodity derivatives could be used by banks to mitigate their risk in lending to farmers. To achieve this, they will have to buy options on futures.
6. The Forward Contracts (Regulation) Act, 1952 be amended and the FMC should evolve a framework for introducing "options" trading in agricultural commodities in India.
7. Banks may be permitted to have independent proprietary position in commodity futures linked in a macro way to their credit portfolio. However, suitable risk control measures may have to be adopted by banks.
8. At present, purely cash-settled contracts are not available in India. The banks trading or dealing in commodity contracts should, therefore, be prepared to make or accept delivery of physical goods. While no restriction may be placed in this regard, banks may be persuaded to preferably close their positions and cash settle the contracts.
9. Banks may be granted general permission to become professional clearing members of commodity exchanges

subject to the condition that they do not assume any exposure risk on account of offering clearing services to their trading clients. At least for the present, banks may not be permitted to act as trading members in the commodity exchanges.

10. While banks may continue to hold their equity stake in the commodity exchanges in order to provide them financial strength and stability, they may reduce/divest their equity holding to a maximum permitted level of 5 percent over a period of time so as to avoid any conflict of interest.

4.15 Regulatory Framework and Supervision

4.15.1 Asset Classification for State Government Guaranteed Advances: Revised guidelines on asset classification norms for State Government guaranteed exposures (i.e. advances and investments), as applicable to commercial banks, were issued to SCBs and CCBs on January 20, 2005 which are to be implemented in a phased manner. Accordingly, it was decided to delink the asset classification and provisioning requirements in respect of State Government guaranteed loans and advances from invocation of State Government guarantee and treat such exposures for asset classification purpose in the same manner as applicable to exposures not guaranteed by the State Governments. However, with a view to enabling banks to have a smooth transition in the matter, the revised prudential norms in respect of State Government guaranteed exposures (*i.e.* both advances and investments) will be implemented in a phased manner in two stages.

With effect from the year ending March 31, 2006, State Government guaranteed advances and investments in State Government guaranteed securities would attract asset classification and provisioning norms, if interest and/or instalment of principal or any other amount due to the bank remains overdue for more than 180 days. In the second stage, which beginning from the year ending March 31, 2007, State

Government guaranteed advance and investment in State Government guaranteed securities would attract asset classification and provisioning norms, if interest and/or instalment of principal or any other amount due to the bank remains overdue for more than 90 days.

4.15.2 Additional Provisioning Requirement for NPAs: For the sake of convergence in policies governing all banks, guidelines for additional provisioning for all advances classified as *doubtful for more than three years* were issued on March 01, 2005, to be implemented in a phased manner from April 01, 2007. In terms of the guidelines, for the unsecured portion of the advance, which is not covered by the realisable value of tangible security to which the bank has a valid recourse and the realisable value is estimated on a realistic basis, provision will be to the extent of 100 percent, as hitherto. The secured portion, on the other hand, would be divided into two categories. Outstanding stock of NPAs classified as *doubtful for more than three years* as on March 31, 2007 would need to be provided for in a phased manner up to 100 percent till March 31, 2010. Also, 100 percent provisioning would need to be made for the advances classified as *doubtful for more than three years* on or after April 1, 2007.

4.15.3 Prudential Guidelines on Agricultural Advances: As mentioned in the Annual Policy Statement of the RBI for the year 2004-05, prudential norms on income recognition, asset classification and provisioning with respect to agricultural advances were modified on July 12, 2004 with a view to aligning the repayment dates with harvesting of crops. Accordingly, effective September 30, 2004 a loan granted for short duration crops is required to be treated as NPA if the instalment of the principal or interest thereon remains unpaid for two crop seasons beyond the due date. A loan granted for long duration (with crop season longer than one year) crops is required to be treated as NPA, if the instalment of principal or interest thereon remains unpaid for one crop season beyond the due date.

4.15.4 Inspections: NABARD undertakes inspection of RRBs, SCBs and CCBs in accordance with the powers vested under Section 35(6) of the Banking Regulation Act, 1949 (AACS). Besides, NABARD conducts voluntary inspection of SCARDBs, Apex Weavers' Co-operative Societies and State Co-operative Marketing Federations. The frequency of statutory/voluntary inspections by NABARD was increased from 2005-06. The statutory inspections of CCBs and RRBs with positive net worth as also the voluntary inspections of Apex Co-operative Societies/Federations would continue to be conducted once in two years. With the introduction of annual inspections, the system of conducting quick inspections has been dispensed with.

The Board of Supervision (BoS) constituted by NABARD in 1999 to provide guidance and direction on matters relating to supervision of SCBs, CCBs and RRBs meets periodically and deliberates on such issues as listed below.

1. Review of insolvent SCBs and CCBs.
2. State-wise review of the functioning of co-operative credit institutions.
3. Review of off-site supervisory system (OSS).
4. Review of frauds, misappropriation, embezzlements, and defalcations.
5. Review of progress in implementation of the recommendations of the Advisory Committee on Flow of Credit to Agriculture and Related Activities (Chairman: V.S. Vyas).
6. Review of functioning of StCBs and SCARDBs based on inspection findings.
7. Procedure for receipt and follow-up of compliance reports on inspection findings.
8. Risk management systems in co-operative banks and RRBs.
9. Review of financial position of RRBs with deposit erosion of 25 percent or more.

10. Making applicable the revised prudential norms to SCARDBs and PCARDBs.

The Board has often expressed concern over (a) deterioration in the financial position of many co-operative banks, (b) non-compliance by several banks with the provisions of Section 11(1) of the Banking Regulation Act, 1949 (AACS), relating to minimum capital requirement and (c) absence of penal provision against the banks not adhering to the RBI's guidelines for asset classification and provisioning norms.

4.16 Problem of Triangular Regulation of Rural Co-operatives

In the case of the rural banking sector, apart from the presence of the Registrar of Co-operative Societies for incorporation/registration-related regulation, banking regulation is further split between the RBI, which has the regulatory powers, and NABARD which is vested with the supervisory responsibility. The shortcomings of this segregation of regulatory and supervisory roles is compounded by the fact that NABARD has limited powers of enforcement of its supervisory findings, for which it has to depend on either its own persuasiveness or seek action through interventions by the RBI or the State Government.

The *duality of control* over the co-operative institutions is a contentious issue. The Task Force on Co-operative Credit System (Chairman: Jagdish Capoor), 1999 addressed the issue of duality of control over co-operative credit institutions and suggested to remove the overlap of controls and endowing functional autonomy and operational freedom to co-operatives. The Task Force suggested to draw an Action Plan to redefine the roles and responsibilities and areas of regulation through delegation of powers in respect of all the players in the field, *viz.* the State Government, RBI, NABARD and co-operative institutions. In view of the weaknesses persisting in the co-operative banks, a system of preparation of institution-specific development action plans and execution of Memorandum of Understanding have been initiated since 2003- 04.

4.17 Agricultural Credit: Recent Policy Announcements

Concerned over the slower growth of agriculture credit, the Government announced a comprehensive policy on June 18, 2004. The policy envisaged a 30 percent increase in credit to agriculture sector in 2004-05 over an estimated credit flow of ₹ 80,000 crore in 2003-04. The implementation of the policy was entrusted to public sector banks, private sector banks, regional rural banks (RRBs) and co-operative banks. The policy indicated that each rural and semi-urban branch of commercial banks, on an average, would take up at least two to three new investment projects in the area of plantation and horticulture, fisheries, organic farming, agro-processing, livestock, micro irrigation, sprinkler irrigation, watershed management, village pond development and other agricultural activities. NABARD was asked to advise District Level Technical Committees to review the scales of finance to meet the realistic credit needs of farmers, especially for capital intensive agricultural operations.

The Budget for 2004-05, presented in the Parliament on July 8, 2004, proposed doubling of credit to agriculture in three years and announced further measures to achieve the target growth in agricultural credit. These measures included holding the sponsor bank of each RRB squarely responsible for the performance of RRB under its control and an incentive scheme under which RRBs, adopting new governance standards and abiding by prudential regulations, qualified for receiving funds from the Government for their restructuring. The Budget proposed setting up of a Task Force to examine the reforms required in the co-operative banking system including the appropriate regulatory regime.

Consequent upon above mentioned policy measures, the flow of institutional credit to the agricultural sector has increased significantly in recent years (Table 4.1).

Table 4.1: Flow of Institutional Credit to Agriculture and Allied Activities

(₹ crore)

Agency	2006-07	2007-08	2008-09	2009-10	2010-11
Co-operative Banks	42,480 (18)	48,258 (19)	46,192 (15)	63,497 (17)	70,105 (16)
Regional Rural Banks	20,435 (9)	25,312 (10)	26,765 (9)	35,218 (9)	43,968 (10)
Commercial Banks	1,66,486 (73)	1,81,088 (71)	2,28,951 (76)	2,85,799 (74)	3,32,706 (74)
Total	2,29,401	2,54,658	3,01,908	3,84,514	4,46,779

Figures in parentheses indicate percentage of total flow of institutional credit.

Source: Government of India, *Economic Survey*, 2011-12, p. 111, Table 5.8.

4.17.1 Agricultural Debt Waiver and Debt Relief Scheme, 2008: In the wake of suicides by farmers in some parts of the country, indebtedness of the farmers was high on the agenda of the Government. The Government had appointed a Committee (Chairman: R. Radhakrishna) to examine all aspects of agricultural indebtedness. The Committee in its report made a number of recommendations but stopped short of recommending waiver of agricultural loans. However, Government was conscious of the problems being faced by the farmers, especially the small and marginal farmers. Having carefully weighed the pros and cons of debt waiver and having taken into account the resource position, the Finance Minister announced the following scheme of debt waiver and debt relief for farmers:

1. All agricultural loans disbursed by scheduled commercial banks, regional rural banks and co-operative credit institutions up to March 31, 2007 and overdue as on December 31, 2007 were covered under the scheme.
2. For marginal farmers (i.e., holding up to 1 hectare) and small farmers (1-2 hectare), there was a complete waiver of all loans that were overdue on December 31, 2007 and which remained unpaid until February 29, 2008. In respect

of other farmers, there was a one time settlement (OTS) scheme for all loans that were overdue on December 31, 2007 and which remained unpaid until February 29, 2008. Under the OTS, a rebate of 25 percent was given against payment of the balance of 75 percent.

3. Agricultural loans were restructured and rescheduled by banks in 2004 and 2006 through special packages. These rescheduled loans, and other loans rescheduled in the normal course as per RBI guidelines, were also eligible either for a waiver or an OTS on the same pattern.
4. The implementation of the debt waiver and debt relief scheme was to be completed by June 30, 2008. Upon being granted debt waiver or signing an agreement for debt relief under the OTS, the farmer was entitled to fresh agricultural loans from the banks in accordance with normal rules.
5. Government estimated that about 3 crore small and marginal farmers and about 1 crore other farmers would benefit from the scheme. The total value of overdue loans waived was estimated at ₹ 50,000 crore and the OTS relief on the overdue loans at ₹ 10,000 crore.

In addition to above, Government has initiated several measures to galvanize the institutional credit system to make it more responsive to the needs of farmers. Some of the important measures initiated in this regard are as under:

1. Banks have been advised to simplify procedures for documentation for agricultural loans.
2. As part of the measures announced by the RBI for financial inclusion, banks have been advised to open *no frills* accounts and issue simple overdraft facility against such accounts. Banks have also been advised to issue General Credit Cards up to ₹ 25,000 without insisting on security and end use of funds.
3. Banks have been advised to undertake, on a pilot basis, 100 percent financial inclusion in at least one district in each State. Based on the success of the pilot, the State

Level Bankers Committee in the States will draw a time-bound plan for achieving 100 percent financial inclusion in other districts of the State.

4.18 Summing Up

Historically, rural co-operative credit institutions (or simply rural co-operatives) have played an important role in providing institutional credit to the agricultural and rural sectors. The structure of rural co-operative banks is not uniform across all the States of the country. Some States have a unitary structure with the State level banks operating through their own branches, while others have a mixed structure incorporating both unitary and federal systems.

India is a country with a population of 121 crore (2011 Census) of which around 70 percent resides in around 6 lakh villages. There are around 95,000 PACS in the country. On grounds of outreach, co-operatives cannot be ignored. The outreach is significant not merely in absolute numbers but also in terms of location of outlets. The number of PACS located in hilly terrains, deserts and other areas with poor access far exceed the number of rural branches of commercial banks and RRBs.

Though the network of commercial banks and RRBs has spread rapidly, their reach in the countryside both in terms of the number of clients and accessibility to the small and marginal farmers and other poorer segments is far less than that of co-operatives.

In spite of their suitability and useful role in building up a just socio-economic rural life, co-operative societies suffer from various weaknesses and their performance has been far from satisfactory in certain respects. The heavy overdues of co-operative societies are a cause for concern. The rising overdues have reduced the borrowing and lending activities of these societies. The increasing incidence of defaulting has brought bad name to these societies.

Co-operative societies have paid inadequate attention to

the needs of landless workers and the rural artisans. The influential people in the villages have been the main beneficiaries of co-operative credit. Of late, there has been a tendency on the part of political leadership to write off the loans of the farmers. The RBI has repeatedly expressed concern in this regard because the non-repayment of loans by the existing borrowers adversely affects recycling of funds and the credit chances of prospective borrowers. A national approach on this issue is required so that co-operative credit system may fulfil the task assigned to it.

Positive impact of reforms, as has been witnessed in the case of commercial banking sector, may take longer to get manifested for co-operative banks given the late start of the reform process in this sector. Unless such a positive scenario evolves for the co-operative banking sector in the near future, the financial health of many of these banks would continue to remain a cause of concern.

It is imperative that the government takes initiatives to expand the network of institutional credit facilities in the rural areas and that the credit needs of the small and marginal farmers are met through earmarking credit for the group. Extension and marketing initiatives need to focus on this segment. At the same time, group initiatives need to be encouraged and awareness among the group has to be increased. The procedural formalities also have to be made less stringent to make the system more user-friendly for the largely illiterate group.

Given the distress among the farmers, it is important that a safety-net programme is introduced to ensure a minimum income for the farmers. Also the risk factor has to be mitigated through adequate insurance and credit facilities. At the same time, the outreach and efficiency of the institutional credit sources have to be improved. This is important to protect the small and marginal farmers who still heavily rely on private moneylenders who charge high interest rates and follow unscrupulous means to perpetuate indebtedness.

End Notes

1. Reserve Bank of India, *Report on Currency and Finance,* 2001-02, p. VI-18.
2. Government of India, *Economic Survey,* 2005-06, p. 63.

5

Micro Credit, Self-help Groups (SHGs) and NABARD

5.1 Credit Facilities for the Poor

Since independence, the Government of India and the RBI have made concerted efforts to provide the poor with access to credit. Despite the phenomenal increase in the physical outreach of formal credit institutions in the past several decades, the rural poor continue to depend on informal sources of credit. Institutions have also faced difficulties in dealing effectively with a large number of small borrowers, whose credit needs are small and frequent and their ability to offer collaterals is limited. Besides, cumbersome procedures and risk perceptions of the banks left a gap in serving the credit needs of the rural poor.

This led to a search for alternative policies, systems and procedures, saving and loan products, other complementary services and new delivery mechanisms that would fulfil the requirements of the poor. It is in this context that micro credit has emerged as the most suitable and practical alternative to the conventional banking in reaching the hitherto unreached poor population. Micro credit enables the poor people to be thrifty and helps them in availing the credit and other financial services for improving their income and living standards.

The proposed Micro Finance Services Regulation Bill defines micro finance services as providing financial assistance to an individual or an eligible client, either directly or through a group mechanism for an amount, not exceeding ₹ 50,000 in aggregate (₹ 1,50,000 if for housing purposes).

5.2 Micro Finance Initiative of NABARD

The micro finance initiative of NABARD, i.e. SHG-Bank

linkage programme has passed through various phases over the last one and half decades, *viz*. pilot testing during 1992 to 1995, mainstreaming during 1996 to 1998 and expansion from 1998 onwards.

Micro credit has emerged as a visible credit channel to the poor as their access to conventional credit channels is constrained by the requirement of collateral and high transaction cost. Micro finance is routed through self-help groups (SHGs). Over the years, SHG–Bank Linkage Programme—which includes commercial banks, regional rural banks and co-operative banks—has emerged as the major micro finance programme in the country. The focus under SHG-Bank Linkage Programme is largely on those rural poor who have no sustainable access to the formal banking system. The target groups, therefore, broadly comprise small and marginal farmers, agricultural and non-agricultural labourers, artisans and craftsmen and other poor engaged in small businesses like vending, and hawking.

The programme has been providing the rural poor access to the formal banking system and has achieved several milestones in terms of gender sensitisation, empowerment and poverty alleviation. The programme provides thrift linked credit support to the members of SHGs. While the programme directly benefits the members, it also helps banks in reducing their transaction costs as well as risk in delivering small loans.

The programme has now assumed the form of a micro finance movement in many parts of the country and has started making inroads in the resource poor regions of the country as well.

5.3 Self-help Group (SHG)-Bank Linkage Programme, 1992

SHG-Bank Linkage Programme was formally launched in the year 1992 as a flagship programme by NABARD and aptly supported by the RBI through its policy support. The objective is to meet the financial needs of the poor by linking SHGs with the formal credit agencies. The programme envisages organisation of the rural poor into SHGs for building their capacities to manage their own finances and then negotiate bank credit on commercial terms. The poor are encouraged to voluntarily come together to save small amounts regularly and extend micro loans among themselves. Once the group attains required maturity of handling larger resources, the bank credit follows.

5.3.1 What is a Self-help Group (SHG)? A self-help group is a group of about 15 to 20 people from a homogenous class who join together to address common issues. They involve voluntary thrift activities on a regular basis, and use of the pooled resource to make interest-bearing loans to the members of the group. In the course of this process, they imbibe the essentials of financial intermediation and also the basics of account keeping. The members also learn to handle resources of size, much beyond their individual capacities. They begin to appreciate the fact that the resources are limited and have a cost.

Once the group is stabilised, and shows mature financial behaviour, which generally takes up to six months, it is considered for linking to banks. Banks are encouraged to provide loans to SHGs in certain multiples of the accumulated savings of the SHGs. Loans are given without any collateral and at interest rates as decided by banks. Banks find it comfortable to lend money to the groups as the members have already achieved some financial discipline through their thrift and internal lending activities. The groups decide the terms and conditions of loan to their own members. The peer pressure in the group ensures timely repayment and becomes social collateral for the bank loans.

5.3.2 Graduation of Mature SHGs into Micro Enterprises: The core needs of savings and credit for consumption and production of SHGs are being met by the banking system. These SHGs have not only availed loans, but have also availed loans more than once. It is being emphasised that a member of the older SHGs would now be in a position to graduate into micro-enterprises by taking up income generating activities. It is a difficult task to find viable micro-enterprises for millions of poor households in rural areas. Though micro-enterprises is not a panacea for the complex problem of chronic unemployment and poverty, yet their promotion is a viable and effective strategy for achieving significant gains in incomes and assets of poor and marginalised people.

However, in the absence of any specific hand-holding strategy to provide financial and non-financial services in an integrated manner, graduation of SHG members from micro-finance to micro-enterprises has not been smooth due to several obstacles. NABARD is, therefore, undertaking a pilot project in select districts, particularly for members of matured SHGs for promotion to the stage of micro-enterprises. NGOs have been selected in each district for implementing the pilot projects.

5.4 Alternative Models of Micro Finance

India has adopted a multi-agency approach for the development of its micro finance programme. All the major credit institutions, *viz.* commercial banks, co-operative banks, RRBs along with non Governmental agencies (NGOs) have been associated with the micro finance programme. The role of the delivering agents and their interface has led to alternative models of micro finance.

Generally, the SHGs need self-help promoting institutions (SHPIs) to promote and nurture them. These SHPIs include various NGOs, banks, farmers' clubs, government agencies, self-employed individuals and federations of SHGs. However, some SHGs have also been formed without any assistance from such SHPIs.

Three distinct linkage models of micro credit are currently being followed in India.

Under Model-I, banks themselves take up the work of

forming and nurturing the groups, opening their saving accounts and providing them bank loans.

Under Model-II, SHGs are formed by NGOs and formal agencies but are directly financed by banks.

Under Model-III, SHGs are financed by banks using NGOs and other agencies as financial intermediaries. In areas where formal banking system faces constraints, the NGOs are encouraged to approach suitable bank for bulk loan assistance.

5.5 Central Government and Micro Finance

It was announced in the Union Budget for 2005-06 that the Government of India intends to promote micro finance institutions (MFIs) in a big way. For this purpose, the Micro-Finance Development Fund (MFDF) was re-designated as Micro-Finance Development and Equity Fund (MFDEF) and the corpus of the fund was increased from ₹ 100 crore to ₹ 200 crore. MFDEF is expected to play a vital role in capitalising the MFIs and thereby improving their access to commercial loans.

The Central Government is considering the need to identify and classify the MFIs and rate such institutions to empower them to intermediate between the lending banks and the clients. To facilitate the process of rating of MFIs, NABARD has decided to extend financial assistance to commercial banks and RRBs by way of grant to enable them to avail the services of credit rating agencies for rating of MFIs.

5.5.1 Micro Finance Development and Equity Fund (MFDEF): Recognising the need for up-scaling the micro finance interventions in the country, the Union Finance Minister, while presenting the budget for the year 2000-01, had created Micro Finance Development Fund (MFDF) with an initial contribution of ₹ 100 crore, to be funded by Reserve Bank of India, NABARD and commercial Banks in the ratio of 40:40:20. In the Union Budget for 2005-06, the Government of India decided to re-designate the MFDF into MFDEF and raised its corpus from ₹ 100 crore to ₹ 200 crore.

To strengthen the efforts of NABARD towards promotional support for micro finance, the Government of India in the Union Budget for 2010-11 further increased the corpus of MFDEF to ₹ 400 crore.

The MFDEF is managed and administered by NABARD under the guidance of an MFDEF Advisory Board. The objective of MFDEF is to facilitate and support the orderly growth of the micro finance sector through diverse modalities for enlarging the flow of financial services to the poor, particularly for women and vulnerable sections of society consistent with sustainability.

The Fund is utilised to support interventions to eligible institutions and stakeholders. The major components of the assistance include promotional grant assistance to Self-Help Promoting Agencies, training and capacity building for microfinance clients and stakeholders of SHG-Bank Linkage Programme, funding support to MFIs, Management Information System (MIS) for microfinance, research, studies and publications.

5.6 Reserve Bank of India (RBI) and Micro Finance

The RBI has been taking a pro-active role in promoting micro-finance. It set up four Groups in 2002 to look into various aspects of micro-financing. Based on the recommendations made by these Groups, the RBI announced that banks should provide adequate incentives to their branches in making the procedures for financing the SHGs simple and easy.

Based on the recommendations of the Vyas Committee, the RBI, in its annual policy statement for 2004-05, indicated that micro finance institutions would not be permitted to accept public deposits, unless they comply with the extant regulatory framework.

In view of the new paradigm shift in micro finance, the RBI is reviewing the issue of micro finance in a comprehensive manner. Accordingly, several initiatives have been taken in the recent period. A Technical Paper on Policy relating to Development, Regulation and Supervision of Micro finance Services was prepared and discussed with the representatives of MFIs on July 18, 2005. Similarly, an Internal Group of the RBI on Rural Credit and Micro-Finance (Chairman: H.R. Khan) was set up to examine the issues relating to micro-finance. The final version of the Report was released to the public in July 2005.

The SHG-Bank linkage programme is now considered by the banking system as a commercial proposition, with advantages of lower transaction cost, near zero NPAs and coverage of maximum number of the rural clientele by the bank branches. It has also led to other quantifiable benefits in business expansion. 27 commercial banks, 81 RRBs and 318 CCBs were participating in the programme at end-March 2010.

5.7 NABARD and Micro Credit

5.7.1 About NABARD: Set up in 1982, National Bank for Agriculture and Rural Development (NABARD), is the apex institution accredited with all matters concerning policy, planning and operations in the field of credit for agriculture and other economic activities in rural areas in India. NABARD serves as an apex refinancing agency for the institutions providing investment and production credit in rural areas.

A. Establishment of NABARD: The Committee to Review Arrangements for Institutional Credit for Agriculture and Rural Development (CRAFICARD) [Chairman: B Sivaraman] set up by the RBI in its report submitted in 1979 recommended the establishment of NABARD. The Parliament through the Act 61 of 1981, approved its setting up.

CRAFICARD, after reviewing the then existing arrangements, came to the conclusion that a new arrangement would be necessary at the national level for achieving the desired focus and thrust towards integration of credit activities in the context of the strategy for Integrated Rural Development Programme (IRDP). Against the backdrop of the massive credit needs of rural development and the need to uplift the weaker sections in the rural areas within a given time horizon, the arrangement called for a separate institutional set up. Similarly, The Reserve Bank had onerous responsibilities to discharge in respect of its many basic functions of central banking in monetary and credit regulations and was not therefore in a position to devote undivided attention to the operational details of the emerging complex credit problems. This paved the way for the establishment of NABARD.

CRAFICARD also found it prudent to integrate short-term, medium-term and long-term credit structure for the agriculture sector by establishing a new bank. NABARD is the result of this recommendation. It was set up with an initial capital of ₹ 100 crore, which was enhanced to ₹ 2,000 crore, fully subscribed by the Government of India and the RBI.

B. Objectives: NABARD was established in terms of the Preamble to the Act, "for providing credit for the promotion of agriculture, small-scale industries, cottage and village industries, handicrafts and other rural crafts and other allied economic activities in rural areas with a view to promoting IRDP and securing prosperity of rural areas and for matters connected therewith in incidental thereto".

The main objectives of the NABARD as stated in the statement of objectives while placing the bill before the Lok Sabha were categorized as under:

1. The National Bank will be an apex organisation in respect of all matters relating to policy, planning operational aspects in the field of credit for promotion of Agriculture, Small Scale Industries, Cottage and Village Industries, Handicrafts and other rural crafts and other allied economic activities in rural areas.
2. The Bank will serve as a refinancing institution for institutional credit such as long-term, short-term for the

promotion of activities in the rural areas.

3. The Bank will also provide direct lending to any institution as may approved by the Central Government.
4. The Bank will have organic links with the Reserve Bank and maintain a close link with in.

C. Major Activities: These are as under:

1. Preparing of Potential Linked Credit Plans for identification of exploitable potentials under agriculture and other activities available for development through bank credit.
2. Refinancing banks for extending loans for investment and production purpose in rural areas.
3. Providing loans to State Government/Non-government Organizations (NGOs)/Panchayati Raj Institutions (PRIs) for developing rural infrastructure.
4. Supporting credit innovations of Non-government Organizations (NGOs) and other non-formal agencies.
5. Extending formal banking services to the unreached rural poor by evolving a supplementary credit delivery strategy in a cost effective manner by promoting Self-help Groups (SHGs).
6. Promoting participatory watershed development for enhancing productivity and profitability of rain-fed agriculture in a sustainable manner.
7. On-site inspection of co-operative banks and Regional Rural Banks (RRBs) and off-site surveillance over health of co-operatives and RRBs.

D. Role and Functions:

1. NABARD is an apex institution accredited with all matters concerning policy, planning and operations in the field of credit for agriculture and other economic activities in rural areas.
2. It is an apex refinancing agency for the institutions providing investment and production credit for promoting the various developmental activities in rural areas.
3. It takes measures towards institution building for

improving absorptive capacity of the credit delivery system, including monitoring, formulation of rehabilitation schemes, restructuring of credit institutions, training of personnel, etc.

4. It co-ordinates the rural financing activities of all the institutions engaged in developmental work at the field level and maintains liaison with Government of India, State Governments, Reserve Bank of India and other national level institutions concerned with policy formulation.
5. It prepares, on annual basis, rural credit plans for all districts in the country; these plans form the base for annual credit plans of all rural financial institutions.
6. It undertakes monitoring and evaluation of projects refinanced by it.
7. It promotes research in the fields of rural banking, agriculture and rural development.

E. Mission: It has the mission of promoting sustainable and equitable agriculture and rural development through effective credit support, related services, institution building and other innovative initiatives.

In pursuing this mission, NABARD focuses its activities on the following:

1. **Credit Functions**: These involve preparation of potential-linked credit plans annually for all districts of the country for identification of credit potential, monitoring the flow of ground level rural credit, issuing policy and operational guidelines to rural financing institutions and providing credit facilities to eligible institutions under various programmes.
2. **Development Functions**: These concern reinforcement of the credit functions and making credit more productive.
3. **Supervisory Functions**: These ensure the proper functioning of co-operative banks and regional rural banks.

F. Role in Training: Section 38 of the NABARD Act provides that the Bank shall:

1. Maintain expert staff to study all problems relating to agriculture and rural development and be available for consultation to the Central Government, the Reserve Bank, the State Governments and the other institutions engaged in the field of rural development.
2. Provide facilities for training, for dissemination of information and the promotion of research including the undertaking of studies, researches, techno-economic and other surveys in the field of rural banking, agriculture and rural development.
3. Provide technical, legal, financial, marketing and administrative assistance to any person engaged in agriculture and rural development activities.
4. Provide consultancy services in the field of agriculture and rural development and other related matters in or outside India, on such terms and against such remuneration, as may be agreed upon.

In this context, the role of training in NABARD and the role played by it for capacity building in client institutions, partner agencies and other developmental agencies is important.

In pursuance of the Bank's mandate as stated in the Act, the Bank provides training facilities for the RFIs and agencies involved in rural development through BIRD and the two RTCs. With a view to broad-base the training and capacity building efforts, the Bank encourages the RFIs to set up their own training systems and provides these training institutes the necessary support to conduct meaningful and quality training. Options and avenues for strengthening the training interventions at the client level are continuously examined so that the human resources in these institutions are developed to take on the challenges, reckon with the competition, improve customer service, expand outreach, develop suitable products and thereby contribute to rural development.

G. NABARD Consultancy Services (Nabcons): Nabcons is a wholly owned subsidiary promoted by NABARD and is engaged in providing consultancy in all spheres of agriculture, rural development and allied areas. Nabcons leverages on the core competence of the NABARD in the areas of agricultural and rural development, especially multidisciplinary projects, banking, institutional development, infrastructure, training, etc., internalized for more than two decades.

In tune with NABARD's mission to bring about rural prosperity, Nabcons has more than just commercial interest in the assignments it undertakes.

H. Bankers Institute of Rural Development (BIRD): Established in 1983 at Lucknow, it is an autonomous institute promoted and funded by NABARD. BIRD was established primarily to cater to the training needs of RRB personnel. The Institute, has, since April 1, 1992, been catering to the training and information needs of rural bankers through its topical training programs/seminars. The Institute's mandate also includes Research and Consultancy in the related areas.

5.7.2 NABARD's Strategy for Popularity of Micro Finance: NABARD is adopting the following strategy to spread the outreach of SHG-Bank Linkage Programme.

1. Widening spatial distribution and intensity of the outreach of the Programme with district oriented planning and strategy.
2. Evolving district-wise plan of action/strategy in consultation with existing stakeholders aiming at promotion and linkage of a minimum of 500 SHGs per district every year.
3. Training and exposure programmes for the staff of the stakeholders.
4. Providing promotional assistance to partners for promoting and nurturing the SHGs generally on an *add-on* basis.
5. Widening the range of SHG promoting agencies.
6. Involving banks at their corporate level, organising training programmes for the regional/zonal managers of commercial banks in association with their Central Offices.

7. Establishing the financing of SHGs as a business proposition for banks.
8. Increasing the participation of the co-operative banks by encouraging them to finance SHGs as *financing co-operatives within the co-operatives*.
9. Associating village communities, people's institutions, rural volunteers and individuals to participate in the programme as SHG promoters.
10. Increasing the quality of the existing SHGs by propagating *self-rating* tools.
11. Large-scale dissemination of the concept and approach among the rural masses.
12. Encouraging the NGOs to play an important role in correcting the regional imbalances in spread of SHG-Bank Linkage Programme.

5.7.3 Tracking the Progress of Micro Finance: In view of the large outreach and pre-dominant position of the micro finance programme, it is important to keep a continuous track of the status, progress, trends, qualitative and quantitative performance comprehensively. To achieve this objective, Reserve Bank of India and NABARD issued guidelines in the year 2006-07 to commercial banks, Regional Rural Banks and co-operative banks to furnish data on progress under micro finance. The data so collected covers various parameters like savings of SHGs with banks, bank loan disbursed to SHGs, bank loan outstanding against SHGs, gross non-performing assets of bank loans to SHGs, recovery performance of loans to SHGs. Further, the banks also furnish the data regarding bank loans provided to Micro Finance Institutions (MFIs). NABARD, has been bringing out the consolidated document annually.

The data furnished by the banks have been analysed on a region-wise, state-wise, agency-wise, bank-wise and also for SHGs exclusively under Swarnajayanti Gram Swarojgar Yojana and exclusive women SHGs.

The major support provided by NABARD under Micro

Finance Development and Equity Fund relates to promotion and nurturing of SHGs by Self-help Promoting Institutions and training and capacity building of the stakeholders in the sector. NABARD is also experimenting innovative projects for further developing the micro finance through Joint Liability Groups.

Since 2006-07, NABARD has been compiling and analysing the data on progress made in micro finance sector, based on the returns furnished by Commercial Banks (CBs), Regional Rural Banks (RRBs) and Co-operative Banks operating in the country. The banks operating, presently, in the formal financial system comprises Public Sector CBs (27), Private Sector CBs (22), RRBs (82), State Co-operative Banks (31) and District Central Co-operative Banks (370). Most of the banks participating in the process of microfinance have reported the progress made under the programme.

NABARD has been instrumental in facilitating various activities under micro finance sector, involving all possible partners at the ground level in the field. NABARD has been encouraging voluntary agencies, bankers, socially spirited individuals, other formal and informal entities and also government functionaries to promote and nurture SHGs. The focus in this direction has been on training and capacity building of partners, promotional grant assistance to Self Help Promoting Institutions (SHPIs), Revolving Fund Assistance (RFA) to MFIs, equity/capital support to MFIs to supplement their financial resources and provision of 100 percent refinance against bank loans provided by various banks for microfinance activities.

5.7.4 Training and Capacity Building: NABARD organizes/sponsors training programmes and exposure visits for the benefit of officials of banks, NGOs, SHGs and government agencies to enhance their effectiveness in the field of micro finance. Training supplements and materials are supplied to banks and other agencies. Best practices and innovations of partner agencies are widely circulated among government agencies, banks and NGOs.

5.7.5 Micro Enterprise Development Programme (MEDP) for Skill Development: MEDP was launched by NABARD in March 2006 with the basic objective to enhance the capacities of the members of matured SHGs to take up micro enterprises through appropriate skill upgradation/development in the existing or new livelihood activities both in farm and non-farm sectors by way of enriching knowledge of participants on enterprise management, business dynamics and rural markets. It is tailor-made and focused on skill building training programme. The duration of training programme ranged between 3 and 13 days, depending upon the objective and nature of training.

The dominant activities in agriculture and allied sector covered under MEDPs were animal husbandry, bee-keeping, mushroom cultivation, vermicompost/organic manure, horticulture, floriculture, etc. whereas predominant non-farm activities taken up under MEDPs were readymade garments, Agarbatti-making, embroidery, bamboo-craft, beauty parlours, etc.

5.7.6 Grant Support to Partner Agencies for Promotion and Nurture of SHGs: NABARD helps in the formation and nurturing of quality SHGs by means of promotional grant support to NGOs, RRBs, DCCBs, Farmers' Clubs and Individual Rural Volunteers (IRVs) and by facilitating capacity building of various partners, which has brought impressive results in the promotion and credit linkage of SHGs.

5.7.7 Support to Activity-based Groups: NABARD introduced a scheme for supporting small-scale activity based groups (ABGs) in 2008-09, wherein capacity building, production and investment credit and market-related support would be extended. The scheme focuses on forming and nurturing the groups engaged in similar economic activities, such as farmers, handloom weavers, craftsmen, fishermen, etc., to improve efficiency of their production and realise better terms from the market through economies of aggregation and scale. The scheme drew upon NABARD's existing modes of support and has both grant and loan components. While grant support covers expenditure on SHGs formation and training, extension services, establishing market linkages, etc. bank loan/s would cover investment activities and working capital needs of the SHGs. Banks are eligible to draw refinance for the loans provided to Activity-based Groups on the same terms as applicable for SHG's financing. In select cases, NABARD provides loans directly to registered SHGs or through the agencies promoting SHGs to establish few initial projects where none exists.

5.7.8 Support to Federations of SHGs: Recognising the emerging role of the SHGs' Federations in nurturing of SHGs, enhancing the bargaining powers of group members and livelihood promotion, NABARD introduced during 2007-08, a flexible scheme to support such Federations, irrespective of their model. The broad norms prescribed for supporting SHG Federations stipulate that the federations should be need-based, member-owned/driven, democratically managed with members at liberty to join, become self-managed over three years, etc. NABARD extends grant support to the Federation for training, capacity building, and exposure visits of SHG members, etc., as also under all of NABARD's existing promotional schemes.

5.7.9 Special Initiative for Scaling-up SHGs/SHG Federations: NABARD has been associated with Rajiv Gandhi Charitable Trust (RGCT) for promotion, credit linkage and formation of SHG Federations in select districts of Uttar Pradesh. The project envisages promotion and credit linkage of 22,000 SHGs, 1,100 cluster-level associations and 44 block-level associations in collaboration with participating banks and implementing NGOs. The project would cover 15 and 29 blocks under Phase I and II respectively in 12 districts of Uttar Pradesh.

5.7.10 Promotional Support to Micro Finance Institutions (MFIs): NABARD has taken the following three major initiatives to support MFIs to strengthen them:

A. Capital Support to MFis: As mentioned earlier, the Micro Finance Development Fund (MFDF) was set up with NABARD by Government of India in 2000-01 with the initial corpus of ₹ 100 crore to be contributed by Reserve Bank of India (40 percent), NABARD (40 percent) and Commercial Banks (20 percent). The MFDF was re-designated as Micro Finance Development and Equity Fund (MFDEF) in 2005-06 and the corpus was increased to ₹ 200 crore and the same was further increased to ₹ 400 crore during 2010-11.

Accordingly, NABARD formulated a scheme called Capital/Equity Support to MFIs in 2007-08 for providing capital/equity support to various types of MFIs to enable them to leverage commercial and other funds from banks. This is expected to help MFIs in providing financial services at an affordable cost to the poor.

During 2009-10, NABARD introduced a new scheme, viz. Capital Support to Start-up MFIs having potential to scale-up their activities but lacking in capital, infrastructural facilities and managerial skills. Micro Finance Organisations (MFOs) and MFI-NBFCs, identified as 'Start ups' on the basis of area of operation, client outreach, lending model, borrowing history etc. are eligible for support under the scheme. Financial support is given in the form of 'subordinated debt' which is sub-ordinate to the claims of all other creditors. The quantum of support is commensurate with the business plan of the MFO/MFI-NBFC but not exceeding ₹ 50 lakh in any case. The rate of interest has been fixed at 3.5 percent to be repaid over a period of 7 years including moratorium of 2 years.

B. Revolving Fund Assistance to MFis: NABARD provides loan funds in the form of Revolving Fund Assistance (RFA), on a selective basis, to MFIs. The RFA provided to these agencies is necessarily to be used for on-lending to SHGs or individuals and the amount is to be repaid along with the service charge between 3.5 percent and 9.5 percent within a stipulated period of 5 to 7 years with one to two years of moratorium period. This enables them to build a 'credit history', which would help them to access credit facilities through the regular banking channels.

C. Rating of MFIs: In order to identify, classify and rate Micro Finance Institutions (MFIs) and empower them to function as intermediaries between the lending banks and their clients, NABARD had introduced a scheme for providing financial assistance by way of grant to CBs, RRBs and Co-operative Banks to avail of the services of accredited rating agencies for rating of MFIs. Banks can avail the services of credit rating agencies viz. CRISIL, M-CRIL, ICRA, CARE and Planet Finance for rating of MFIs and also avail financial assistance by way of grant to the extent of 100 per cent of the professional fees of the credit rating agency. During 2009-10, the scheme has been refined and the grant support has been increased to a maximum of ₹ 3.00 lakh. The facility is available for the first rating of an MFI with a minimum loan outstanding of ₹ 50.00 lakh and maximum loan outstanding of ₹ 10 crore.

5.7.11 Quality and Sustainability of SHGs: NABARD had entrusted a study to Institute for Social and Economic Change (ISEC), Bangalore for studying the quality and sustainability of SHGs in Karnataka. For study purpose, three representative districts, viz. Mysore (well developed), Tumkur (medium), and Bagalkot (less developed), were selected. The major findings of the study were as follows:

1. 96 percent of the SHGs constituted women's group with an average of 17 members per SHG.
2. 90 percent of the members were owning less than two acres of land.
3. Around 40 percent SHGs were credit-linked to RRBs; 30 percent to CBs and 30 percent to Co-operatives.
4. In developed district of Mysore 22 percent of the members lost interest in attending meetings and meetings were held less frequently.
5. Government department promoted groups expected

subsidised loans and depended on Anganwadi workers for maintenance of accounts and further guidance.

6. NGOs and government departments provided better opportunities for training for taking up income generating activities than the banks whose role in the area appeared to be low.
7. Training imparted by NGOs/Government agencies, however, was not of substantial help and useful as training imparted did not match the needs of the members.
8. Training on routine activities like papad and pickle making etc. were not preferred by the members.
9. Average loan amount increased from ₹ 56,307 in the first linkage to ₹ 2,13,333 in the fifth dose in all the districts covered under the study. Maximum loan availed amounted to ₹ 45 lakh for a group-based activity.
10. Nearly 57 percent SHGs availed loans less than three times of their savings, 24 percent between three and five times.
11. Certain problems encountered by the groups were as under:

- 97 percent of the SHGs in Bagalkot district, 81 percent in Mysore district and 70 percent in Tumkur district reported getting inadequate loans.
- Delay in getting loans with the need for frequent visits by the members to the banks.
- SGSY loans being made available in instalments which were equally divided among the members.
- Different interest rates charged by the banks: while commercial banks and RRBs charged 12 percent whereas the DCCBs charged at the rate of 4.5 percent (subsidised by the State Government).

12. Dependency on money lenders was reduced as about 96 percent of the SHGs stopped going to money lenders.
13. Repayment of loans was made regularly on monthly basis.

The SHG BLP has led to social and economic empowerment of the rural poor, such as:

92 percent of the SHG members came out of the four walls

of the their houses and 76 percent of the them were able to interact with officials/give speeches and 28 percent of the members were able to save in banks; the result were seen in decision making in household matter, sending children to school, changing undesirable habits of their spouse, participating in Gram Panchayat election, access to bank credit after joining SHG (98 percent) as compared to mere 2 percent before joining, increase in income by undertaking income-generating activities, etc.

5.7.12 Centre for Micro Finance Research: With the funding support from MFDEF, a Centre for Micro finance Research (CMR) has been setup in Bankers Institute of Rural Development, Lucknow to take up research studies in the field of microfinance with the mission of strengthening microfinance sector through supply of research inputs to facilitate policy initiatives and improvements in design and delivery system that provide poor with sustainable access to quality financial services. The CMR along with four sub-centres viz., Indian Institute of Bank Management (IIBM), Guwahati, Institute of Financial Management and Research (IFMR), Chennai, Institute of Development Studies (IDS), Jaipur and Chadragupta Institute of Management, Patna (CIMP) had initiated several studies on critical issues of microfinance. Grant assistance of ₹ 375.00 lakh was sanctioned to CMR from MFDEF to pursue the above-envisaged activities.

5.7.13 NABARD–German Technical Collaboration (GTZ) in Rural Finance: Under the purview of technical collaboration in Rural Finance Institutions Programme between GTZ and NABARD, technical assistance continued to be extended to NABARD during the year for, inter alia, promotion and development of microfinance as well as improvement in the quality and viability of financial services under SHG-Bank Linkage Programme. Exposure-cum-studies, capacity building interventions and documentation, etc., were undertaken in collaborative process for furtherance of the sector. The report of the 'Committee on Financial Inclusion' has indicated the need for addressing the remittance needs of the poor and NABARD has to play an important role in this. Keeping in view, NABARD with GTZ has undertaken a quick study on present practices of remittance and the team leader was Y.S.P. Thorat (ex-chairman, NABARD). Based on the findings of the study report, a joint appraisal mission on remittance discussed the issue with various partners viz., Ministry of Finance, Government of India, Reserve Bank of India, State Bank of India, India Post, Mr Nandan Nilekani (Unique ID), etc. On the basis of the discussions of the appraisal team, NABARD and GTZ signed 'Agreed Minutes on the Joint Appraisal of the Programme' on 19 January 2010. The NABARD and GTZ have now commissioned a detailed study on "Remittance needs of the poor" in different corridors (Eastern Uttar Pradesh and Mumbai, Intra State between various parts of Maharashtra and Mumbai and Orissa and Kolkata). Findings of the study will be presented before Government of India and Reserve Bank of India for policy changes, if required, for financial inclusion of poor migrant workers particularly rural women.

5.7.14 Joint Liability Groups (JLGs): Based on the studies conducted by NABARD, it was found that financing of JLGs is a good business proposition. It needs simplified documentation, group dynamics, timely repayment culture and prospects of credit enhancement to quality clients. Keeping in view the need and findings of the studies, NABARD has issued comprehensive guidelines on JLGs to Banks focusing on small and marginal farmers, oral lessees, tenant farmers engaged in farm sector and other clients under non-farm activities. NABARD supports banks for nurturing and financing of JLGs for the initial three years. Banks may use the services of JLG-promoting agencies. In addition, NABARD would also extend support for training, exposure visits, experience-sharing, etc., for banks' staff.

SHG-Bank linkage programme has proved to be successful

in providing financial services from the formal banking sector to the poor. However, the issue of linking the small/marginal farmers, tenant farmers/oral lessees, share croppers and the rural non-farm entrepreneurs with the formal banking sector was concern for NABARD as their demand were not met through the SHG as in SHGs, loan amount is linked to savings. NABARD had piloted Joint Liability Groups (JLGs) programme during 2004-05 in eight states of the country with the help of 13 RRBs through the mechanism of joint liability approach. Besides the above pilot project, the Government of Andhra Pradesh through its Agriculture Department primarily designed the initiative by promoting Rythu Mithra Groups (RMGs) on the SHG model. RMGs are also expected to serve as a conduit for technology transfer, facilitate access to market information and assist in carrying out activities like soil testing, training, health camps, assess input requirements, etc., to its members.

Over the last few years NABARD has been propagating the idea of JLGs at various fora. Based on the experience gained in implementation of the pilot project, a scheme for financing JLGs by the Commercial Banks, RRBs and Co-operative Banks has been formulated and circulated to RRBs and Co-operative Banks by NABARD and to Commercial Banks through Reserve Bank of India/Indian Banks Association. The salient features of the scheme are as given below:

A. Objectives: The scheme aims at the following objectives:

1. To augment flow of credit to tenant farmers cultivating land either as oral lessees or sharecroppers and small farmers who do not have proper title of their land holding, through formation and financing of JLGs.
2. To extend collateral free loans to target clients, including rural micro entrepreneurs through JLGs.
3. To build mutual trust and confidence between banks, tenant farmers, entrepreneurs, etc.

B. General Features of JLG: These are the following:

1. JLG is an informal group of preferably 4 to10 individuals but can be up to 20 members as in the case of SHG.
2. The JLG members would offer a joint undertaking for bank loans.
3. The JLG members are expected to engage in similar type of economic activities like crop production.

C. Criteria for Selection of JLG Members: JLGs can be formed primarily consisting of tenant farmers and small farmers cultivating land without possessing proper title of their land/rural entrepreneurs engaged in non-farm activities.

1. Members should be of similar socio-economic status and background carrying out farming activities/non-farm activities and who agree to function as a joint liability group.
2. The members should be residing in the same village/area and trust each other to take up joint liability for group/ individual loans.
3. The members should be engaged in agricultural activity for a continuous period of not less than one year within the area of operations of the bank branch.
4. The group members should not be a defaulter to any other formal financial institution.
5. There should not be more than one person from the same family in the JLG.

D. Security: The group would extend mutual guarantee for the group or individual loan.

E. Formation of JLGs: Banks may initially form JLGs by using their own staff wherever feasible. Banks may also engage business facilitators like NGOs and other individual rural volunteers to assist banks in promoting the concept and formation of groups.

F. Savings by JLG: The JLG is intended primarily to be a credit group. Therefore, savings by the JLG members is voluntary and not compulsory as in the case of SHG. All the JLG members may be encouraged to open an individual "no frills" account. However, if the JLG chooses to undertake savings as well as credit operations through the group mechanism, such groups should open a savings account in the name of JLG with at least two members being authorised to operate the account on behalf of the group.

G. JLG Models: Banks can finance JLG by adopting any one of the following two models:

- **Model A: Financing Individuals in the Group:** The group would be eligible for accessing separate individual loans from the financing bank. All members would jointly execute one inter-se document (making each one jointly and severally liable for repayment of all loans taken by all individuals in the group). The financing bank could assess the credit requirement, depending on the activities being undertaken and credit absorption capacity of the individual. However, there has to be mutual agreement and consensus among all members about the amount of individual debt liability that will be created.
- **Model B: Financing the Group:** The JLG would consist preferably of 4 to 10 individuals and function as one borrowing unit. The group would be eligible for accessing one loan, which could be combined credit requirement of all its members. In case of crop loan, the credit assessment of the group could be based on crop/s to be grown and the available cultivable area by each member of the JLG. All members would jointly execute the document and own the debt liability jointly and severally.

H. Types of Loan: Banks may consider cash credit, short-term loan or term loan or composite loan (working capital with term loan) depending upon the purpose of loan.

I. Margin and Security Norms: No collaterals may be insisted upon by the banks against their loans to JLGs. It may however, be ensured that the mutual guarantees offered by the JLG members are kept on record. Margin as per the norms prescribed by RBI, may be applied.

J. Documents:

- **Model A:** The documents to be obtained include Introduction form, application-cum-appraisal form, mutual guarantee and DPN.
- **Model B:** Documents as applicable to SHGs may be adopted.

K. Financing to JLGs: Financing to JLGs by bank will form part of priority sector lending and banks may include lending to JLGs in their corporate plan and also in the training schedule of officers/staff.

L. Support Extended by NABARD:

- **Grant Support for of JlGs:** To facilitate promotion of JLGs, NABARD provides grant assistance to Banks and other institutions involved in promotion and nurturing of JLGs. JLG promoting institute is expected to formulate a plan for a minimum of 20 JLGs. Grant assistance of ₹ 2000 per JLG will be extended to banks for formation, nurturing and financing of JLGs over a period of three years. The first instalment of ₹ 1000 would be released to the Bank/other institutions after sanction of loan by the bank. The second instalment may be released after commencement of repayment. The third instalment may be released in third year subject to certification of bank with regard to satisfactory repayment. However, the grant to other institutions would be released, based on the certification by the banks as indicated above.
- **Refinance:** NABARD will provide 100 percent refinance assistance to all banks in respect of their lending to JLGs under investment credit and the procedure for claiming refinance from NABARD would be similar to that under SHG-Bank Linkage Programme.

M. Capacity Building: Banks may undertake capacity building measures like conduct of training programmes for stakeholders, awareness and sensitization of JLG concept both for banks own staff as well as the target group. The banks operating staff should be familiar with the concept, benefits for the banks and clients under the programme. NABARD would consider supporting capacity building programmes for Bank's staff and other publicity measures, such as publication of pamphlets/ leaflets, use of media (print as well as others), etc. for greater awareness and orientation.

5.8 Recommendations of the Group on Rural Credit and Micro Finance, 2005

As a follow-up to the announcement in the Union Budget, 2005-06, the RBI constituted this Internal Group (Chairman: H.R. Khan) which in its Report submitted in July 2005 observed that there is an imperative need to work out efficient mechanisms involving external entities to cater to the under-serviced areas and the rural poor.

The Group felt that extended outreach to the under-serviced areas and the rural poor would facilitate acquisition of a large number of customers, *albeit* small ones with substantial potential for large increase in business volumes and profit as banking with the poor is rather profitable banking. The major recommendations of the Group are set out below.

1. For providing comprehensive financial services encompassing savings, credit and remittance, insurance and pension products in rural areas, the Group recommended two models, *viz.*, the Business Facilitator Model and the Business Correspondent Model as proactive response.
2. Under the Business Facilitator Model, it was envisaged that banks could use a wide array of civil society organisations (CSOs) and others for supporting them by undertaking non-financial services. The Facilitators would provide support services for effective delivery of financial services such as (a) borrower identification, (b) collection, processing and submission of applications, (c) preliminary appraisal, (c) marketing of the financial products including savings, (d) post-sanction monitoring, (e) promotion and nurturing SHGs/Joint Liability Groups (JLGs) and (f)

follow-up for recovery.

3. NGOs, farmers clubs, functional co-operatives, IT enabled rural outlets of corporates, postal agents, insurance agents, well-functioning panchayats, rural multi-purpose kiosks/village knowledge centres, agri-clinics/business centres financed by banks, Krishi Vigyan Kendras, Khadi and Village Industry Commission (KVIC)/Khadi and Village Industries Commission Board (KVIB) units may function as the Business Facilitators.
4. Under the Business Correspondent Model, institutional agents/other external entities may support the banks for extending financial services. The Business Correspondents would function as "pass through" agencies to provide credit related services such as disbursal of small value credit, recovery of principal/ collection of interest and sale of micro insurance/mutual fund products/pension products besides the other functions of Business Facilitator Model.
5. Registered NBFCs with significant rural presence, NGO-micro-finance institutions (MFIs) set up under the Societies/Trust Act, Mutually Aided Co-operative Societies (MACS) with a charter to undertake financial functions, IT enabled rural outlets of corporates with appropriate contractual agreements with the principal, well running primary agricultural credit societies (PACSs) and post offices may function as the Business Correspondents.
6. The micro credit portfolio of the regulated MFIs may be made eligible for direct finance from NABARD; a line of credit may be extended by NABARD to provide liquidity assistance in view of the co-variant nature of credit risk of the MFIs.
7. Institutions such as NABARD and SIDBI may provide bulk lending support to start-up MFIs and funds of State/ Central Development/Finance Corporations, if feasible, may be channelised through NABARD to identified MFIs.
8. Accounting standards for SHGs and NGOs may be developed, codified, and standardised by NABARD as a

promotional initiative in consultation with the Institute of Chartered Accountants of India (ICAI).

9. NABARD, in consultation with Ministry of Information and Technology, may draw up a time bound action plan to set up Rural Kiosks/Village Knowledge Centres, partly funded from RIDF. The remaining cost may be borne by the Central/State Governments on a shared basis.
10. The MFIs may be rated to help banks/financial institutions to decide about engaging them as their agents and funding them. The rating agencies need to be accredited with an appropriate authority.
11. NABARD, SIDBI and major banks may consider promoting independent rating agencies by way of equity contributions. Financial support may be provided to the accredited rating agencies to cover their operational deficits for a period of three to five years and the expenses in this regard may be met from the Micro Finance Development and Equity Fund (MFDEF).
12. Non-deposit taking MFIs may attempt self-regulation by forming State level associations.
13. A separate and exclusive regulatory and supervisory framework for MFIs may not be required for the present.
14. Considering the high transaction costs and the emphasis on timely availability of credit, it may not be appropriate to fix any ceiling on interest rates and service fees charged by MFIs.

5.9 Summing Up

Micro finance sector has traversed a long journey from micro savings to micro credit and then to micro enterprises and now entered the field of micro insurance, micro remittance and micro pension. This gradual and evolutionary growth process has given a great opportunity to the rural poor in India to attain reasonable economic, social and cultural empowerment, leading to better living standard and quality of life for participating households. Financial institutions in the country continued to play a leading role in the micro finance programme. They have joined hands proactively with informal delivery channels to give micro finance sector the necessary momentum.

The Self-help Group (SHG)-Bank Linkage Programme has become a well-known tool for bankers, developmental agencies and even for corporate houses. SHGs, in many ways, have gone beyond the means of delivering the financial services as a channel and turned out to be focal point for purveying various services to the poor. The programme, over a period, has become the common vehicle in the development process, converging important development programmes. With the small beginning as Pilot Programme launched by NABARD by linking 255 SHGs with banks in 1992, the programme has reached to linking of 69.5 lakh saving-linked SHGs and 15.8 lakh credit-linked SHGs and thus about 9.7 crore households are covered under the programme as on March 31, 2010, envisaging synthesis of formal financial system and informal sector.

To sum up, the micro credit programme, which was formally heralded in 1992 with a modest pilot project of linking around 500 Self-help Groups (SHGs), has made rapid strides in India exhibiting considerable democratic functioning and group dynamism. The micro credit programme in India is now the largest in the world. Since independence, the Government of India and the RBI have made concerted efforts to provide the poor with access to credit. Despite the phenomenal increase in the physical outreach of formal credit institutions in the past several decades, the rural poor continue to depend on informal sources of credit. Institutions have also faced difficulties in dealing effectively with a large number of small borrowers, whose credit needs are small and frequent and their ability to offer collaterals is limited. Besides, cumbersome procedures and risk perceptions of the banks left a gap in serving the credit needs of the rural poor.

6

Urban Co-operative Banks (UCBs)

6.1 Importance of UCBs

The co-operative banking system forms an integral part of the Indian financial system. It comprises urban co-operative banks and rural co-operative credit institutions. Urban co-operative banks have a single-tier structure whereas rural co-operatives have a two- or three-tier structure.

The single tier urban co-operative banks (UCBs)—also referred to as primary co-operative banks—play an important role in meeting the growing credit needs of urban and semi-urban areas of the country. The UCBs, which grew rapidly in the early 1990s, showed certain weaknesses arising out of lack of sound corporate governance, unethical lending, comparatively high levels of non-performing loans and their inability to operate in a liberalised environment. Accordingly, some of the weak UCBs have been either liquidated or merged with other banks.

Co-operative banks in India are more than 100 years old. These banks came into existence with the enactment of the Agricultural Credit Co-operative Societies Act in 1904. Co-operative banks form an integral part of the banking system in India. These banks operate mainly for the benefit of rural areas, particularly the agricultural sector. Co-operative banks mobilise deposits and supply agricultural and rural credit with a wider outreach. They are the main source of institutional credit to the farmers. Co-operative banks are chiefly responsible for breaking the monopoly of moneylenders in providing credit to agriculturists. They have also been an important instrument for various development schemes, particularly subsidy-based programmes for the poor. Co-operative banks operate for non-agricultural sector also but their role is small.

Though much smaller as compared to scheduled commercial banks, co-operative banks constitute an important segment of the Indian banking system. They have an extensive branch network and reach out to people in remote areas. They have traditionally played an important role in creating banking habits among the lower and middle-income groups and in strengthening the rural credit delivery system.

Urban co-operative banks play an important role in meeting the growing credit needs of urban and semi-urban areas. UCBs mobilise savings from the middle and lower income groups and purvey credit to small borrowers, including weaker sections of the society. Scheduled UCBs are under closer regulatory and supervisory framework of the RBI.

Unfortunately, financial reforms have not impacted the functioning of co-operative banks. This was brought out clearly in the following observation of the Reserve Bank of India, "Since the introduction of reforms, there has been very little perceptible improvement in either stability or efficiency of co-operative banks. In particular, the asset quality and profitability of scheduled Urban Co-operative Banks (UCBs) showed some deterioration in the reform period. Positive impact of reforms, as has been witnessed in the case of commercial banking sector, may take longer to get manifested for co-operative banks given the late start of the reform process in this sector." [1]

The financial reforms process initiated in 1991 has tried to achieve regulatory convergence among various financial intermediaries in view of their systemic importance. Therefore, the basic objectives and instruments of reforms for co-operative banks have been the same as for State Co-operative Banks (SCBs). However, given the special characteristics of co-operative banks, they have been extended certain dispensations in terms of pace and sequencing of reforms.

UCBs have grown rapidly since the early 1990s. During the phase of rapid expansion, however, the sector showed certain weaknesses arising out of (a) lack of sound corporate governance, (b) unethical lending, (c) comparatively high level of loan defaults and (d) inability to operate in a liberalised and competitive environment. The RBI, therefore, has been striving to harness the growth of UCBs with appropriate application of prudential regulation and supervision to safeguard the interests of depositors.

Keeping in view the weak financial position of many UCBs, the RBI has undertaken a series of measures directed towards strengthening of the UCBs. Since March 31, 1993, the UCBs have been advised to adhere to the prudential norms which include, *inter alia*, the following.

1. Applying capital adequacy standards.
2. Prescribing an asset-liability management framework.
3. Enhancing the proportion of holding of Government and other approved securities for the purpose of Statutory Liquidity Ratio (SLR) stipulation.
4. Restriction on bank finance against the security of corporate shares and debentures.
5. Limiting the exposure to capital market investment.

In view of the challenges arising from the functioning of the UCBs for the financial system, the RBI appointed a High Power Committee (Chairman: K. Madhava Rao), 1999 to review the performance of UCBs and to suggest necessary measures to strengthen this sector. Based on the recommendations of this Committee, measures have been initiated to strengthen the existing urban banking structure.

6.2 Vision Document and Medium-Term Framework (MTF) for UCBs

Various entities in the urban co-operative banking sector display a high degree of heterogeneity in terms of deposits/asset base, areas of operation and nature of business. In view of its importance, it is imperative that the sector emerges as a sound and healthy network of jointly owned, democratically controlled and professionally managed institutions. In order to achieve these objectives, the RBI has taken a series of policy initiatives in recent years. The most significant initiative in this regard was the Vision Document and Medium-Term Framework (MTF) for UCBs. With a view to protecting depositors' interests on the one hand, and enabling UCBs to provide useful service to local communities on the other, the Medium-Term Framework (MTF) seeks to achieve the following objectives.

1. To rationalise the existing regulatory and supervisory approach keeping in view the heterogeneous character of the entities in the sector.
2. To facilitate a focused and continuous system of supervision through enhancement of technology.
3. To enhance professionalism and improve the quality of governance in UCBs by providing training for skill upgradation and also by including large depositors in the decision making process/management of banks.
4. To put in place a mechanism that addresses the problems of dual control, given the present legal framework and the time-consuming process in bringing requisite legislative changes.
5. To put in place a consultative arrangement for identifying weak but potentially viable entities in the sector and provide a framework for nursing them back to health including, if necessary, through a process of consolidation.
6. To identify the unviable entities in the sector and provide an exit route for such entities.

The above framework is implemented through the following measures:

1. A differentiated regulatory regime as opposed to a *one-size-fits-all* approach.
2. A two-tier regulatory regime: (a) simplified regulatory regime for unit banks and single district banks with deposits less than ₹ 100 crore; and (b) regulation for all other banks on the lines of commercial banks.
3. As the strategy to deal with UCBs may need to be State-

specific, a State Level Task Force for Urban Co-operative Banks (TAFCUB) is to be constituted comprising senior officials from the RBI, State Governments and local/central co-operative Federations.

4. TAFCUB would be responsible for (i) identifying weak but viable UCBs and devise a time-bound programme for revival; and (ii) recommending (a) the nature and extent of financial support, (b) future set up of unlicensed banks, and (c) the manner and timeframe for exit of unviable banks.
5. To address issues/difficulties relating to dual control within the existing legal framework, it has been proposed to evolve a working arrangement in the form of Memorandum of Understanding (MoU) between the RBI and the State Government.

6.3 Regulation and Supervision of UCBs: Strengthening Measures

The regulation and supervision of the urban co-operative banks (UCBs) was brought within the ambit of the RBI's statutory control under the Banking Laws (as Applicable to Co-operative Societies) Act, which came into force from March 1, 1966. The regulatory powers conferred on the RBI with regard to co-operative banks are limited. While the principles of supervision with regard to co-operative banks have been formulated and implemented by the RBI in respect of UCBs under the Banking Regulation Act, 1949, the Act does not apply to primary agricultural credit societies and land development banks, thus leaving them under the regulatory purview of the State.

Instances such as the Madhavapura Mercantile Co-operative Bank's failure brought to the fore the need to have stringent regulatory control over the co-operative banking system. In order to strengthen the supervisory mechanism, the RBI extended the Off-site Surveillance System (OSS) to all non-scheduled UCBs having deposit size of ₹ 100 crore and above. A supervisory reporting system was introduced for the scheduled UCBs from March 2001 as a first step towards setting up of OSS for all UCBs. The capital adequacy norms were introduced in a phased manner from March 2002. Better risk management through avoidance of concentration of credit risk, off-site surveillance for non-schedule UCBs and following up of Know Your Customer (KYC) guidelines have also been introduced to strengthen the UCBs.

A total ban has been imposed since October 2003 on grant of loans and advances to directors of UCBs, their relatives and concerns in which they have interest with a view to preventing certain irregularities. The RBI has also directed that UCBs should undertake usual due diligence in respect of investments in non-SLR securities. The RBI introduced a new system of grading of UCBs in April 2003, which is based on their CRAR, level of net NPAs, record of losses and compliance with regulatory environment. Similarly, a system of supervisory rating for UCBs under the CAMELS model has also been introduced. Initially, it was implemented for scheduled UCBs but subsequently its simplified version was extended to non-scheduled UCBs in March 2004.

Despite the structural and cultural differences between UCBs and commercial banks, the above measures suggest that the RBI has been exercising its regulatory and supervisory powers to ensure that the co-operative credit structure is strengthened on the lines similar to the regulation and supervision of commercial banks.

The RBI is entrusted with the responsibility of regulation and supervision of the banking-related activities of UCBs under the Banking Regulation Act, 1949 As Applicable to Co-operative Societies (AACS). Other aspects such as incorporation, registration, administration, management and winding-up of UCBs are supervised and regulated by the respective State Governments through Registrars of Co-operative Societies (RCS) under the Co-operative Societies Acts of the respective States. UCBs with a multi-state presence are registered under the Multi-State Co-operative Societies Act, 2002 and are regulated and supervised jointly by the Central Government through Central Registrar of Co-operative Societies and the RBI.

Thus, current legislative framework provides for dual control over UCBs. For resolving problems arising out of dual control regime, a draft legislative bill proposing certain amendments to the Banking Regulation Act, 1949, based on the recommendations of the High Powered Committee on UCBs, was forwarded to the Government. Pending the amendment to the Act, the RBI is entering into a regulatory arrangement with the State Governments through Memorandum of Understanding (MoU) to facilitate proper and coordinated regulation and supervision of UCBs. MoUs have already been signed between the RBI and three States that have a large network of UCBs, *viz.* Andhra Pradesh, Gujarat and Karnataka. As a follow-up to the signing of MoUs, the RBI has constituted State Level Task Force for Urban Co-operative Banks (TAFCUBs) in these States.

6.3.1 Memorandum of Understanding (MoU) with the State Governments: The MoUs contain the following commitments by the State Government and the RBI.

The State Governments, through the MoU, agree to:

- Introduce long form audit report for statutory audit and modify their audit rating models to bring them in alignment with the gradation system adopted by the RBI for UCBs.
- Provide for statutory audit by Chartered Accountants (CAs) for UCBs with deposits over ₹ 25 crore and special audit by CAs, if required by the RBI, for any UCB.
- Put in place 'fit and proper' criteria for Chief Executive Officers (CEOs), based on guidelines of the RBI.

The RBI, as a signatory to the MoU, is committed to:

- Constitute a State Level TAFCUB, comprising Regional Director of the RBI, Registrar of Co-operative Societies (RCS) of the State, a representative of Central Office of

Urban Banks Department of the RBI, a representative of the State Government and a representative each from the State and National Federation of UCBs. TAFCUBs would identify and draw up time bound action plans for the revival of potentially viable UCBs and recommend non-disruptive exit for non-viable ones.
- Facilitate human resources development and IT initiatives in UCBs.

MoUs signed between the RBI and the respective State Governments also envisage the signing of another MoU between the Registrars of Co-operative Societies of the States and respective Regional Directors of the RBI. This MoU stipulates the broad measures to be taken by the signatories for implementing the recommendations of the TAFCUB for each of the potentially viable/non-viable UCBs that are placed for consideration of TAFCUB.

The MoU, *inter alia,* also provides that the RBI would consult RCS before cancelling or refusing licence under the Banking Regulation Act, 1949, of a UCB covered by the MoU, i.e. in States with which MoUs have been signed. The RCS would comply without delay any requisition by the RBI for supersession of the Board or for winding up of any UCB.

6.3.2 Licensing of New Banks/Branches: Consequent upon the easing of licensing norms in May 1993, more than 800 licences were issued for setting up urban co-operative banks. However, close to one-third of these newly licensed UCBs became financially weak within a short period. There was, thus, a need to moderate the pace of growth of this sector, particularly given the vexatious issue of dual control over UCBs. The RBI proposed certain amendments to the Banking Regulation Act, 1949 (AACS) to overcome the difficulties arising out of dual control. Pending enactment of these amendments, it was announced in the Annual Policy Statement for 2004-05 that issuance of fresh licences would be considered only after a comprehensive policy on UCBs, including an appropriate legal and regulatory framework for the sector, is put in place and a policy for improving the financial health of the urban co-operative banking sector is formulated. Accordingly, at present, applications for banking licence, including licence for opening of new branches, are not considered.

6.3.3 Income Recognition, Asset Classification and Provisioning Norms: In line with the international best practice and extant practices in commercial banks in India, the RBI decided to reduce the time period for reckoning an advance as non-performing from the existing 180 days to 90 days with effect from March 31, 2004. However, subsequently keeping in view the representations received from co-operative federations/banks, small loans up to ₹ 1 lakh were exempted from the purview of the 90 days norm and continued to be governed by 180 days norm. This exemption was granted only up to March 31, 2006. It was also decided to grant additional time of two years, in comparison with commercial banks, to meet the 100 percent provisioning required for advances identified as doubtful for more than three years.

Further, taking into consideration representations received from UCBs, it was decided to permit certain categories of UCBs to classify loan accounts as NPAs based on 180 days delinquency norm instead of 90 days norm. These included unit banks, i.e. banks having a single branch/HO and banks having multiple branches within a single district with deposits up to ₹ 100 crore. The relaxation was given up to the financial year ending March 2007 and banks were advised to build up adequate provisions to comply with the 90 days delinquency norm after the stipulated date.

The RBI also decided to delink the asset classification and provisioning requirements in respect of State Government guaranteed advances and investments from the invocation of the State Government guarantee. Accordingly, asset classification and provisioning norms on State Government guaranteed advances were made applicable in the same manner as exposures not guaranteed by the State Governments from the year ending March 31, 2006.

6.3.4 Exposure Norms: With a view to avoiding concentration of credit risk, UCBs were advised to fix the prudential exposure limits at 15 percent and 40 percent of the *capital funds* in the case of a single borrower and a group of borrowers, respectively. Banks were also advised that *capital funds* for the purpose of prudential exposure norms would be in relation to bank's total capital funds and the exposure for the purpose includes both credit and investment exposure (non-SLR).

6.3.5 Off-site Surveillance: The on-site financial inspection carried out by the RBI continues to be one of the main instruments of supervision over UCBs. The off-site surveillance system (OSS) for supervision was made applicable to all scheduled UCBs from March 2001. The returns for OSS were reviewed by the RBI and a revised set of 8 returns was prescribed from March 2004. The OSS returns of UCBs are designed to monitor compliance and obtain information from them on areas of prudential regulation. The main objective of the OSS returns is to obtain relevant information on areas of prudential interest, address the management information needs, strengthen the management information system (MIS) capabilities within the reporting institutions and to sensitise bank managements about concerns of the supervisory authority.

Compliance monitored through these returns covers assets and liabilities, earnings, asset quality, sector/segment-wise analysis of advances, concentration of exposures, connected or related lending and capital adequacy. These concerns earlier were being addressed through periodical on-site inspections of banks undertaken at intervals ranging from one to two years. The OSS system was extended to non-scheduled banks with deposit base of over ₹ 100 crore from June 2004.

6.3.6 Know Your Customer (KYC) Guidelines: Know Your Customer (KYC) guidelines were issued to UCBs by the RBI in the context of the recommendations made by the

Financial Action Task Force (FATF) on Anti-Money Laundering (AML) standards and Combating Financing of Terrorism (CFT). UCBs were advised to ensure that a proper policy framework on KYC and also AML measures is formulated and put in place with the approval of their Boards. UCBs were also advised to ensure full compliance with the provisions of these guidelines before December 31, 2005.

6.3.7 Priority Sector Lending: UCBs are required to lend 60 percent of their total loans and advances to the priority sector of which 25 percent should go towards weaker sections.

A. Housing Loans under the Priority Sector: In order to improve flow of credit to the housing sector, it was decided that UCBs with the approval of their Boards may extend direct finance to the housing sector up to ₹ 15 lakh per beneficiary of a dwelling unit, irrespective of location, against the earlier limit of ₹ 10 lakh, as part of their priority sector lending.

6.3.8 Disclosure Norms: In consonance with the best practices and in the interest of the members and depositors, it was decided that disclosure of the details of the levy of penalty on a bank would be put in public domain through a press release by the RBI. The UCBs were also advised that the penalty should be disclosed in the *Notes on Accounts* to their balance sheets in their next Annual Reports.

With a view to indicating the exact status of co-operative banks as also to avoid confusion among members of public, all UCBs were advised to display their full name on stationery item, publicity material and name board in the form in which it appears in the Certificate of Registration issued by the Registrar of Co-operative Societies and the licence granted by the RBI.

6.4 Mergers/Amalgamations of UCBs

With a view to encouraging and facilitating consolidation and emergence of strong entities and as well as for providing an avenue for non-disruptive exit of weak/unviable entities in the co-operative banking sector, guidelines were issued to facilitate merger/amalgamation in the sector. The RBI, while considering proposals for merger/amalgamation, confines its approval to the financial aspects of the merger taking into consideration the interests of depositors and financial stability. The RBI considers proposals subject to the post-merger entity meeting the prescribed following prudential norms.

1. When the net worth of the acquired bank is positive and the acquirer bank assures to protect entire deposits of all the depositors of the acquired bank.
2. When the net worth of acquired bank is negative but the acquirer bank, on its own, assures to protect deposits of all the depositors of the acquired bank.
3. When the net worth of the acquired bank is negative and the acquirer bank assures to protect the deposits of all the depositors with financial support from the State Government extended upfront as part of the process of merger.

6.5 Relaxation of Investment Portfolios of UCBs

UCBs were given some relaxation in the prudential norms for their investment portfolio in September 2004. They were allowed to exceed the limit of 25 percent of total investment under held till maturity (HTM) category provided (a) the excess comprises only SLR securities, and (b) total SLR securities held in HTM category are not more than 25 percent of their net demand and time liabilities (NDTL) as on the last Friday of the second preceding fortnight.

Taking into account the difficulties faced by UCBs in meeting the provisioning requirements, it was further decided, as a special case, to consider relaxing the provisioning requirements both for scheduled UCBs and non-scheduled UCBs. Accordingly, scheduled UCBs were advised that they may crystallise the provisioning requirement arising on account of shifting of securities from HFT/AFS categories to HTM category consequent to the issue of guidelines dated September 2, 2004 and amortise the same over a maximum period of five years commencing from the accounting year ended March 31, 2005, with a minimum of 20 percent of such amount each year.

As regards non-scheduled UCBs, they were allowed to shift securities from HFT/AFS categories to HTM category at book value, subject to the following conditions. First, in case the book value is higher than the face value, the difference between the book value and the face value, i.e. the premium may be amortised in equal instalment over the remaining period to maturity. If the security was obtained at a discount to face value, the difference should be booked as profit only at the time of maturity of the security. Second, the securities transferred under this special dispensation should be kept separately under HTM category and should not be transferred back to the HFT/AFS category in future in terms of the existing instruction of transfer of securities from HTM category. Third, in normal course, such securities under HTM category should not be sold in the market and redeemed on maturity only. However, in exceptional circumstances, if such securities are to be sold, profit on sale of investments in this category should be first taken to the *profit and loss account* and thereafter be appropriated to the *capital reserve*. Loss on sale will be recognised in the *profit and loss account* in the year of sale.

6.6 Restructuring of Scheduled UCBs with Negative Net Worth

A policy regarding restructuring of scheduled UCBs with negative net worth has also been formulated by the RBI. The RBI has begun a consultative process with a few scheduled UCBs with negative net worth by involving officials of the concerned State Governments and banks with a view to revitalising and rehabilitating them. The emphasis is on a time-bound programme by identifying the contours of their rehabilitation plan and setting up monitorable milestones. The RBI will be closely monitoring the achievements of the banks *vis-à-vis* the targets set at regular intervals and initiate appropriate action with a view to protecting depositors' interest and avoiding systemic problems. Issues relating to large depositors, part conversion of deposits into equity, reduction of non-performing assets, human resources and technological development and the support from the State Governments would be examined. The option of merger/amalgamation could also be explored, wherever necessary. The RBI would limit its examinations and approvals to the banking and regulatory issues to satisfy itself that the restructuring package is in the interests of the depositors and the public at large. The RBI would also take into account various other parameters such as infusion of funds, sacrifice by stake holders, restructuring of liabilities, recovery of NPAs, regulatory support and forbearance, governance, business plan, and filing of applications and documents.

6.7 Problem of Dual Control in Co-operative Banking

The single most important regulatory and supervisory weakness that persists in the co-operative banking sector is the prevalence of dual control. While incorporation/registration and management-related activities are regulated in the states by the Registrar of Co-operative Societies or the Central Registrar of Co-operative Societies (for multi-state co-operative banks), banking-related activities are under the regulatory/supervisory purview of the Reserve Bank of India (RBI) or NABARD. The basic issue is that co-operation is a state subject under the Indian Constitution and as such *co-operatives* as a form of organisation are governed by the State Co-operative Societies Act, irrespective of whether they are banks or other forms of co-operative entities.

This duality of control and the absence of a clear demarcation of functions between the regulators have engaged the attention of a number of committees in the past. While in the case of commercial banks the RBI has the powers under the Banking Regulation Act, 1949 to deal with crucial aspects of functioning such as supersession of the board of directors, appointment of liquidators, initiating action for removal of the CEO/Chairman of a bank, instituting special audits, and conducting statutory audit through external chartered accountants. In the case of co-operative banks these powers are subordinated in a way by the requirement that all such actions would require the intervention/approval of the Registrar of Co-operative Societies of the respective State Governments or the Central Registrar of Co-operative Societies, as the case may be.

This duality of control affects the quality of supervision and regulation, and it also affects the functioning of co-operative banks. The regulatory weaknesses foster inefficiency and impede the development of governance principles. Moreover, it burdens the banks with multiple levels of compliance and reporting requirements.

6.7.1 Impairment in Governance and Management: A unique feature of the co-operative banking system in India is that borrowers have a significant say in the management of the bank. This follows from the fact that only borrowers of the co-operative bank are eligible to be its members, contributing to share capital. As the Board Members of the bank are elected by borrowers, it results in the policies of the bank not always being in congruence with the interests of depositors. In view of the propensity of these banks to pursue borrower-oriented policies rather than policies that should be in favour of protecting interest of depositors, it has often been suggested that the involvement of depositors in the management of these banks should be enhanced by encouraging membership of depositors on par with borrowers.

Another reason for impairment of governance in the co-operative banking structure is attributed to interference in matters related to appointment of directors on the basis of political affiliations rather than on merit. This manifests itself in lack of professional expertise at the board level and interference in decision-making, particularly in respect of loan sanctions. This impairs the financial health of co-operative banks.

6.8 Working Group on IT Support for Urban Co-operative Banks

In today's financial systems, usage of Information Technology is fundamental to the survival and growth of the institutions. IT usage not only help banks hold and reduce their cost of operations, several developments in the information and communication technology (ICT) enable the institutions to offer highly profitable products and services to their constituents. IT has become not just an enabler, but also the distinguishing and differentiator; it also provides competitive advantage and edge to its user. Further, current regulatory and supervisory compliance demands that the institutions have a very sound usage of IT systems for their operations.

The Vision Document for Urban Co-operative Banks (UCBs), released in March 2005, proposed signing of Memorandum of Understanding (MOU) between RBI and Central and respective State governments for establishing a consultative approach to supervision and regulation of UCBs. The Reserve Bank has so far signed such MOUs with 16 State Governments and the Central Government.

In terms of the MOUs, the RBI is committed to facilitate IT initiatives in UCBs. In furtherance of the commitment made under the MOUs, Governor announced in the Mid-term Review of the Annual Policy 2007-08, that 'a working group comprising representatives of the Reserve Bank, State Governments and the UCBs sector' would be constituted 'to examine the various areas where IT support could be provided by the Reserve Bank.' Accordingly, the RBI constituted a Working Group on IT Support for Urban Co-operative Banks (Chairman: R. Gandhi) on December 19, 2007 with the following Terms of Reference:

1. To review the current level and use of IT infrastructure in

UCBs.

2. To structure a model/benchmark level of IT infrastructure for UCBs in general or for identified sub groups of UCBs.
3. To prepare a suggested roadmap of building such an infrastructure by the UCBs.
4. To identify areas and ways in which IT support may be provided by the RBI.
5. To make recommendations on the nature, scope and delivery mechanism for IT support to UCBs by the RBI.

6.8.1 Findings of the Working Group: There exists a wide disparity with regard to the usage of Information Technology by the Urban Co-operative Banks. As on March 31, 2007, 16 out of 1853 banks had implemented Core Banking Solutions, while about 50 banks did not even have computers. The remaining banks exist somewhere along the continuum between those that had CBS on the one hand, and those without even PCs on the other.

Most banks have solutions based on Total Branch Automation. Several banks have implemented locally developed and customised application solutions. While some big UCBs have in-house IT wings to take care of development and maintenance of systems, most banks have outsourced these services.

Anecdotal evidences are there about the problems faced by these banks because of their small size, lack of adequate IT knowledge, lack of adequate IT savvy manpower and small time vendors. They had suffered because small vendors could not provide satisfactory AMC and adequate post-implementation support for making changes in the software on account of their inability to retain skilled staff or sometimes because of the small scale of their operations, which rendered them unviable. Moreover, such legacy systems, set up by small vendors, were not standardized and therefore made migration to new systems more cumbersome and expensive than even acquiring a new one.

The acquisition of non-standardized software/software

developed by local/regional level vendors is fraught with the following risks:

1. **Vendor Disappearance:** Vendors who developed software for small banks are often small-time operators and are not available for support, modifications and change management subsequently. Their mortality rate is often high. Eventually, the software became obsolete and redundant.
2. **Loss of Key Personnel by Vendor:** Some times, the vendor is available but the key personnel, who were involved in the development of software, are no more with the vendor. The vendor finds it difficult to extend the required level of the support without its skilled personnel as being small it has little flexibility in the absence of backup staff. As they often also do not follow standard practice of software development and documentation, the maintenance and updation of source-codes becomes difficult for the new personnel.
3. **Lack of Regulatory Compliance Modules:** Almost all the small-vendor developed software systems do not contain important regulatory provisions such as compliance to KYC norms, etc.

The Group also observed that there were several large banks which had their own data centres and were offering core banking solutions to the smaller banks and that a few successful cases of sharing of data centre facilities among banks were also known. However, as awareness of IT among UCBs was not pervasive, several banks seemed reluctant to keep their data in the data centres owned by other bank/banks.

6.8.2 Problem Analysis and Possible Solutions: Considering the increasing penetration of commercial banks in what till recently were the niche areas of UCBs (such as middle and low income housing finance/retail loans etc.), the need to computerize the operations of even the smallest UCBs has become imperative to improve customer service and ensure survival. While deliberating upon the level of computerization of UCBs, the Group noted that in a country like China, all the two-lakh odd branches of all the banks had been computerized.

The Group, while noting with satisfaction that the front line UCBs have taken advantage of what the ICT can offer, also observed that a very large proportion of UCBs have not done the same. Among UCBs, considering the high concentration of very small banks, lack of uniformity in the levels of computerization and inadequate awareness about effectiveness of computers in enhancing competitiveness, the Group felt that it is necessary to articulate the minimum IT infrastructure which should exist in each UCB regardless of its size, location or profitability.

This minimum level of IT infrastructure, the Group felt should include the following:

1. Computerized front-end i.e. customer interface;
2. Automatic backend accounting (through software);
3. Computerized MIS reporting; and
4. Automated regulatory reporting.

The above minimum benchmark for computerization does not include 'networking' among branches, since the sector is largely dominated by unit banks or banks with only a few branches.

The Group then discussed about various methods by which a bank can create IT infrastructure for its use. In view of the variance in size, financial strength and IT capabilities of UCBs, the Group also considered the possibility of sharing of IT infrastructure at the state level as state was operationally a logical unit for UCBs which are under the regulation of state governments and RBI.

While an arms' length distance between banks owning the data centre and the database of other UCBs using the facility is technologically feasible, it also needs to be recognized that the long-term sustainability of such an arrangement is an issue, as banks are essentially in the business of banking and activities like development and maintenance of Data Centres and providing software support to financial institutions are focussed functions of IT firms.

6.8.3 Issues in Computerization and Support:

A. Desired Level of IT in a Bank, Irrespective of Size, Location and Profits: The Group opined that the minimum level of IT infrastructure in a bank should be a computerized front office services, back-office accounting, MIS and regulatory reporting.

B. Available Solutions: Several solution providers from big firms to middle range players and banks etc., existed in the market. Peer group banks working jointly for developing facilities like data centre for use by group members could also come together to provide solutions for the smaller banks. Even local developers were offering inexpensive solutions to banks which were workable in the short/medium term. However, choosing standardized products was essential for ensuring reliability and continued support.

C. Cost Factor: Costs of the ASP models have been discussed earlier. However, the costs mentioned above were the 'list costs' of the firms and would be negotiable, particularly if banks got together and bulk orders were to be placed. Different payment terms were also available which included a small charge every month combined with per transaction fee which could possibly be of interest to the smaller banks. In addition to the ASP model, the outright purchase offering also existed.

D. Approach to be Adopted: In respect of the small banks, particularly the unit banks, it was felt that the best method for computerization could be through the ASP model wherein a few software vendors could be short-listed by an agency like IDRBT and the banks could select the vendor from out of the list, based on their geographical location and convenience. There was another view, however, that the independent application model might also be considered, should a bank be capable and desirous.

E. Who Should be Supported and How? The Group

deliberated upon the need for mandating the minimum level of IT usage by UCBs. It was observed that so far, mandates had been given by the Reserve Bank for regulatory purposes only, but if necessary, Reserve Bank could explore the possibility of laying down prescriptions for business purposes too.

Prima facie banks that were making losses or very meagre profits or those that are very small in size and therefore do not have the financial strength to acquire the IT infrastructure set by RBI, require support. However, in case support is extended only to the weak or small banks, the better performing or growing banks may tend to interpret that they were indirectly suffering because of their good performance or growth as RBI was not extending support to them for their IT efforts. Even though, in fact, the better performing banks may not be needing support, this approach of providing support to only those which are loss making or small may give a wrong and unintended signal to better performing banks.

This dilemma can therefore be addressed by ensuring that the support is not seen as a grant from Reserve Bank which was suggested by NAFCUB, as the banks must feel importance of participating by owing what they get. In any case, interest free payment over a period of time itself provides the built-in subsidy element. Similarly, the Committee felt that 3 years' subsidy on monthly rentals, as proposed by NAFCUB, may not be required.

Instead it could be in the form of, say, an interest free conditional loan. The repayment could be structured for different categories of banks. For loss making banks, for example, there could be a moratorium on repayment till the bank turned around. RBI could also attach conditions and link declaration of dividend to the repayments. In such a case, while the loss making banks would not have any problem in accepting the loan, the profit making banks that avail of it would have an incentive to pay back quickly so that they can declare dividend. Another area of support that Reserve Bank may provide to all banks could be in the area of training which could range from PC application to purchase/sale of securities over the Negotiated Dealing System.

Further, financial support may be needed for purchasing and/or leasing in adequate and benchmarked hardware, required for setting up the system envisaged by the Group. The terms of the loan could be the same as that for acquisition of software, discussed earlier, as the existence of appropriate hardware in every bank is a very important plank in the over-all proposal of ensuring a minimum standard of computerization in all UCBs.

F. Routing the Financial Support: On the issue of strategy for routing financial support to UCBs, the options were as under:

1. Providing funds directly to banks for outright purchase of customised software and hardware.
2. Paying the vendors who provide the software, on behalf of the UCB.
3. Funding a national-level institution like IDRBT and routing the support through it.

In this context, it may be mentioned that in case of the first option i.e. providing finance to individual banks, it would be difficult to manage as effecting timely payment and monitoring the proper end use of the funds would be a major issue. RBI would also not be able to enforce the agreement between the vendor and the bank as RBI or its agency like IDRBT would not be a party to the agreement. Option 2 would mean a direct support to a vendor rather than to banks. Therefore, in Option 3, the ASP model, the agreement could be tripartite. In this option i.e. providing support through IDRBT, it needs to be mentioned that the institution was created by RBI for providing services to banking and financial sector in India and it is already providing applications such as SFMS to many banking entities on similar lines. Further, IDRBT's budgetary deficit is fully financed by the Reserve Bank and therefore it is very easy and logistically simple for the Reserve Bank to extend financial support to the UCBs through IDRBT. IDRBT could shortlist vendors for procuring the ASP model for urban co-operative banks, as IDRBT could provide IT consulting and could also monitor the implementation of the SLA. As such, the 3rd Option is considered to be very practical. Further, the ASP approach will make it easier to negotiate the price as consolidating the demand would provide economies of scale for both the vendor and the purchaser. ASP model would be a way of ensuring that even the smallest banks acquired standard software with continued support through reputed vendor.

There was also a view that banks which decided to select vendors independently should also be supported by RBI. Representatives of the sector felt that banks that had already selected or were in advanced stage of vendor selection for acquiring Core Banking Solutions stood to benefit from the support provided by RBI and should not be limited in the choice of vendor for availing the support. The Group debated this and concluded that such an option can be considered only for those banks which are well capitalised and with good track record, on whom we have confidence and comfort that the end use of funds are assured, and that they have IT savvy personnel to implement/oversee and deal with the vendors and for whom investing in an outright purchase option is financially a preferable option. The group felt that only banks which have deposits of over ₹ 100 crore and are making profits for the last 3 years and have CRAR of over 9 percent should be supported for such outright purchase.

6.8.4 Recommendations: Usage of Information Technology for financial systems in the modern world is fundamental to the survival and growth of the institutions. IT usage not only helps banks hold and reduce their cost of operations, several developments in the information and communication technology (ICT) enable the institutions to proffer highly profitable products and services to their constituents. IT has become not just an enabler, but also the distinguishing factor and differentiator. It also provides competitive advantage and edge to its users. Further, current regulatory and supervisory compliance demands that the institutions have a very sound usage of IT systems for their operations.

A. Minimum Information Technology Infrastructure in UCBs: Considering the concentration of small UCBs, the lack of uniformity in the levels of computerization and inadequate awareness about the efficacy of computers in enhancing competitiveness, the Group felt it necessary to articulate the minimum IT infrastructure which should exist in each UCB regardless of its size, location or profitability. This minimum level of IT infrastructure should include the following:

1. Computerized front-end i.e. customer interface.
2. Automatic backend accounting (through software).
3. Computerized MIS reporting.
4. Automated regulatory reporting.

B. UCBs to be Supported: While maximum support is required for the small/weak banks, if support is extended only to the weak or small banks, the better performing or growing banks may tend to interpret that they were indirectly suffering because of their good performance or growth as RBI was not extending support to them for their IT efforts. As such, the group felt that support should be structured in such a way that it can be offered to all.

C. Nature of Support: In order to implement the minimum level of IT infrastructure by the UCBs as indicated in Recommendation No. 1, Core Banking Solution (CBS) would be required to be adopted by the banks. The model of CBS may be according to the size and spread of the banks.

The models for acquiring the IT infrastructure could be one of the following:

(a) Application Service Provider (ASP) Model: In respect of the small banks, particularly the unit banks, it was felt that the best method for computerization could be through the ASP model as the problems of software development and maintenance, training and retention of IT professionals, installation and maintenance of complex and costly hardware and other logistics like data centres etc would be addressed by the service provider without need for much initiative or involvement of the UCB. An agency like IDRBT could short-list/select one/few vendors and be the conduit and service quality assuror to the banks. The payment model for the ASP option includes a one time payment and a small charge every month combined with per transaction fee, which could also be suitable for the smaller banks. Moreover, in ASP model, initial investment would be less and by combining the requirements of a large number of banks the cost could be further reduced.

(b) Outright Purchase Model: If banks seek to go for outright purchase of the Core Banking, including data centre, the cost would be in the range of ₹ 1.5 crores to ₹ 2 crores for 5-10 branches per bank. Further, availability and retention of IT savvy professionals are also to be ensured. Besides, the bank should be strong enough to enforce service quality by the vendor. The Group feels that only those banks which are well capitalised and with good track record, on whom we have confidence and comfort that the end use of funds are assured, and that they have IT savvy personnel to implement/oversee and deal with the vendors and for whom investing in an outright purchase option is financially a preferable option should be given the option to choose this model. As such, banks which have a business of more than ₹ 100 crores, CRAR of over 9 percent and have been profit making for the past 3 years could be provided support for outright purchase.

(c) Delivery Mechanism: As indicated above, the support will be available for all UCBs. However, it should not be given in the form of a grant; support may be in the form of a loan and not subsidy.

Experience shows that subsidy tends to reduce seriousness regarding the end use of funds. Financial support may be extended as follows:

1. Support could be in the form of interest free loan, repayable in 7 years, with one year moratorium. UCBs

would be eligible for loan for software as also for purchase of hardware.

2. In the case of big banks preferring to go for outright purchase of software and hardware, interest free with only service charge of ½ percent to 1 percent to be charged by the SCB routing the loan may be considered.
3. In respect of weak/sick banks, the 'moratorium' may be for two years. In case the UCB defaults on its repayment obligations even after that, a view may be taken at that point regarding other options like continuation of management, non-disruptive exit of the bank etc.
4. For the banks which have to adopt ASP Model, routing of the interest-free loan by the Reserve Bank could be through IDRBT, which could prepare Systems Requirement Specifications, select vendors, prepare development/testing and implementation plans, and vetting the SLA (Service Level Agreement) between users i.e. UCBs and the service providing entity, to ensure smooth implementation and post-implementation support by the vendor.
5. For the banks which elect to have outright purchase of the application system, the Group felt that the Reserve Bank may not be able to extend direct loans due to monetary policy implications. However, NABARD has a separate fund for IT usage in co-operative sector, a portion of which can be routed to UCBs, through SCCB/DCCBs.
6. If required, IDRBT may develop an area of expertise within itself to cater to the IT needs of small banks, including UCBs. National and State Federation of co-operatives may also think of creating such IT facilities for UCBs in the long run for the benefit of the sector.

(d) Conditionality:

1. The aforementioned facilities will be made available only for UCBs located in the MOU states.
2. Even if the UCB is a loss-making one, it would still have to honour repayment obligations in respect of the interest-

free loan/loan from NABARD.

3. In case any UCB needs customization/change in the package for particular functionalities, it may put in a request to IDRBT, which will make arrangements for the same. However, such changes/enhancements will have to be paid for by the concerned UCB.
4. In case of banks which already have software in their existing branches, interest-free loan would be available for meeting cost of upgradation and/or expansion, under the same terms and conditions.
5. A bonus could be considered for the banks which repay the instalments on time and/or earlier. The bonus could be in the form of waiving the last installment.

6.9 Working Group on Umbrella Organization and Revival Fund for Urban Co-operative Banks

There are a large number of Primary (Urban) Co-operative Banks (UCBs) in the country forming a heterogeneous group in terms of size and spread. Many of these banks are very small in size and reach. They compete with larger participants in the same banking space. Over the years, a number of UCBs have become weak and non-viable thus posing systemic risk to the UCB sector. They lack avenues for raising capital funds since they cannot go in for public issue of shares nor can they issue shares to members at a premium. At the same time, there are a number of UCBs in the sector that are financially strong and viable. Some sort of co-operative bonding and mutual support system could make the sector strong and vibrant. Looking at various successful federal models internationally, especially in Europe and USA, a need was felt for an umbrella organization that would be in a position to channelize their resources, aggregate their needs and also lend credibility through mutual support in the financial market.

In this backdrop, it was decided by the RBI to constitute a Working Group (Chairman: V.S. Das) on May 28, 2008 to suggest measures including the appropriate regulatory and supervisory framework, to facilitate emergence of umbrella organization(s) for the UCB sector in the respective states. Further, the Standing Advisory Committee for UCBs has opined that the Working Group may also look into the issues concerning creation of Revival Fund for the sector.

6.9.1 Terms of Reference of the Working Group:

1. To study the regulatory and supervisory structure of umbrella organizations of financial co-operative institutions/banks, as prevalent in other parts of the world, especially in relation to raising of capital and intra co-operative group support system.
2. To study the existing structure and legal framework for UCBs in India and to examine the need and scope for a federated structure/umbrella organization for UCBs at the state level.
3. To suggest appropriate supervisory and regulatory framework to facilitate emergence of such umbrella organisation(s) for UCBs, taking into consideration the international experiences and systems.
4. To study and suggest modalities for setting up an appropriate mutual assistance/revival fund for urban co-operative banks and the nature of support that could be provided by such fund.

6.9.2 Recommendations:

A. Need for Umbrella Organization: Urban Co-operative Banks in India cater to the financial needs of the middle and lower middle class people in metropolitan, urban and semi-urban centres. They operate on a standalone basis, unlike rural co-operatives in India, which have a three tier structure. These banks are large in number, though of varied asset size, ranging from small to medium. Although they compete with commercial banks, their share in total deposits is barely 4 percent. There is a significant part of the UCB sector that lacks professionalism and is unable to keep pace with rapid advancements in IT, modern banking systems and financial products. The sector also has significant number of banks which are weak and need financial support. There have been occasions when, due to contagion effect, banks have encountered liquidity problems. Being in the nature of co-operative societies, the UCBs' ability to augment their capital is also restricted, thereby hindering their growth.

The organizational structure of UCBs, their small size and limited area of operation add to their vulnerability. Further, in the wake of advances in information and communication technology, payment and settlement systems and services, they need to widen their range of services to run on professional lines and match the services provided by commercial banks.

Internationally, co-operative banks, popularly called Credit Unions, operate in networks and have an entity which provides a wide range of services to them, such as, fund management services, lines of credit, asset management, payment and settlement system gateway, ATM networks, credit card, investment, securitisation, capital raising and other financial services. These entities act as Umbrella Organizations and the networks provide co-operative solidarity. International experience has shown that the presence of such an Umbrella Organization has contributed towards the member Credit Unions being stable, sound and efficient entities.

B. Umbrella Organization at the National Level: The Working Group carefully went into the important issue of whether in India we should have an Umbrella Organization at the national level or whether each state should have its own Umbrella Organization. While countries such as Canada and USA have provincial Umbrella Organizations, Australia and European countries have preferred to consolidate and have national level organizations.

UCBs in India are not evenly spread across the country. They have predominant presence in five states, viz. Andhra Pradesh, Gujarat, Karnataka, Maharashtra and Tamil Nadu accounting for about 89 percent of the total business of the sector. Further, UCBs in Maharashtra alone had about 64 percent of the total business. In contrast, their presence was minimal in many states. Considering the regional spread and market share of UCBs, the Working Group is of the opinion that having multiple umbrella organizations for UCBs in India or state-wise umbrellas may be neither feasible nor desirable. Therefore, the Working Group is of the view that there should be one Umbrella Organization at the national level for the entire UCB sector.

C. Functions of the Umbrella Organization: The Umbrella Organization should act as a central credit institution for UCBs, like similar organizations abroad for Credit Unions. It should provide a wide range of services such as providing loans and advances, refinance, payment and settlement services, IT services, ATM network services, investment banking, fund management, management consultancy, capacity building services and even capital support. The UCB sector was found to be particularly keen that the organization provides payment and settlement services and liquidity assistance. This may possibly be emanating from the concern arising in the context of implementation of the new eligibility norms for MICR clearing, RTGS, SGL/CSGL accounts and making them out of reach for a large number of UCBs and lack of avenues for temporary liquidity assistance (even against SLR securities) in case of need and urgency; more so in case of run like situations. Similarly, many small UCBs are looking forward to a centralized agency for buying, selling and managing Government securities on their behalf in view of their lack of skill and expertise in the areas. The Working Group recommends that the Umbrella Organization should provide a whole range of services to member UCBs, as described above.

D. Form of Organization of the Umbrella Organization: The Working Group observed that non-banking financial companies (NBFC) could perform most of the functions of Umbrella Organization. The minimum startup capital for such companies has been stipulated at ₹ 2 crore, for the present, as per the Reserve Bank's policy for issue of certification for registration. The Working Group is of the view that even though contribution to share capital of the Umbrella Organization would be voluntary, the initial startup capital could easily be garnered from UCBs.

It would be better to build the edifice, brick by brick, with low startup capital and augment the capital funds over the years, rather than to commit huge capital funds from the co-operative sector, which itself is facing difficulties in raising capital.

Further, at present, the Reserve Bank has been vested with adequate power to regulate and supervise NBFCs. The current RBI regulations, however, do not permit NBFC to undertake certain activities and place restrictions on certain others; more importantly, the Payment and Settlement services.

Considering that access to Payment and Settlement gateways and dealing platforms for securities through Umbrella Organization are the most sought after services, the Working Group was of the view that it would be within the powers of the Reserve Bank to grant regulatory permissions/ forbearances wherever necessary, depending upon the type of functions. NBFCs may be broadly divided into deposit taking and non-deposit taking. The term "deposit", however, does not include amount of money received from banks and financial institutions and further, the term "public deposit" excludes certain categories of deposits. The NBFCs that are authorized to accept/hold public deposits need to have minimum net owned Funds and they are required to maintain certain specified percentage (15 percent) of the public deposits in liquid assets in the form of approved securities and unencumbered term deposits with scheduled commercial banks. These NBFCs should achieve minimum investment grade credit rating for accepting public deposits. The regulations for the deposit taking NBFCs are tighter than that of non-deposit taking. On the contrary, a non-deposit taking NBFC enjoys more freedom in undertaking its business, more particularly deployment of its funds. Keeping in view the extant regulations applicable and the relative merits of deposit taking and non-deposit taking NBFCs, the Working Group is of the opinion that to start with, a non-deposit taking NBFC may be the most suitable form of organization and recommends that Umbrella Organization may be initially set up as a non-deposit taking NBFC. The Umbrella Organization in the form of a non-deposit taking NBFC would, however, access money from UCBs and others, which are not treated as public deposits. The conversion of the Umbrella Organization to a banking company could be considered in due course in the light of experience gained.

E. Authorized Capital, Subscribed/Paid up Capital: The Working Group deliberated at length on the modus operandi of raising share capital for the Umbrella Organization. It was felt that share capital of the Umbrella Organization should be closely held by the UCBs and subscription should be voluntary. However, some members strongly felt that contribution to the share capital of the Umbrella Organization should be made compulsory for UCBs and the Reserve Bank could consider issuing direction to UCBs in this regard. The Group discussed on the pros and cons of the proposal and was of the view that though equity participation by all UCBs should be encouraged; there could be constraints to make it compulsory for UCBs. The Group was of the view that both the options should be kept open. The National and State Federations should educate UCBs about the benefits of having an Umbrella Organization and also play a big role for its set up and raising of capital.

F. Sources of Working Capital: To begin with, the capital funds would normally go to finance fixed assets of Umbrella Organization and the balance amount could be used for financing activities. Umbrella Organization would also need some source of working capital. Being a non-deposit taking NBFC, it would have access to the following sources for its working capital:

1. Borrowings from banks/financial institutions.

2. Deposits: term deposits from UCBs.
3. Debt instruments: bonds/debentures.
4. Refinance: against financial assets (loans and advances) including securities.
5. Other miscellaneous sources.

The Umbrella Organization would need to have access to deposits from UCBs, which could be a major source of working capital for carrying out its business. A significant number of UCBs have low credit deposit ratios and they park their surplus funds with DCCB/SCB and commercial banks. Umbrella Organization, being the central credit institution for UCBs, may be able to tap these deposits for its financing and investment activities.

G. CRR and SLR: The Working Group feels that it would be attractive for UCBs to place deposits with Umbrella Organization if these deposits are treated as CRR/SLR. The Umbrella Organization would definitely need such deposits to meet its working capital requirements. The Working Group, therefore, recommends that the Reserve Bank may consider exempting UCBs placing term deposits with the Umbrella Organization from maintenance of SLR in the form of Government and other approved securities up to 15 percent of their NDTL. The Working Group also feels that this would serve as an incentive for UCBs to take up membership of the Umbrella Organization. The Working Group feels that the Reserve Bank which has been instrumental in promoting several developmental and financial institutions should consider the recommendation positively and favorably as the Umbrella Organization is being conceptualized to provide the much needed stability to the UCB sector that would also contribute to financial stability.

H. Business Profile and Sources of Income: Profitability of the UO's operations is very crucial and, therefore, in most countries, the central credit institutions have a significant asset portfolio outside the captive business. Further, its ability to raise capital and debt in the market would also depend upon the strength of its balance sheet. The Working Group, therefore, recommends that UO should delicately balance its commitment towards UCB sector and the need to keep its asset portfolio strong and healthy.

As the Umbrella Organization would function as a central credit institution, it would orient its business to provide various services to the member UCBs (loans and advances, refinance, payment and settlement services, IT services, ATM network services, investment banking, fund management and capital support). This would fetch it revenue in the form of interest, commission, exchange, etc. It is felt that the income derived from services extended to the UCB sector may not be sufficient to sustain the Umbrella Organization. The large and strong UCBs may not avail some of the services. However, small and medium sized UCBs are expected to avail most services for their clients and for themselves, as they may not be eligible for carrying out such activities on their own. The Umbrella Organization's asset portfolio would predominantly comprise loans and advances, which would involve more than the normal risk as many of the UCBs are small entities and have local operations. The Umbrella Organization could also lend to non-UCBs. It would also need to have a healthy investment portfolio.

I. Management: It goes without saying that an Umbrella Organization, such as the one under design should be run on thoroughly professional lines and observe the best practices insofar as corporate governance is concerned. The Working Group recommends that the Memorandum and Articles of Association of the company (Umbrella Organization) should specifically provide for appointment of independent directors. In order to achieve this objective, the fit and proper criteria for the Board of Directors and Executive Board/CEO may be prescribed either in the Memorandum and Articles of Association, or by the regulators.

CEO should be a professional of repute, with deep knowledge and understanding of the UCB sector, combined with business acumen of a finance company to inspire confidence in the Umbrella Organization. The Working Group leaves it to the Reserve Bank for putting in place a suitable system, standards and stringent fit and proper criteria to ensure that the position of CEO is held by a competent person. The Working Group is also of the considered view that the Reserve Bank should nominate on the Board a suitable officer, at least during the initial formative years of the Umbrella Organization, Subsequently, the Reserve Bank may have an Observer on the Board. This would not only lend the Umbrella Organization greater credibility, but its nominee's guidance would also be useful in adherence to best corporate governance practices, regulations and formulation of appropriate business strategies and products.

J. Emergency Liquidity and Solvency Support: Occasionally, UCBs confronted by financial distress, caused by temporary liquidity problems, need emergency liquidity support systems to come to their rescue. Similarly, UCBs classified in Grade III and IV with meager or entirely eroded net worth needs solvency support for their revival. Representatives from the UCB sector, during the meeting with the Working Group emphasized the need for addressing these pressing issues.

The Working Group, while appreciating the need for evolving a mechanism to address the aforesaid twin issues, is of the view that it should not be the mandate of the Umbrella Organization to provide such emergency liquidity and solvency support to UCBs as it may be difficult for it to meet the quantum of financial assistance that may be required in this regard. Further, solvency support is subject to high risk and low or nil return and envisages a fairly long period of pay back. Neither the sector, nor the Umbrella Organization, being a non-deposit taking NBFC, would be in a position to fund the recapitalization needs of problem UCBs. However, arrangements need to be put in place to address and resolve these problems.

K. Emergency Liquidity Support: The Working Group believes that due to lack of homogeneity, uneven geographical spread of UCBs, cultural differences, affinity to state federations and state laws on co-operation, the bonding of UCBs at the State level is strong. Empirical evidence also demonstrates that the contagion effects are localized and solidarity amongst the co-operatives at the State level is far greater than at the national level. The emergency liquidity supports need to be provided to UCBs in financial distress and, in most cases, such facility would be without collateral and for a short term. The uncollateralized emergency liquidity support would carry more than the normal counter party credit risk. Therefore, a thorough understanding of the local polity, the management and operations of the distressed UCB, its problems and prospects would be necessary. The Working Group is of the view that a State level institution would not only have better appreciation of the financial needs of the distressed UCB, but also pull resources for supporting the UCB concerned. Therefore, the Working Group recommends State-specific Emergency Fund Facility Schemes.

L. Revival Fund: The presence of a large number of weak and sick UCBs (about 399; 23 percent of the total), which need solvency support, call for an urgent need for creation of a Revival Fund. If UCBs with negative net worth were to be brought to positive net worth, an enormous sum of about ₹ 2,500 crore may be required. While RBI may pursue a menu of options, including mergers, with or without DICGC support, and financial restructuring for turn around of these banks, possibly, an amount of ₹ 2000 crore may still be necessary. However, such a fund could only be raised out of contribution from the net profits of UCBs. The total net profit of the sector being about ₹ 1,000 crore, mobilization of this magnitude of resources from the sector may not be feasible. The Working Group has observed that though the Central/State Governments have been supporting the revival of the rural co-operatives, such support was not extended to UCBs.

Therefore, in the absence of capital contribution from the Central/State Governments, the Revival Fund for solvency support to UCBs would not be feasible. The Working Group also believed that the providing solvency support to UCBs from contributions from the profits may be resisted by the sector and the contribution would be too little to rescue sick UCBs. Therefore, it would be more appropriate to provide both short and medium term finance from the Emergency Fund. UCBs not complying with the prescribed CRAR may be supported from the Emergency Fund by way of subscription to Tier II instruments issued by these banks.

6.10 Summing Up

The financial sector reforms have been components of the overall economic reforms undertaken in a phased manner from 1991 by the Government of India. A look has to be taken at the reform process and what it means to the co-operative credit institutions. These reforms also envisaged improving the efficiency and productivity of the co-operative credit delivery system which in turn would accelerate the requisite credit flow to the productive sectors of the economy.

The major objectives of these reforms in the co-operative sector were as under:

1. To make the institutions competitive by removing external constraints having a bearing on their operations.
2. To improve their financial health.
3. To ensure transparency in their business operations.
4. To improve their profitability.
5. Institutional building and strengthening.

Positive impact of reforms, as has been witnessed in the case of commercial banking sector, may take longer to get manifested for co-operative banks given the late start of the reform process in this sector. Unless such a positive scenario evolves for the co-operative banking sector in the near future, the financial health of many of these banks would continue to remain a cause of concern.

It is significant to note that introduction of reforms and the consequent increase in competition has resulted in some convergence in operations of commercial banks and co-operative banks, especially scheduled UCBs. Furthermore, while most of the loss-making commercial banks are relatively small, in the case of UCBs some of the large banks are incurring losses and this has increased the vulnerability of the whole segment. Detection of irregularities in a few UCBs in the recent past has raised concerns about the conduct of the management in co-operative banks. For this purpose, the RBI has suggested the establishment of a unified supervisory authority for UCBs and the related amendment to the Banking Regulation Act, 1949.

End Note

1. Reserve Bank of India, *Report on Currency and Finance,* 2001-02, p. VI-18.

7

Problems and Challenges Faced by the Co-operative Sector

Co-operatives in India came into being as a result of the Government taking cognizance of the agricultural conditions that prevailed during the latter part of the 19th century and the absence of institutional arrangements for finance to agriculturists, which had resulted in mounting distress and discontent. Small, local, locally worked institutions, co-operative in form, which would satisfy the postulates of proximity, security and facility for providing credit, were seen as the answer to this situation. However, subsequent events during both pre- and post-Independence period have led to a vast growth of co-operatives covering various sectors of the Indian economy.

Though India can claim to have the world's largest and most diverse co-operative movement, barring some exceptions co-operatives in India, in general, are fraught with a number of problems and challenges. Apart from certain inherent weaknesses, they are constrained by the overwhelming role of the government as well as prescriptive and restrictive legislation and have been unable to retain an autonomous and democratic character.

The problems and challenges that co-operatives face today are numerous. These encompass the functional aspects of co-operatives namely Membership, Governance and Operations which could be considered as internal to the organization. These problems are further compounded by two important external factors, namely politicization of co-operatives and the control/interference by governments. These are discussed below in detail.

7.1 Ensuring Active Membership

Theoretically and conceptually, a co-operative comes into being as a result of a common need of members. The need could either be for a service, which serves as an input into his activity or to service his output. The member owns the co-operative conjointly with other members and is expected to act with due diligence to fulfil his membership duties and responsibilities. If co-operatives are to succeed, it is important that members are well informed of not only their rights but also obligations and the need to participate actively in the affairs of the co-operative.

Ensuring active member participation and enabling speedy exit of non-user members has remained a daunting task for co-operatives. Unfortunately, over the years, we have come to a state where a large number of co-operatives are either unable to cope with the needs of members or the members have in general become passive and apathetic and do not use the services offered. Quite a number of co-operatives have also become irrelevant to their members' needs. Poor member participation has also been due to lack of effort to enhance member equity in co-operatives and near absence of member communication and awareness building efforts.

This situation has been further aggravated due to the lack of provision in Indian co-operative law to ensure that members are users and for removal of inactive members expeditiously and on a regular basis. The Co-operative Acts allow a person who is not doing business with co-operative to continue being enrolled as a member and eligible to participate in meetings, exercise voting rights and to elect/be elected on the Board. Consequently, it is found that in several co-operatives non-users apart from continuing as members, participate in elections and even get elected to hold positions on the Board of Directors/Chairman.

Co-operative Acts in general stipulate removal of membership only by the General Body through a special resolution. Calling a General Body meeting and expelling members is a long drawn process and coupled with this due to political compulsions the problem of removing a large percentage of inactive members has not been addressed with the required seriousness.

7.2 Lack of Recognition of Co-operatives as Economic Institutions

A fundamental issue having substantial bearing on the governance of co-operative institutions is the lack of recognition of co-operatives as economic institutions meant to serve the needs of its members. The general perception has been that co-operatives are instruments of government meant for public good and therefore need to be supported by the government.

Co-operatives must, therefore, be seen as autonomous, economic institutions of user members engaged in production, distribution or other services. They have to be competitive to survive as viable entities, without which they cannot serve their members.

The general lack of a well defined and explicitly stated official and legal recognition of co-operatives in most co-operative laws is, and without doubt, the root cause of many of the problems that afflict the sector. Further, both members of co-operatives and the public at large do not consider co-operatives as economic institutions at par with other business organizations in view of the predominant role being played by the government through exercise of vast powers that the law provides.

7.3 Structure of Co-operatives

The design of a co-operative is an important factor in determining the manner in which it is governed, its success and viability. While designing a co-operative enterprise, one needs to consider factors such as local socio-political conditions, local economy, leadership, structure, by-laws, norms and rules, critical linkages with federal and other organizations, macro policies etc.

Most co-operatives in the country have come into being through a top-down approach or based on a blue print model and are a result of target-based programmes/actions taken by the higher tier organizations and State departments. Besides, there are numerous instances of suppression of local initiatives and ignoring the perceived needs of the members while structuring the co-operatives. Higher tier co-operatives in most cases have hardly retained any co-operative character and operate like Parastatals and frequently with little or no member involvement.

Lack of initial knowledge about the multi-faceted choices in designing/re-designing co-operatives seriously affects governance, inhibits growth and can result in wrong choices. This is particularly so where there is no clear focal and dynamic leadership.

7.4 Board and Management Interface and Accountability

Co-operatives have a two-tier management structure of the Board and its executives, all in the ultimate analysis responsible to the General Body. The effectiveness of a co-operative depends in large part on the quality of partnership between its Board and Chief Executive. The Board should concern itself with long-term or strategic planning; organizational (as opposed to operational) policies; representation and relationships with members, government, other business and the public at large; resource mobilization; monitoring of the organization's performance; and the selection, supervision/direction of the Chief Executive. The Chief Executive must be responsible for achievement of plan objectives; the efficient, economical and effective use of resources; recommending possible business strategies to its Board; recruitment, supervision and evaluation of employees; coordination of departments and groups; etc.

In general, co-operative Boards suffer from lack of long-term perspective, market and business orientation, understanding of the co-operative way of business and how it differs from other enterprises, awareness about the environment (e.g. globalization) and using the knowledge for furthering member interest. In addition, they are also not able to cope with the changing needs of members and be responsive to member needs.

Ensuring accountability at all levels necessitates vesting the required authority (delegation) and clearly defined roles and responsibilities. Unfortunately, in a large number of co-operatives, Board and executive functions are not clearly demarcated, often leading to identity conflicts. Boards are generally found to be assuming operational responsibilities and disinclined to delegate powers and responsibilities to Managers. Striking a balance between Board and Executive functions is a crucial element which determines the success of a co-operative enterprise. The law too does not clearly define the roles, responsibilities and accountability at different levels.

7.5 Professionalization and Accountability

In a business environment the importance of professionally trained and qualified manpower cannot be overemphasized. However, this is one of the weakest areas of co-operatives where the practice of posting government officials in managerial positions in co-operatives for brief tenures has been growing. Many States have common cadre of employees who are deputed to the co-operatives. Most often, these officials have no understanding of the business, either by training or practice and they are deputed for too short a tenure to acquire adequate understanding. There are also numerous instances where the officers posted by the government to hold key positions such as Chief Executive are changed too frequently resulting in a lack of accountability and thus affecting the business of the co-operatives. The laws also do not provide the required autonomy to co-operatives in matters related to staff strength, remuneration payable, service conditions etc.

Co-operatives are also unable to attract and retain competent professionals (particularly in areas such as marketing and finance) since apart from their lack of financial ability to pay market based compensation they are also unable to provide a stimulating and conducive work culture and environment including freedom for operations with the required delegation of authority. The need for change and adoption of sound HR policies assumes great importance, particularly with a rapidly growing private sector.

7.6 Lack of Capital

Lack of capital, both equity and debt, is a key constraint in the development and growth of co-operatives. In the case of value-added businesses the problem is further compounded due to their high capital requirements. The need for equity in all forms of organization arises out of the requirement of containing the financial risk of debt within reasonable limits. Equity also ensures member stake and interest in the co-operative. It is the sharing of risk in their venture, through substantial financial stake, that is likely to enhance member interest and participation as well as control in the affairs of co-operatives. In the absence of member funding, the stake of members in the success of the business of their co-operatives is not high, which makes co-operatives vulnerable to poor governance and mismanagement.

Most co-operatives suffer from lack of member capital and consequently low leverage in raising debt required for the growth of the business. In fledgling co-operatives, the problem is particularly acute since they have no reserves to fall back on and nor do the members, most of whom are marginal and small operators, have the wherewithal to contribute substantially to initial capital. Low levels of equity imply a higher debt equity ratio with the accompanying hazards of actual cash flows being possibly inadequate to service the debt.

Unallocated reserves/retained earnings are the highest quality funds available to functioning co-operatives. However, to avoid payment of income tax, co-operatives most often follow the practice of paying price differentials to members for their supply, which has severely undermined capital formation in co-operatives. Further, co-operatives are generally constrained to minimize retained earnings, as the co-operative Act and Rules virtually treat retained earnings as out of the purview of members' funds.

While corporate entities can raise equity as well as borrow from the market by placing appropriate instruments, co-operatives do not have access to capital markets. Any effort to broaden the equity base—through introduction of instruments other than the shares to be subscribed only by members—opens up the debate about the ownership, voting rights, co-operative principles etc.

The concept of share holding in co-operatives suffers in competitive attractiveness when compared to shares in corporate entities.

1. The principle of one-person one-vote precludes any advantage to holders of a larger number of shares in the affairs of a co-operative.
2. The principle of limited return on capital results in denying co-operatives access to capital.
3. The value of a share to a member has no correlation with the performance of the co-operative, as he gets back only the face value of his share.
4. Shares of co-operatives have no liquidity as there is no trading platform for transfer of shares.

Thus, co-operatives are finding it increasingly difficult to augment their capital to the required levels through the existing available avenues, i.e. seeking more share contribution from their members and retained earnings.

A problem affecting the capital of a co-operative is one relating to recoveries of debt. The high level of under recoveries of primary credit societies has not only adversely affected their own growth, but also the financial results of higher tier financial co-operatives. The problems of non-credit co-operatives are not materially different. A large number of non-credit co-operatives are also either defunct or sick, the major reasons being similar to those of credit co-operatives.

There has been extensive debate on whether government should participate in the share capital of co-operatives. Government financial support is often justified on grounds that co-operatives cannot raise capital from capital markets and a majority of the members are unable to contribute share capital in the quantity required to run the co-operatives efficiently. However, equity contribution from government has invariably impacted on the autonomy of co-operatives and is a matter which does not merit compromise.

In the globalized economic order, co-operatives as economic entities cannot remain isolated. In order to be competitive they have necessarily to grow and for that, augmentation of capital at the required pace is also necessary, as capital adequacy is one of the important parameters to judge the strength of an economic business entity.

7.7 Linkages and Competitiveness

Though a tiered structure in co-operatives is intended to bring about effective linkages, both forward and backward and maximize benefits to the primary membership, this has not often been achieved. Since co-operatives at each level are distinctive legal entities, myopic assertions of freedom have prevented greater integration leading to high transaction costs. More and more co-operatives at primary as well as higher levels are transacting business with non-members; higher tier co-operatives are frequently competing in business with their constituent members and networking amongst co-operatives a rare feature to be seen. Lack of or ineffective linkages have been adversely impacting the business performance of the co-operatives and their competitiveness.

In the current liberalized and globalized economic environment, co-operatives need a level playing field in order to cope with the emerging competition, sustain growth and meet member needs and services effectively. Unfortunately, constrained by restrictive laws, co-operatives lack functional autonomy including the required freedom in matters such as, area of operation, appointment of staff, deciding on remuneration payable, pricing, mobilization of funds, investment of funds and flexibility in business operations.

7.8 Accessibility to Finance/Credit by Members

Lack of credit facilities to a large segment of rural population, particularly the poor and marginalized, is a concern that needs to be addressed.

Although there is no hindrance in co-operative law for share croppers/tenant farmers/agricultural labourers to be members of co-operatives, they are unable to avail loans in the absence of clear ownership title to land/collateral, and hence remain for all practical purposes outside the co-operative credit system. This marginalized segment does not have access to the commercial banking system for the same reasons.

The weather cycle and the crop cycle do not always match and hence particularly in drought prone areas, farming is, and is likely to be, at best, a marginally viable if not non-viable proposition. From time to time, governments have been resorting to one-time debt settlements and/or re-scheduling of overdue loans, but these are not permanent solutions to the basic problem of a perpetual cycle of indebtedness, which needs to be addressed.

7.9 Sickness in the Co-operative Sector

Of over 5 lakh co-operatives in the country at different levels, a large number today are not viable, while many are practically dormant. A large number of the non-viable co-operatives are, in fact, on the verge of sickness or incipient sickness. The sickness is particularly visible in the processing sector, of which sugar, textiles and vegetable oil account for a sizeable portion.

Though the government has been providing financial

assistance for rehabilitation of sick co-operatives into a healthy enterprise, it has not always met with encouraging results. It must be recognized that most co-operatives function in the agricultural sector where the risk element is relatively high and the returns on investment low and they, therefore, start off with an initial disadvantage. It is also important for us to appreciate that the co-operative form of enterprise may not be the most suitable for all sectors and commodities. While there should no doubt be a clear voluntary exit policy for co-operatives which are not amenable to revival, sick co-operatives with the potential for improvement need to be supported through appropriate agencies and funding possibilities.

7.10 Aligning Governance with Objectives

In an organizational context, governance refers to the institutional framework that defines the structure and linkages, behaviour, interaction, rules of conduct, conflict resolution, incentives and disincentives for behaviour. In co-operatives, governance issues are primarily focused on the structure of the Board and its relationship with members, managers and the State. Sadly, the most important function of governance, which is that of aligning the tasks in tune with the basic objective with which a co-operative is organized, has received very little attention.

7.11 Politicization of Co-operatives and Interference by Government

Although co-operative democracy is based on common economic interest and as such is entirely different from political democracy, over time co-operatives have been increasingly politicized. Co-operative institutions in the country with their vast outreach have become powerful instruments of political mobilization. Instances of a political party in power assuming control over large sized co-operatives through methods such as appointing an active member of the party to the position of chairman, nominating persons of its choice on the board, issuing directions to them and the official nominees to vote for a particular candidate as chairman have become common. Further, when elections are held, they are fought on party lines with panels of political parties keenly contesting to gain control of the organization. This has led to factions in the board, conflicts in governance and management and lack of consensus in decision making. Also, factors such as personal/political interests of board members and use of the co-operative for political patronage have weakened the co-operative sector and affected their ability to function as competitive and professionally managed business entities.

Mass enrolment of members of co-operatives is also resorted to, prior to elections. Changes in law to suit political ends are also to be found when there is a change of government. In many instances, politicians who are chairmen of co-operative boards refuse to call for elections, continuing to be entrenched in positions of authority.

Audit of co-operatives is conducted by the registrar and in several states it is not found to be timely as well as satisfying the present day requirements/standards and challenges.

This state of affairs is largely on account of the enormous powers that the government and registrar are vested with by the Act. Apart from paving the way for politicization, with the laws governing co-operatives becoming progressively more restrictive, the functional autonomy and democratic character of the co-operatives have been seriously compromised. Some of the restrictive provisions and powers of the government/registrar which are contained in the State Co-operative Societies Acts and which often lead to perpetuation of politicization and government interference in co-operatives are as under:

1. Refusal to register co-operatives on various grounds.
2. Compulsorily amend by-laws, divide, merge, amalgamate co-operatives.
3. Give directions to a co-operative(s) in public interest.
4. Appoint supervisory staff and set up common cadres,

approve wages and staff service conditions.
5. Nominate persons on the management committee/board.
6. Conduct/postpone elections.
7. Classify co-operatives and deal with them en masse for the purposes of amalgamation, common cadres, service conditions, business, etc.
8. Supersede committees/boards, disqualify members and committee members, compel admission of members, and reinstatement of expelled members.
9. Rescind resolutions of the committee/board.
10. Grant exemption to a co-operative or a class of co-operatives from any of the provisions of the Act.
11. Prescribe rules to be followed.
12. Restriction on simultaneously holding office in a number of co-operatives.
13. Restriction on the terms of office bearers of the co-operative.

All these powers militate against the voluntary and autonomous nature of co-operatives. There are numerous instances of misuse of powers such as supersession of boards, postponement of elections, granting exemptions and issuance of directives to meet political ends etc.

In short, following can be listed as major problems being faced by co-operatives of various types:

1. Inability to ensure active membership, speedy exit of non-user members, lack of member communication and awareness building measures.
2. Serious inadequacies in governance including that related to Boards' roles and responsibilities.
3. A general lack of recognition of co-operatives as economic institutions both amongst the policy makers and public at large.
4. Inability to attract and retain competent professionals.
5. Lack of efforts for capital formation particularly that concerning enhancing member equity and thus member stake.

6. Lack of cost competitiveness arising out of issues such as overstaffing, a general top-down approach in forming co-operatives including the tiered structures.
7. Politicization and excessive role of the government chiefly arising out of the loop holes and restrictive provisions in the Co-operative Acts.

In addition to the above, there is also a serious problem of a large number of co-operatives that are sick/non-viable.

7.12 Summing Up

Growth of co-operatives sector has not been uniform in all parts of the country. The primary reasons for this situation are control of co-operatives by dominant vested-interest groups, poor management, dependence of co-operatives on higher tiers and government for financial assistance and limited range of business activities. The function of thrift has not been given due importance by co-operatives leading to resource crunch and ultimately to their inability to serve the poor.

One of the major issues concerning the co-operative sector is the professionalisation of management. If the co-operatives have to compete in a more open economic regime, the State Governments will have to professionalise the management of co-operatives and especially the co-operative processing units, This is crucial for overall co-operative development vis-à-vis other sectors. For achieving this, it will be necessary to convince the State Governments of the need for granting functional autonomy to co-operatives.

8

Measures to Strengthen Co-operatives

The success of co-operatives ultimately depends upon their ability to perform their functions—whether they relate to production, finance, marketing, distribution or construction—efficiently and to the satisfaction of the members and the community. The loyalties of the members can be retained not on the basis of monopoly, agreements or under duress but on the strength of the goodwill secured by rendering service.

8.1 Improvement of Personnel

A unit of business, whatever its form, cannot survive if it does not fulfil properly the tasks which it undertakes. It also ceases to grow if the management is not watchful for new opportunities. In the agricultural sector for instance diesel engines and electric motors are being increasingly used for providing irrigation in some areas while in others tractors are utilised for cultivation and reclamation. A progressive co-operative, besides supplying seeds, fertilisers and other requisites, would provide spare parts, repair and servicing facilities at reasonable cost. These and similar measures in other fields can be adopted only if the staff consists of competent and trained men. Co-operatives are sometimes organised and administered by those who lack both the qualifications and the experience necessary for the job. This factor alone accounts for a large number of failures of co-operatives and the uneven development of the movement, in the country.

The importance of efficient management cannot, therefore, be too much stressed. Being a movement essentially dependent on the ability of persons in humble walks of life, who are often amateurs in the handling of business operations, the need for training and education is greater than for those who have ample resources and business experience. The co-operative society is, besides a democratic body, each member of which is equally important. Hence the need, recognized from the earliest days of the movement in foreign countries, for diffusing knowledge of the principles and practice of co-operation among all ranks of co-operators.

Many of the managerial and supervisory functions call for specialised knowledge and technical skill. The co-operatives ought to recruit qualified men and get the existing staff adequately trained.

8.2 Co-operative Education and Training

Government of India has been implementing a Central Sector Scheme for Co-operative Education and Training through the National Co-operative Union of India (NCUI) and the National Council for Co-operative Training (NCCT) since Third Five Year Plan (1961-66). The programmes relating to co-operative education are being implemented by the NCUI.

NCUI has been implementing the Central Sector Scheme for Co-operative Education in co-operatively underdeveloped States/underdeveloped area of developed States. The Government of India is providing 100 percent grants-in-aid to NCUI for implementing the Special Scheme of Intensification of Co-operative Education in Co-operatively underdeveloped States. At present NCUI is running 44 projects.

The Co-operative Training Programmes are being conducted by NCCT through its 5 Regional Institutes of Co-operative Management, 14 Institutes of Co-operative Management, located in different states and Vaikunth Mehta National Institute of Co-operative Management, Pune. Government of India provides financial assistance in the form of grants-in-aid to NCCT for conducting co-operative training programmes.

From the year, 2004-05, Government introduced a new component in the Central Sector Scheme for Assistance to

Junior Co-operative Training Centres (JCTCs) in conducting training programmes. JCTCs are financed and run by the State Co-operative Unions/State Governments.

8.3 Co-operative Education and Training Activities in the North-Eastern Region

The Government of India is implementing a special scheme for intensification of co-operative education in co-operatively underdeveloped states including the North-Eastern Region through NCUI with 100 percent financial assistance. NCUI has established 8 field projects, namely Aizwal (Mizoram), Bishnupur, West Imphal (Manipur), Jorhat, Kamrup (Assam), Kohima (Nagaland), Shillong (Meghalaya) and West Sikkim in the North-Eastern Region. These projects have made tangible impact in improving the income of members of self-help groups and co-operatives.

8.4 Assistance to National Co-operative Development Corporation (NCDC) for Co-operative Development: Government of India implements its co-operative development programmes, inter alia, through (NCDC). The programmes/schemes being implemented through NCDC are (a) integrated co-operative development projects in selected districts, (b) assistance to co-operative marketing, processing and storage programmes in co-operatively underdeveloped/least developed States/Union Territories and (c) share capital participation in growers'/weavers' co-operative spinning mills under the restructured central sector scheme. Under this scheme, subsidy component is provided by the Government of India and the loan component is arranged by NCDC through its own sources.

NCDC is a non-equity based development financing institution created exclusively for the co-operative sector with the objective of planning and promoting programmes for production, processing, marketing, storage, export and import of agricultural produce, food stuff and certain notified commodities and services on co-operative principles. With amendment of the NCDC Act in 2002, scope of activities of NCDC has widened to cover livestock, cottage and village industries, handicrafts, rural crafts and certain notified services besides enabling NCDC to lend directly to co-operative societies on furnishing security to its satisfaction. With notification of additional services like tourism, hospitality, transport, electricity and power, rural housing, healthcare, hospitals and education co-operatives, the scope of NCDC funding has further broadened. The Central Government has, however, prescribed an overall ceiling of 25 percent of annual budget of NCDC for financing all activities under notified services so that focus of NCDC continues on financing of co-operatives in agriculture and allied sector.

8.5 Co-operative Spinning Mills

In order to improve the economic condition of the cotton growers as well as handloom and powerloom weavers and to consolidate the gains achieved so far, Government, through NCDC, provides financial assistance to the spinning mills and ginning and pressing units in the co-operative sector.

NCDC is implementing Restructured Central Sector Scheme for share capital participation in growers'/weavers' co-operative spinning mills. Loans are met out of funds of the NCDC and subsidy is provided by Government of India under this scheme.

8.6 Co-operative Storage and Cold Storage

Government, through NCDC, has been making systematic and sustained efforts to assist co-operatives in creating additional storage capacity aimed at facilitating expanded operations of co-operative marketing of agriculture produce, distribution of inputs and sale of consumer articles.

Similarly, Government, through NCDC, has been providing financial assistance to State Governments and also directly to the co-operative societies for establishment of cold storages aimed at facilitating expanded shelf life of potatoes and other fruits and vegetables.

NCDC provides financial assistance to the extent of 90 percent of the block cost to the State Governments for setting up, modernization, expansion, rehabilitation of cold storages and ice plants by co-operatives. In case of direct funding, assistance to the extent of 75 percent is provided. NCDC has also dovetailed its cold storage programme with National Horticulture Board (NHB) and acts as a nodal agency to route subsidy to State Governments/Co-operatives for cold storage projects. In such cases, quantum of assistance provided by NCDC is reduced by the subsidy available under the Capital Investment Scheme (CIS) of NHB. The scheme provides enhanced back-ended subsidy @ 40 percent of the project cost for general and 55 percent in case of hilly and scheduled areas for maximum storage capacity up to 5,000 ton per project at normative cost @ ₹ 6,000/7,000/8,000 per ton as per prescribed standards under the scheme.

8.7 Integrated Co-operative Development Projects (ICDP): Government has made systematic efforts to develop primary co-operatives as multi-purpose entities to provide a package of services to rural communities. With this in view, NCDC is implementing ICDP scheme in selected districts in the rural areas.

8.8 Co-operatives in Underdeveloped States

The process of economic development in the country brought to light certain regional disparities and imbalances in some parts due to inherent factors like topography, agro-climatic conditions and poor infrastructure. During formulation of the Fifth Five Year Plan (1974-79), the limitations of this approach came to the fore and as a consequence, the concept of co-operatively underdeveloped States evolved to ensure balanced regional development.

The categorization of States for funding by NCDC was

reviewed by the Planning Commission in November 2004. Accordingly, Andhra Pradesh, Uttar Pradesh, Madhya Pradesh and Goa were also placed under the category of co-operatively underdeveloped States. Similarly, Jharkhand, Bihar and Jammu and Kashmir were classified as co-operatively least developed States, in addition to the existing States. Now 10 States and 2 UTs have been categorized as co-operatively underdeveloped and 11 States as least developed.

8.9 Strengthening of National Level Co-operative Federations

The progressive expansion and diversification of the co-operative movement has led to organization of national level co-operative institutions in different fields of economic activity with a view to accelerating the pace of co-operative development and also to strengthen co-operatives in their economic activities in a coordinated manner. National level co-operative federations have been playing a significant leadership role. Most of these federations are promotional in nature excepting a few which are involved in commercial activities. Government provides both policy direction and financial support to these federations. The objective of the scheme is to assist the national level federations in undertaking promotional and research activities, bringing about improvement in infrastructural facilities and also to assist in building up their equity base.

8.10 Revitalization of Co-operatives

With phenomenal expansion of co-operatives in almost all the sectors, signs of structural weakness and regional imbalances have also become apparent. The reason for such weakness would be attributed to the large percentage of dormant membership, heavy dependence on Government assistance, poor deposit mobilization, lack of professional management, mounting overdues, etc. Concrete steps have been initiated to revitalize the co-operatives to make them vibrant democratic organizations with economic viability and active participation of members. The steps taken for revitalization of co-operatives include (a) enunciation of a National Policy on Co-operatives, (b) revamping of co-operative credit structure and (c) reforms in co-operative legislation for providing an appropriate legislative framework for sound and healthy growth of co-operatives.

8.11 Market Intervention Scheme (MIS)

Government is implementing Market Intervention Scheme (MIS) for procurement of agricultural and horticultural commodities generally perishable in nature and not covered under Price Support Scheme. The MIS is implemented in order to protect the growers of these commodities from making distress sale in the event of bumper crop when there is glut in the market and the prices tend to fall below economic levels/cost of production. Procurement under MIS is made by NAFED as Central agency and by the State designated agencies. Losses, if any, incurred by the procuring agencies are shared between Central Government and the concerned State Government on 50:50 basis (75:25 in case of North-Eastern States). However, the amount of loss to be shared between Central Government and the concerned State Government is restricted to 25 percent of the procurement cost. Profit, if any, earned by the procuring agencies is retained by them.

8.12 Constitution (One Hundred and Eleventh Amendment) Bill, 2009

Since most farmers in India belong to the category of small and marginal farmers, the strengthening of co-operatives is seen as a measure to empower them. An amendment to the Constitution, for the purpose of empowering co-operatives through voluntary formation, autonomous functioning, democratic control and professional management, has been mooted. After the approval of the Government, the Constitution (One Hundred and Sixth Amendment) Bill, 2006 was introduced in the Lok Sabha on May 22, 2006. The Lok Sabha referred this Bill to the Standing Committee on Agriculture for its examination and report. The Standing Committee's Report was submitted in Lok Sabha on August 20, 2007. This report was considered by the Government and it was decided to move official amendments to the Bill. Accordingly, official amendments to the Bill were moved in the Lok Sabha. However, the Bill could not be discussed in the Lok Sabha for passing. The Bill lapsed on dissolution of 14th Lok Sabha on May 18, 2009.

It was decided to reintroduce the Bill for amendment to the Constitution. Accordingly, the Constitution (One Hundred and Eleventh Amendment) Bill was introduced in the Lok Sabha on September 30, 2009. The Bill was referred to Standing Committee of Parliament on Agriculture which considered the Bill and submitted its report to the Lok Sabha on September 3, 2010. The suggestions made by the Standing Committee were considered by the Government and it was decided with the approval of the Cabinet to move official amendments to the Constitution (One Hundred and Eleventh Amendment) Bill, 2009. Accordingly, notices were sent for moving the official amendments. The process is under way.

8.13 Summing Up

Co-operatives are often criticised for being dominated by vested interests. The solutions sought so far have been in the nature of limiting the number of terms of office etc. While these measures are useful as far as they go, they still do not impinge on the basic question of commitment of an office bearer to the objectives of the society. An office bearer of a marketing society, who does not market his own produce through his marketing co-operative, is hardly likely to have any stake in the performance of that society. Likewise, an office bearer of a credit co-operative bank, who is himself a defaulter in payment of dues is hardly likely to pursue recovery discipline in his society. It will be necessary to take a close look at the bye-laws of various types of co-operatives and to suitably revise these, wherever necessary to ensure that such commitments are built into the bye-laws as to eliminate mere office seekers from the management of the society. In fact, dairy co-operatives of the Anand Pattern have a specific clause built into the bye-laws about the supply of milk to the co-operative for a certain minimum number of days in a year as an essential qualification for office. A similar provision needs to be built in the bye-laws of other type of co-operatives also.

9

Co-operatives and Globalization

Co-operatives in India have mostly played the role of an agent of the government. Co-operatives are seen to be the institutions that carry the State programmes to people, and in turn get State support.

9.1 Occupying New Spaces

Globalization and liberalization of economic policies creates new spaces in two forms. First, the governments are withdrawing from different domains hitherto solely or generally occupied by them creating vacant spaces, be it in manufacturing or service sector. Secondly, additional opportunities are continuously being created in newer areas, under the new economic environment. Many of these domains are not regarded as being commercially attractive. However, they are very important for people and communities and there is definitely a demand for these services. As such, the challenge would be to make them commercially viable and profitable. Traditional areas of social sector such as education, health, transportation, water supply, forest management, electricity are some of the areas where co-operative solutions could be superior to either public or private approaches to utility management. In fact privatization efforts in India are already on in this area. Co-operatives have been working in all these areas and have the potential to prove their strength and hence they could be effective alternatives to privatization.

Further co-operatives could play a major role in newer areas such as precision farming, sun farming, water harvesting, micro finance. Other potential areas are information technology, communications, tourism and hospitality etc., the demand for which is ever growing and which could provide alternative means of livelihood for co-operative members. Outsourcing of services would also be the practice as firms grow in size and specialization. Such outsourcing would expectedly lead to savings in transaction costs. Entering such services through the co-operative route could prove an attractive alternative employment generating avenue.

9.2 Providing an Institutional Form for the Displaced

Globalization would also result in restructuring leading to displacements occurring due to exit policies, labour re-engineering, closure of less competitive units, adoption of new technologies and consequent down sizing, mergers, acquisitions etc. including displacement from the agricultural sector. Displaced specialists could form co-operatives for providing essential specialized services, which institutions would be increasingly outsourcing. There has been a sharp reduction in the population dependent on agriculture and landless labourers have increased in number. The alarming rate of unemployment among youth continues. Collective endeavours through co-operatives of such marginalized sections of the people can work, as many services would still be required by existing concerns which may not wish to have such service providers on their pay roll.

9.3 Constructive Competitors

Cartels or pre-determined market sharing by private enterprises can jeopardize free and fair trade. Co-operatives could provide the role of the constructive competitors. This could be either through a stand-alone co-operative or by entering strategic partnership with the private sector in the form of co-operative-private sector collaborations etc. Co-operatives by their very presence would help to maintain the balance in terms of price and quality. For this reason co-operatives need to enter all those areas where full domination by the private corporate might eventually spell bad news to the consumers.

9.4 Safeguarding the Interest of Agriculture and Rural Areas

Agriculture will continue to be very important in terms of percentage share of dependent population. The logic of agriculture would be applicable to almost the entire rural population. Self-help initiatives by farmers in the area of cultivation, marketing, accessing agricultural inputs, finding jobs for the landless labourers, displaced rural artisans etc., would continue to be a major role for the co-operative sector. None else is equipped to handle this.

9.5 Facilitating the Millennium Development Goals (MDGs)

The Government of India has its commitment to the UN, of achieving the MDGs within a specified time frame. In many of the specified areas, the country is clearly lagging behind. Rural health (and in particular maternal health) and combating contagious diseases (medical co-operatives), gender equity (women co-operatives), and poverty reduction (agricultural and tribal co-operatives) are some of the crucial areas under MDGs, where the co-operative sector can play the lead role.

9.6 Preserving the Cultural and Ethical Values of the Country

Co-operatives are the best channels to keep the spirit of collectivism and democracy afloat. The presence of a large network of social organizations, like co-operatives, would aid in the generation and utilization of social capital and more the social capital, greater would be the possibility of development. Therefore, co-operatives have a futuristic role of fostering collectivism and preserving the social capital base of the country.

9.7 Summing Up

It is thus clear that co-operatives have a significant role to play in the future settings of the Indian economy. In fact they have a more important role to play in the future compared to their agency role of the past. It is only the presence of a strong and wide network of co-operatives that can make the process of globalization less painful and global integration smooth. It is the co-operatives again who are equipped to work as pressure groups to voice views of the people in the market.

10

Summing Up

The 1990s witnessed a paradigm shift towards market oriented economic policies and a careful dismantling of obstacles in its wake. This has helped the smaller, emerging economies gain access to world markets, emergent technologies and collaborations. This has also given them a window to the developed world and helped them understand the significant role of globalisation as an instrument, which could be utilised not just to achieve economic efficiency, but also eradicate poverty.

Co-operatives are one of primarily, autonomous, economic institutions of user members united voluntarily to meet their common economic, social, cultural needs and aspirations through a jointly-owned and democratically-controlled enterprise. They are self-reliant and self-sustaining institutions functioning in a free, fair and transparent way in keeping with the principles and values of the co-operative movement. To arrest the practice of concentration of power in a few hands to the detriment of the larger member community, education for awareness building should be an integral part of a co-operative.

Agro-processing of fruits and vegetables is a potential area for development of co-operatives of the farmers. These processing units should, ideally, be part of integrated projects linking production with agro-processing and supporting by products. The major weaknesses of the co-operative fruit and vegetable processing units are under-utilisation of capacity and inefficient technical and financial management.

The recent changes introduced by the Government in several fields provide an opportunity for co- operatives to play a much larger role in several areas such as marketing of agricultural produce, creation of marketing infrastructure, establishment of agro-processing units etc.

Co-operatives in India being a State subject have been and continue to be variously governed through multiple individual State Acts. The Acts endow governments with draconian powers which have in many cases militated against the very concept of a co-operative. Supersession of elected boards of co-operatives and appointment of special officers for long periods without elections are examples of the interference of state governments in co-operative functioning.

The global economy, and in particular the Indian economy, is passing through transformation. The positive dimension of globalization includes liberal economic policies, reduction of state intervention, and easy access to monetary capital and consequently new opportunities for economic participation. This is already evidenced in India in the form of increased economic growth and state withdrawal from many economic and social domains. On the other hand, there is apparently a misplaced perception developing in India that co-operatives may not be able to deliver in the context of the globalized market conditions and the changes that are taking place as a result.

Under the circumstances, there is a need for resurgence of co-operatives as important players. Co-operatives have tremendous opportunities because (a) they have a special identity, (b) they have both social and economic objectives, (c) they are value- and community-based, (d) they are people-oriented and (e) they have a network of linkages through the co-operative movement.

In terms of the decent work paradigm, co-operatives could lead the way by demonstrating what is really meant by freedom, equity, security and human dignity. Thus, co-operatives by being true to their basic principles provide locally-based answers to globalization. Therefore, contrary to the belief that globalization impedes the growth of co-operatives, they are the vital agencies to face the challenges posed by globalization.

From the Eighth Five Year Plan (1992-97) onwards, co-operatives have found no mention in the Five Year Plans drawn up by the Planning Commission. It is important that due recognition is given to co-operatives as a third sector of the economy and its development, particularly in terms of its marginalized and weaker segments.

Part II
Edited Extracts from India's Five Year Plans on Co-operative Movement

First Five Year Plan: 1951-56

The First Five Year Plan (1951-56), outlined in detail the vision of the co-operative movement in India and the rationale for emphasizing co-operatives and panchayats as preferred organizations for economic and political development. The Plan emphasized the adoption of the co-operative method of organization to cover all aspects of community development. It provided for setting up of urban co-operative banks, industrial co-operatives of workers, consumer co-operatives, housing co-operatives, diffusion of knowledge through co-operative training and education and recommended that every government department follow the policy of building up co-operatives.

Development of the Co-operative Movement

After the experience of the limited success of merely regulatory laws like the several anti-usury measures, an effort at building up by mutual association the people's own credit institutions was sponsored by government. In the then prevailing atmosphere of economic passivity on the part of the State this official sponsoring of a special form of organization was considered to be a great event. The first piece of co-operative legislation was the Co-operative Credit Societies Act of 1904, which was amended in 1912 to permit the formation of societies for purposes other than credit. As a result, societies for a variety of purposes began to be organized.

This process of diversification was, however, slow in its pace, until the special needs of the period of the Second World War, and the subsequent years of reconstruction invested co-operative organizations with a special importance and significance. When individualism was the order of the day, co-operation represented a defensive act of association on the part of individual citizens. But with the adoption of the principle of social regulation, the co-operative societies, which from their commencement in this country have been socially sponsored and supported, came to occupy a more positive role. In a regime of planned development, co-operation is an instrument, which while retaining some of the advantages of decentralisation and local initiative will yet serve willingly and readily the overall purposes and directives of the plan. This has been amply proved by the recent experience of India, as also of other countries, like the UK which have entered upon an era of democratic planning. The co-operative form of organization can no longer be treated as only a species within the private sector. It is an indispensable instrument of planned economic action in a democracy.

The broad features of the history and evolution of co-operation in India are unmistakable. With 1,81,000 Societies, a membership of about 14 million and a working capital of ₹ 276 crore the movement constitutes an important economic and social force in the country. It has shown a steady quantitative expansion, especially during the last five years. Even more striking than the expansion in numbers and size, is the growing diversity of functions assumed by co-operative societies. Besides agricultural societies of all types, viz. credit, processing, marketing, farming, irrigation, consolidation etc., there are industrial co-operatives, labour societies, consumers' co-operatives in rural as well as in urban areas, housing societies; processing factories; and urban banks. However, agricultural societies still constitute more than 80 percent of the total and of these credit societies are still by far the most numerous. The non-credit and the non-agricultural forms are, however, making steady progress The conditions created by the Second World War, the emphasis on intensive and rapid rural development in the post-War reconstruction programmes of State Governments, arid the channelling of state aid activity through co-operative institutions have been responsible for this trend.

An increasing measure of responsibility for organising and financing rural economic development is being shouldered by co-operatives. Both the natural evolution of co-operative activity, and the impetus of the special need created in several parts of the country by agrarian legislation regulating the business of money-lenders, scaling down of debts, restricting rents and abolishing landlordism are responsible for the striking increase in the operations of co-operative credit societies. Co-operation is in fact being transformed steadily yet surely, from a tolerated exception into a general rule. In industry, commerce, transport and retail distribution co-operatives are gaining experience and strength. Different State Governments sometimes emphasize different fields of co-operative activity in keeping with local conditions. There can be no doubt, however, that a new awareness of an opportunity to build up a form of business organisation more suited to the conditions and needs of the times than the joint stock company has come over the people of small means everywhere. The joint stock company is too cumbersome as an organization for the small producer, agricultural or industrial. What is needed and what the co-operative society has provided is a simpler form of organization more suited to the needs of the people to be served and therefore likely to be more acceptable.

We have in several parts of this report expressed our preference for the co-operative organisation of the economic activities of the people, especially of those activities, e.g. agriculture, marketing, cottage and processing industries and internal trade, which form the most important part of the developmental schemes included in the Plan. As an instrument of democratic planning, combining initiative, mutual benefit and social purpose, co-operation must be an essential feature of the programme for the implementation of the Five Year Plan. As it is the purpose of the Plan to change the economy of the country from an individualistic to a socially regulated and co-operative basis, its success should be judged, among other things, by the extent to which it is implemented through co-operative organisations. The Planning Commission in consultation with the State Governments, co-operative organizations, and the Reserve Bank intends to formulate a more specific programme for the expansion of the movement in all the sectors in respect of which co-operative organisation has been considered suitable.

Co-operatives and Panchayats

We are anxious to ensure that in the agricultural part of our Plan the village as a whole should be actively associated in framing targets, in suggesting suitable methods for achieving them, in evolving and directing a suitable organisation for day to day working and in checking periodically the progress made. A willing and constructive participation of the people can alone ensure the success of the Plan. While a general stirring of the aspirations of the people is to be noticed all over the country, the establishment and successful working of village organisations remain to be achieved in many parts. Latterly there has been a welcome earnestness on the part of State Governments for the establishment of Panchayats as civic and developmental bodies charged with the general responsibility of attending to the collective welfare of the village community. Panchayats have an indispensable role to play in the rural areas. As representing the best interests of all sections of the community their status is unique. Many activities such as, framing programmes of production for the village, obtaining and utilising governmental assistance for the betterment of the village such as the construction of roads, tanks etc., encouraging villagers to improve the standards of cultivation, organising voluntary labour for community works and generally assisting in the implementation of economic an social reform legislation passed by the States, will naturally fall within the purview of the panchayat.

On the other hand, for the working of individual programmes of economic development, where not only the general interest but also the specific responsibility and liability of a member have to be ensured, a more integrated and binding form of association is needed. Specific and practical tasks of reclaiming land, of providing resources for better cultivation, of marketing the produce of the villagers, both agriculturists and artisans, can be best performed through co-operatives. The co-operative agencies will naturally have to conform to the principles of business management, namely, of satisfactory service and economical working. That they are not profiteering associations and that they function for mutual service makes them desirable agents of democratic planning. It is therefore very necessary that Co-operative agencies in the village should have the closest possible relationship with the principal democratic body namely, the panchayat. Though in the discharge of their functions the two bodies have specific fields to operate, in a number of common functions by having mutual representation and by having common ad-hoc committees, it will be possible to build up a structure of democratic management of developmental plans through both the organisations, the panchayats and the co-operative societies. We therefore suggest that in so far as institutional reform is an essential part of the implementation of the Five Year Plan, emphasis in due proportion and in appropriate fields should be placed both on panchayats and on co-operative societies.

Multi-purpose and Credit Societies

The States as a whole are conscious of the importance of developing co-operative societies as a means of re-organisation of rural life. Among co-operative bodies working in rural areas, the multi-purpose society has quite rightly come to occupy an important place. It has come to be realised that division of the needs, activity and assets of a villager into mutually exclusive parts such as credit, production, sale etc. is somewhat artificial. At any rate, it has been agreed that for the future an attempt should be made to have in each village a co-operative organisation which will cater for the multiple needs of its members. In some parts of the country efforts are now being made to transform many of the credit societies, which historically have been the most important co-operative organisations, into multi-purpose societies, the emphasis now being placed on the concentrated and all-sided development of rural areas would suggest the desirability of encouraging such transformation. Pending this development the credit societies will continue to play a vital role in rural economy. In fact it is dim-cult to over-estimate the importance of the services that rural societies could render in the sphere of credit organisation.

Recently there has been a noticeable increase of money incomes in the agricultural sector of the economy. Much of the development that will be brought about under the Five Year Plan will strengthen this tendency. While therefore, on the one hand, larger sums will come to be disbursed in rural areas, it is of the utmost importance to see that monies so spent do not go outside the system of organised credit. In other words, rural savings and monies generally in the hands of the rural population have to be kept flowing into credit organisations. A co-operative society is calculated to do this much better than almost any other organisation. In the Co-operative form of organization the provision of resources such as credit goes with the practice of thrift. Even if a village co-operative is too small to open a savings account for its members it can induce them either to open accounts with the postal savings banks or the Central Co-operative Banks. It can also function as an authorised agent for savings, Promoting savings schemes sponsored by the State or Central Governments. The establishment of credit societies in villages is thus a sine qua non of the organisation of credit in the context of planned investment in the developmental schemes approved in the Plan.

In the past the village credit societies have been accustomed to secure their finance from central financing agencies operating in urban centres and utilising mostly capital resources made available by the urban classes. In keeping with the normal financial structure an apex co-operative bank has also been established almost in all States. The State Governments have lately taken a more active part in assisting financially the apex banks. The Reserve Bank which as the Central Bank of the country is interested in the creation of a co-ordinated and sound system of rural credit as recently liberalised its procedure for accommodation to co-operative banks. The advances to the cultivators through the institutional agencies (i.e. the Government and the co-operatives, the latter with the assistance of the Reserve Bank) should be steadily increased so as to reach the limit of at least ₹ 100 crore per annum by the end of the Plan year 1955-56. If, however, the credit structure of the country is to be geared to an increasing pace with economic activity in rural areas an intensive effort at integrating all the channels of credit for the common purpose is needed.

Sale and Purchase Societies

The purchase of the agriculturist's requirements and the sale of his produce are key activities in the business of farming and their importance is likely to be even more crucial in a socially regulated economy. Due to his inability to secure a fair deal at these two stages the average agriculturist is denied the full fruits of his industry. The organisation therefore of co-operative sale and purchase societies and of other marketing organisations is vital both for its direct and indirect benefits. With credit and marketing co-operatively organised all over the country not only would the success of the present initial Plan be more adequately assured but the stage will be set for a much more ambitious and constructive programme of rural development.

The emphasis of the Plan is on augmenting agricultural production. In this sphere co-operation has a very significant contribution to make. Co-operatives can help to increase the effectiveness of extension work. Other services which a cultivator needs for efficient utilization of his land can also be made available through co-operative agencies. Such aids as seeds, fertilisers, and implements on which depends the profitable exploitation of the resources of the soil can be effectively placed at the disposal even of the small farmer by co-operative societies. In fact, in the field of agriculture co-operation comprises almost every activity that is connoted by the term agricultural organization. It is the best medium for promoting a progressive agriculture. Major items of agricultural development e.g. consolidation of holdings, soil conservation and provision of facilities for irrigation as well as current needs such as protection of crops from pests, diseases and animals can be most effectively served through co-operative organizations.

Co-operative Farming

In most parts of the country for ensuring economic cultivation an increase in the unit of cultivation is necessary. Here again, co-operative farming has direct relevance. Without under-mining the sense of proprietorship and the incentive to industry that it gives, co-operative farms can produce all the advantages that a larger unit possesses. A community which has been accustomed to the advantages of co-operative association in other vital matters of its business will be more successfully approached for establishing a co-operative farm than is possible in a community in which co-operation has made little headway. While the controversy between voluntary and compulsory formation of co-operative farms may at this stage be avoided, it can be suggested that in any area where a majority of holders representing at least half of the total area under cultivation desire to establish a co-operative farm, legislative means should be at their disposal to proceed with the formation of a co-operative farming society for the whole village. The State on its part should do everything in its power to encourage the establishment of such farms and to promote their satisfactory working afterwards. Farming through a co-operative calls for a number of individual and corporate virtues on the part of members. It will therefore be some time before co-operative farms reach a developed stage. If during the period of the First Five Year Plan, in representative areas of different States a good number of societies are established as going concerns, we can proceed more confidently to expand that pattern of cultivation in the next Five Year Plan.

Co-operation and Community Projects

For the intensive and all-sided development of the villages the community projects have recently been launched in the various States. The purpose and the organisation of the projects have been touched on elsewhere in this Report. We have recommended that; in all the aspects of community development co-operative methods of organisation should be adopted to the maximum possible extent. As is obvious, the ultimate justification of (immunity projects will depend on the extent to which the people are enabled to make self reliant efforts to carry out all their activities in an improved, business-like and progressive manner. While the leadership and assistance of departmental and external sources will to son extent help in initiating the process of community development, for the development to be permanent and expanding the people must be active participants in the whole process. It is not easy to conceive how, in the absence of co-operative organisation of their business and of their social activities, this desirable object of community projects can be realised.

While the working of these projects is no doubt likely to vary from area to area in keeping wit the local environment, a broad co-operative pattern should be considered essential. As in other spheres of co-operative expansion, the programme of reform should take account of the financial and personnel resources that will be made available by departmental as well as institutional agencies. It is, however, essential that in every community project area a programme for all round co-operative development .should be drawn up. The establishment of various types of co-operative societies after educating the local public regarding their benefit will be the best means of enlisting the active support of the people on a voluntary basis for works of improvement on an organized scale.

Industrial Co-operatives

In the rural areas the needs of employment will not all be met by farming. The Plan contemplates several improvements such as irrigation, soil conservation, and reclamation which may succeed in giving fuller employment to agriculturists than what they have at present. But limitations of nature will in many instances require that the agriculturists should turn to some other occupations during the slack seasons. Besides these part-time workers there are in the villages several classes of artisans who under the pressure of competition from organised industry are finding it difficult to maintain their traditional employments. While the formation of agricultural co-operatives is by now a familiar experience, industrial co-operatives are still in their infancy. Their activity is so directly in touch with the moving events of a competitive market that the uncertainties of their business often loom larger than their basic importance.

Moreover, co-operative financing and marketing agencies have yet very limited experience of doing business with industrial co-operatives. As a result of these factors, the future of industrial co-operatives is yet not well-established as appears to be the case with agricultural co-operatives. As we have recommended elsewhere, we desire that cottage and small scale industries should have for themselves well-marked fields which are not encroached upon by large-scale industry. This principle will no doubt have to be translated into more specific and concrete terms as a result of further investigations and experience. When this is done the conditions for the successful operation of industrial co-operatives will be more assured. In the mean while, it is desirable that co-operatives organised for the several trades be established on a sound footing.

While it is possible and indeed desirable that the special advantages recommended by us elsewhere should be made available to the members of these co-operative societies, their place in the industrial structure of a planned economy will ultimately depend on their efficiency. Nothing should be done which will undermine the initiative and self-confidence of the members of these societies. Aids in respect of power, implements, raw materials, technical advice and marketing facilities should all be made co-operatively available to these societies. It is not necessary for us in the present context to suggest how the organisation of the industrial co-operatives themselves should develop from the village to the State level. We expect that according to the experience of each State, some form of federal organisation will in due course evolve. But in respect of the capital needs of these co-operatives it must be emphasised that provision for finance will have to be made commensurate with the extent to which the industrial co-operatives are expected to fulfil given targets of production. Whether the existing co-operative financing agencies can continue to offer finance for industrial activities which are somewhat special and, if so, to what extent is a matter in respect of which further enquiry by the States concerned, as also by the Reserve Bank, will have to be undertaken.

We note that many of the States are establishing industrial finance corporations, designed for the most part for meeting the financial needs of comparatively small-scale units of industry. The Plan also provides ₹ 15 crore for assisting small-scale and cottage industries. We would recommend that financial aid from this provision and from such corporations should by preference be made available to co-operatively organised industries. With artisans' industry co-operatively developed and with a number of processing factories established on a co-operative basis, a growing portion of rural economic activities will come within the co-operatives sphere. For reasons mentioned earlier in this chapter, such development will conform to the requirements of democratic planning and will make it possible at later stages of planning to formulate more comprehensive schemes of economic progress.

Urban Co-operatives

While in the immediate future extension of co-operation is most urgently called for in the rural area, where agricultural operations play a dominant part, the urban sector of the co-operative movement has also to develop along systematic lines, if in due course it is to make its contribution to planned development. In urban areas there are a number of artisans of small means who find it difficult to organise themselves in keeping with the requirements of modern times. It is to be desired on social as well as on economic grounds that members of this class should be enabled to reorganise themselves to be able to take full advantage of modern scientific methods. Small industries co-operatively using advantages like power and special techniques will be able to make a significant contribution to the industrialisation of the country. We have elsewhere expressed our preference for a decentralised type of industrialisation and how far we can go in the direction of decentralisation without loss of economic advantage will depend to a very large extent on the capacity of artisans to organise themselves on a co-operative basis. The utility of co-operation in the urban areas extends to the credit and other needs of small entrepreneurs and cottage workers. Urban banking conducted on co-operative lines has a very important role to play in this field. Co-operative banks are more democratic and more amenable to local control than even small sized joint stock banks, and hence urban banking closely associated, with other forms of urban co-operation ought to be more purposefully developed.

In urban areas special importance must be attached to consumers' co-operatives. Unfortunately, we notice that as yet, the development of consumers' co-operatives has not made enough progress in the country. Under the influence of rationing and governmental distribution of scarce goods, a number of consumers' societies have no doubt come into being. They have, however, as a class failed to extend their usefulness beyond these limits. Their future, therefore, in the event of removal of controls on distribution of essential articles is somewhat uncertain. The success of consumers' co-operation will primarily depend on the enthusiasm and preference that the co-operators themselves succeed in creating among their fellow citizens. It should, however, be possible for the State to adjust its policies in such a way that the legitimate interests of consumers' co-operative societies are not ignored by those departments of the Central and State Governments which have to attend to their claims. It would in our opinion be in the best interest of the planned development of distributive trades that an attempt be made to build up consumers' co-operatives over as wide a field of distribution as possible. Here again, the questions of finance and credit are likely to be very important. We must, however, remember that to the extent to which co-operatives replace private business, capital engaged in the latter will tend to be released. If a common credit policy is made effective for all credit agencies a transfer of functions will gradually but effectively bring about an appropriate transfer of financial resources.

A problem of urban areas in regard to which co-operation has a special significance has been touched upon by us in our chapter on housing. While "it is not necessary in this place to cover the same ground again, it must be stated that with the strong urge towards urbanisation that industrialisation is bound to promote, housing assumes crucial importance. While institutional activity such as that undertaken by governmental departments, civic bodies and employers' associations, will meet the situation to a certain extent, a considerable burden of the construction of houses, especially for the middle and lower income groups, will fall on their own co-operative organisations. From the choice of a site to the letting out or use of house-room when it is ready, the work of these housing societies will impinge on a number of departments. It should be the policy of these departments to assist in the formation and progress of these societies.

Improvement of Personnel

The success of co-operatives ultimately depends upon their ability to perform their functions—whether they relate to production, finance, marketing, distribution or construction—efficiently and to the satisfaction of the members and the community. The loyalties of the members can be retained not on the basis of monopoly, agreements or under duress but on the strength of the goodwill secured by rendering service. A unit of business, whatever its form, cannot survive if it does not fulfil properly the tasks which it undertakes. It also ceases to grow if the management is not watchful for new opportunities. In the agricultural sector for instance diesel engines and electric motors are being increasingly used for providing irrigation in some areas while in others tractors are utilised for cultivation and reclamation. A progressive co-operative, besides supplying seeds, fertilisers and other requisites, would provide spare parts, repair and servicing facilities at reasonable cost. These and similar measures in other fields can be adopted only if the staff consists of competent and trained men.

Co-operatives are sometimes organised and administered by those who lack both the qualifications and the experience necessary for the job. This factor alone accounts for a large number of co-operatives' failures and the uneven development of the movement, in the country. The importance of efficient management cannot, therefore, be too much stressed. Being a movement essentially dependent on the ability of persons in humble walks of life, who are often amateurs in the handling of business operations, the need for training and education is greater than for those who have ample resources and business experience. The co-operative society is, besides a democratic body, each member of which is equally important. Hence the need, recognized from the earliest days of the movement in foreign countries, for diffusing knowledge of the principles and practice of co-operation among all ranks of co-operators.

Many of the managerial and supervisory functions call for

specialised knowledge and technical skill. The co-operatives ought to recruit qualified men and get the existing staff adequately trained. The present facilities for the training of higher personnel are not adequate and we have provided a sum of ₹ 10 lakh for their improvement. We also trust that the State Governments will arrange for the training of other staff, and of workers for the co-operative movement.

Even though almost all the States have a co-operative department, many of them have to be helped to equip it to shoulder the new, diversified and complex responsibilities now envisaged. Until recently the main statutory functions of the department were registration, audit and inspection. Consequently the bulk of the staff was well versed in these activities. Now that the co-operatives are being recognised and utilised as an important instrument of economic planning, the staff of co-operative departments, without spoon feeding or interfering too much in the working of the Societies, should be able to provide effective guidance and knowledge and not merely, be auditors and inspectors of the Government. In short a constructive attitude and determination to make a success of the co-operatives must pervade the Government departments and the people.

In the past there have been occasional complaints to the effect that while the State generally sponsors co-operative societies and desires to accord them preference, in actual practice agencies, other than co-operatives, often receive better treatment from a number of departments. There is also a tendency, in some of them, to regard only the co-operative department as responsible for co-operative development. It has already been indicated that the various forms of co-operative activity impinge on a number of departments. Therefore, unless every department and every Ministry accepts and adopts the policy of fostering co-operative methods of business, rapid and enduring results cannot be obtained. For instance the Central and State Public Works and Irrigation Departments spend fairly large amounts on works programmes every year.

Except in one or two States most of the works are entrusted to contractors.

We consider that every department should follow the policy of building up co-operatives which may eventually replace the contractors or other middle men. It is, however, not our intention that co-operatives should be bolstered up indefinitely, irrespective of the quality or cost of the service they offer. At the same time it is only reasonable to expect that in their formative years they should be ungrudgingly helped by the State to utilise the opportunities offered to them and enabled to consolidate their strength.

Second Five Year Plan: 1956-61

The Second Five-Year Plan (1956-1961), emphasized "building up a co-operative sector as part of a scheme of planned development" as being one of the central aims of National Policy. It aimed at enabling co-operatives to increasingly become the principal basis for organization of economic activity. The Plan drew up programmes of co-operative development based on the recommendations of the All India Rural Credit Survey Committee (AIRCS). It was envisaged that every family in a village should be a member of at least one co-operative society.

Linking of credit and non-credit societies to provide better services to the farmers was also targeted. State partnership with co-operative institutions at various levels, the essential basis of which was to be assistance and not interference or control, was recommended and for facilitating State partnership in co-operatives, the Plan also recommended the establishment of a National Agricultural Credit Long-term Operations Fund. The National Co-operative Development Fund was also established by the Central Government, during this period, to enable states to borrow for the purpose of subscribing share capital of non credit co-operative institutions in the country.

Co-operative marketing and processing of agricultural produce formed an important part of the Integrated Scheme of Co-operative Development in the Second Plan. About 1900 primary marketing societies were set up and State Marketing Federations were established in all the States, as well as the National Co-operative Marketing Federation at the Centre. Marketing co-operatives along with the agricultural co-operatives played a major role in promoting the Green Revolution by providing credit and inputs to farmers as well as processing their increased outputs.

Co-operation and National Planning

Economic development along democratic lines offers a vast field for the application of co-operation in its infinitely varying forms. Our socialist pattern of society implies the creation of large numbers of decentralised units, both in agriculture and in industry. These small units can obtain the advantages of scale and organisation mainly by coming together. The character of economic development in India with its emphasis on social change, therefore, provides a great deal of scope for the organisation of co-operative activity. The building up of a co-operative sector as part of the scheme of planned development is, thus, one of the central aims of national policy.

The limit to the range of activities to which the principle of co-operation can be applied is set by the fact that a primary co-operative group should be reasonably small for its members to know and trust one another. For certain purposes a number of small groups may, and indeed must, combine into larger organisations, but, in the last analysis, the strength of co-operation comes from relatively small and homogeneous groups which function actively. If strong primary units exist at the base, effective organisations can also be built up at higher levels. The structure as a whole can then undertake activities and provide services which require large resources and organisation. From this aspect the fields which mark themselves out as being specially appropriate for the co-operative method of organisation are agricultural credit, marketing and processing, all aspects of production in rural areas, consumers' co-operative stores, co-operatives of artisans and labour and construction co-operatives. In these fields the objective is to enable co-operative increasingly to become the principal basis for the organisation of economic activity.

In areas which offer special opportunities for its development, the co-operative form of organisation has advantages which neither the system of private enterprise nor that of State ownership can match. In particular, it offers a means of achieving results valuable to the community by drawing equally upon incentives which are social and incentives which are individual. Where it succeeds, co-operation brings large gains to the community, but the human factors involved in it are complex and in some ways it is much more difficult for the co-operative form of organisation to succeed than it is for a completely socialised enterprise or for an individual entrepreneur. It is therefore necessary to take effective measures to enable co-operation to succeed, whenever possible, and especially in fields which are assigned to it in the scheme of national development.

This aspect has received careful consideration in the report of the Rural Credit Survey organised by the Reserve Bank of India. Programmes of co-operative development for the second live year plan have been drawn up broadly on the lines recommended in the Rural Credit Survey. These do not yet cover the entire field of co-operation. In some directions further programmes have to be worked out; in others targets and other details have to be determined carefully as the plan goes into action. Because of historical circumstances in India, agricultural credit accounts for the greater part of development in the field of co-operation during the past fifty-years. The provision of adequate credit on reasonable terms is undoubtedly a most important part of co-operation, but the movement has wider and more far-reaching aims.

To a large extent, in rural co-operation the crucial unit is the village. In implementing the programme of rural co-operation, there are three aspects to which special attention has to be given. Firstly, credit is only the beginning of co-operation. From credit, co-operation has to extend to a number of other activities in the village, including co-operative farming. In co-operation hard and fast rules of development! Cannot be made and every step is determined by the experience of the people. The second aspect is that every family in a village should be member of at least one co-operative society. The third aspect is that the co-operative movement should aim at making every family in the village creditworthy. At present, even in areas in which the movement has spread most, only 30 to 40 percent of families are able to satisfy the tests laid down. The primary co-operative society and the village panchayat have to work in unison if the needs of all the families in the village are to be met.

The appropriate size of a primary rural society has to be considered both from the aspect of credit and from the point of view of co-operative development generally. Ultimately, it is the aim, as stated above, that co-operation should extend to all activities in the village including cultivation. More than 3,80,000 villages have populations of 500 or less and the question of combining small villages into units with the population of about 1,000 deserves to be examined. It is necessary to have villages which are small enough to have a sense of solidarity and yet not so small that personnel cannot be provided for the essential services organised for their benefit. Considerations which bear on the organisation of convenient village units are also relevant to the consideration of the size of the primary co-operative society. Its area of jurisdiction should, on the one hand, be large enough to make it an efficient unit and, on the other, it should not be so large that it might become difficult to secure amongst members the knowledge, the sense of mutual obligation and concern for rehabilitation of the weaker sections of the community and the intimate contact between the committee of management and individual families without which co-operation cannot make a real impact on rural life.

Co-operatives, like village panchayats, are institutional agencies for achieving social cohesion. In a country whose economic structure has its roots in the village, co-operation is something more than a series of activities organised on co-operative lines; basically, its purpose is to evolve a system of co-operative community organisation which touches upon all aspects of life. Within the village community there are sections of the populations who need special assistance. Co-operation should therefore mean an obligation towards all families in the village community and the development of land and other resources and of social services in the common interest of the village as a whole. This is the underlying approach in setting co-operative village management as the main direction of reorganisation in the rural economy.

With the rapid growth of towns and closer integration between the rural and the industrial economy there is a large and expanding Held for the development of co-operation in urban areas. In the past urban co-operation has received inadequate attention. In retail and wholesale trade, transport, small industry, banking, housing and construction, for instance, much can be achieved through efficient organisation along co-operative lines. When co-operation develops sufficiently, producer, marketing, consumer and other forms of co-operatives become parts of an inter-related and inter-dependent co-operative sector with close links also with other aspects of the economy and the distinction which now exists between rural and urban co-operation becomes less significant.

Review of Progress

When co-operation was first introduced under the Co-operative Credit Societies Act, 1904, it was confined to the organisation of the co-operative credit societies in urban and rural areas with a view to relieving indebtedness and promoting thrift. The Co-operative Societies Act, 1912, permitted the registration of co-operative societies for promoting non-credit activities as well as federations of primary societies into organisations at higher levels. Both in the field of credit and of non-credit activities the co-operative structure consists of primary societies at the base in villages or towns, central organisations at the district level and apex organisations at the State level.

The development of agricultural credit organisations falls broadly into two parts, those concerned with short and medium-term finance and those which are intended to provide long-term finance. In the first group there were in June, 1954, 22 State co-operative banks, 499 co-operative central banks and 1,26,954 agricultural credit societies with a total membership of 5.8 million. These various organisations operated in 1953-54 with total owned funds amounting to about ₹ 39 crore, deposits of about ₹ 71 crore and working capital of about ₹ 161 crore. Fresh advances by agricultural credit societies were of the order of about ₹ 30 crore. Institutions for long-term agricultural finance were developed to a much smaller extent, being confined to 10 central and 304 primary land mortgage banks with a total working capital of about ₹ 24 crore. On the non-agricultural side the principal credit institutions were 716 urban banks with a total working capital of about ₹ 33 crore, 8,389 co-operative credit societies with a membership of about 2.7 million and 3,651 societies of salaried employees and wage earners.

In recent years greater attention has been given to the development of non-credit organisations, but it cannot be said that in non-credit activities, except at selected centres, co-operation has made any large impression. In the field of agricultural marketing there were in June, 1954, 16 State marketing societies, 2,125 marketing unions and federations and 9,240 primary marketing societies with a total annual turnover in 1953-54 of about ₹ 52 crore.

In some States during the first plan irrigation societies and milk supply societies have shown encouraging results. There were in 1953-54, 937 irrigation societies, 65 milk supply unions and 1,473 primary milk supply societies. In 1953-54 there were also 234 land colonisation societies and 601 co-operative farming societies.

In the non-agricultural field perhaps the largest measure of success has been achieved in the formation of handloom weavers' societies of which there were in 1953-54, 5,748. The number of looms included "in these societies has increased during the First Plan from 6,26,119 to about a million and is to be increased to about 1.45 million by the end of the Second

Five Year Plan. In consumers' co-operation only a fraction of the ground has been covered so far, the number of primary stores being 8,251 and of wholesale stores 86 with a total turnover of less than ₹ 40 crore. Other non-credit societies which have come into existence during recent years and a proportion of which are working fairly well are 2,036 housing societies, 536 labour, contract societies, 124 forest labourers societies and 78 transport societies. There were also 4,643 health and better living societies, almost entirely in rural areas.

Reorganisation of Rural Credit and Marketing

The main proposals of the Committee of Direction of the Rural Credit Survey have been accepted in broad principle by the Central Government, by the Reserve Bank of India and by representatives of the co-operative movement. These form the general basis on which programmes of development for the second five year plan have been drawn up. The most important departure from earlier programmes which the Rural Credit Survey envisaged was that the State should enter into partnership with co-operative institutions at various levels. It was felt that such financial partnership would provide additional strength to co-operatives and make available to them in fuller measure assistance and guidance from the Government. The principle of State partnership will apply especially at the apex and the central bank level and in a more flexible manner at the primary level. It has been made clear that the essential basis of State partnership is assistance and not interference or control.

With a view to facilitating the partnership of the State in co-operatives the Reserve Bank has established a National Agricultural Credit (long-term operations) Fund with an initial contribution of ₹ 10 crore. Contributions of ₹ 5 crore per annum will be made during the period of the second plan so that by 1960-61 the Fund will have a capital of ₹ 35 crore. From this Fund loans are to be advanced to States to enable them to subscribe to the share capital of co-operative credit institutions. A second Fund, known as the National Co-operative Development Fund is to be established by the Central Government. From this Fund States will be able to borrow for the purpose of subscribing to the share capital, of non credit co-operative institutions. Assistance towards the construction of godowns, staff for co-operative societies and for strengthening the administration of co-operative departments will also be provided from this Fund.

Another feature of the scheme of reorganization proposed in the Rural Credit Survey is that credit and non-credit societies should be linked to one another so that the agriculturist can be provided with credit for seeds, manures, agricultural implements and essential consumer goods and is also helped in disposing of his produce. In view of the range of operations contemplated, the Rural Credit Survey recommended that large-sized credit societies serving groups of villages should be formed by amalgamation of the existing small societies and societies constituted for the first time should conform to the pattern recommended by the Survey. The general pattern of organisation for a larger co-operative society is that it would have a membership of about 500, the liability of each member being limited to five times the face value of the capital subscribed by him. The society would have a minimum share capital of about ₹ 15,000 and would serve an appropriate number of villages, grouped together for the purpose and together providing (wherever possible) a total annual business of about ₹ 1.5 lakh. By 1960-61 it is proposed that 10,400 such larger sized credit societies, each with a trained manager, should be established.

Rural credit societies, whether already existing or established afresh, are to be affiliated to the primary marketing society serving a mandi area Agriculturists will receive loans for agricultural operations from credit societies. They will also obtain from them their requirements either for cash or against approved credit limits. Credit societies will collect the produce of their members for disposal through the marketing society.

They will purchase the stocks required by them from marketing societies and distribute them to their members. Primary marketing societies are to be federated together in an apex marketing society serving the State as a whole.

In the development of rural credit perhaps the greatest difficulty in the past has been that a substantial proportion of agriculturists are non-credit worthy according to the rules and conditions for advancing loans which were generally prescribed. To meet this situation it is proposed that loans should be advanced by credit societies on the basis of production programmes and anticipated crops. A maximum credit limit will be fixed for each member and within this limit he will be permitted to obtain loans according to his requirements. To ensure proper use of funds loans will be given as far as possible in kind, in the form of seed, fertilizer, etc. Where cash loans are given, the payment may be in instalments. Members of credit societies will be persuaded to agree .in advance to market their produce through the primary marketing society.

Warehousing will provide an important institutional link between the activities of credit and non-credit societies which have been described above. Primary marketing societies as well as the better organised credit societies will have to construct godowns on a large scale. As recommended by the Rural Credit Survey, it is proposed to establish a Central Warehousing Corporation and warehousing corporations for States. These corporations will function under the direction of the National Co-operative Development and Warehousing Board. The maximum authorised share capital of a State warehousing corporation is expected to be about ₹ 2 crore but the issue capital will vary according to the requirements of different States.

It is proposed that the Central Warehousing Corporation should subscribe half the capital and the other half should be found by the State Government. It is anticipated that 16 warehousing corporations will be set up and in the course of the second five year plan they will establish about 250 warehouses at different centres with a total storage capacity of about a million tons. Suitable centres for setting 'up warehouses are being selected. The Central Warehousing Corporation is expected to have a total capital of ₹ 10 crore, of which the Central Government through the National Co-operative Development and Warehousing Board may subscribe ₹ 4 crore and the rest may be subscribed by the State Bank of India, scheduled banks, co-operative institutions, etc. The Central Warehousing Corporation is expected to set up large-sized warehouses at about 100 important centres. Warehouse receipts will be treated as negotiable instruments on the security of which banking institutions ran provide credit to those who deposit agricultural produce in warehouses.

In the Second Five Year Plan, provision has been made for developing co-operative processing on a substantial scale, especially for producing sugar, ginning cotton, crushing oil and balling jute.

As recommended in the Rural Credit Survey, the Imperial Bank of India was converted into State Bank of India. The State Bank of India has a statutory obligation to open 400 new branches during the first five years of its existence or such extended period as the Central Government may specify. As a first step, 100 places have been selected. Besides, 31 branches will be opened in accordance with the expansion programme on which the Imperial Bank was engaged prior to nationalisation. In addition to the provision of banking and of credit facilities in rural areas, the State Bank will be able to provide better remittance facilities and larger amounts of market finance.

Producers' and Other Co-operatives

The measures outlined in the preceding section for the development of rural credit marketing and processing will assist the formation and development of producer co-operatives in agriculture. Strong co-operative financial institutions will find it possible to provide increasing assistance also to industrial co-operatives. It has been suggested that during the second five year plan such essential steps should be taken as will provide sound foundations for the development of agrarian co-operatives, so that within a period of 10 years or so a substantial proportion of agricultural lands are cultivated on co-operative lines. The following action has been recommended.

1. In each district and later in each national extension and community project area experimental or pilot projects in co-operative farming should be undertaken with a view to evolving better methods of management and organisation. These centres should be developed into practical training centres for co-operative, agricultural and' other extension workers.
2. As far as possible, surplus areas which become available on the imposition of ceilings on agricultural holdings should be settled along co-operative lines.
3. Farms smaller than the prescribed basic holding should be brought into co-operatives to which surplus lands are allotted, provided their owners agree to pool their lands. When consolidating holdings, lands belonging to persons with very small holdings should be located as near as possible to the pooled lands, so that those cultivators who may not join co-operative farms immediately may find it convenient to do it so at a later stage.
4. Special attention should be given to existing co-operative farming societies, many of which are functioning indifferently, and steps should be taken to put as many of them as possible into good condition, so that their success may serve as an incentive to others to form co-operative farming societies.
5. Groups of persons should be encouraged to form co-operative farming societies, which should be assisted.
6. In tribal areas, where communal ownership is still the common practice, as settled cultivation is introduced, steps

should be taken to develop agriculture on co-operative lines.

7. An extensive programme for training in co-operative farming should be organised.

In consultation with States, in the course of the next year, it is proposed to work out detailed targets for the second five year plan for developing agrarian producer co-operatives.

In village industries there is perhaps greater scope for producer co-operatives than, for instance, in small-scale industries and handicrafts, where supply and marketing co-operatives may play a larger role. In the handloom industry, broad targets for developing industrial co-operatives have been worked out. In other village and small industries also steps should be taken as early as may be possible to formulate programmes for developing co-operatives and providing staff to assist them.

Although there is considerable scope for it, a consumers' co-operative movement has so far failed to develop. During the war and the immediate post-war period, in respect of articles in short supply for which controls existed, co-operative distribution societies were formed both in urban and rural areas on a fairly extensive scale. With the removal of controls, however, a proportion of these societies ceased to exist. In urban areas, except in a few States, co-operative departments have not operated to any great extent. A network of consumers' co-operative stores in urban areas will be a source of strength to the consumers' co-operative-movement in rural areas as well as to producer co-operatives.

Although targets for developing the consumers' co-operative movement have not been worked out so far, it is recommended that problems in this field should receive closer study and programmes worked out. After a period it may become possible to work out specific targets. Measures which are proposed to be undertaken for the development of co-operative marketing of agricultural produce will pave the way for the re-organisation of the rest of rural trade on co-operative lines. There is little doubt that if the bulk of rural trade is organised on business lines through co-operative agencies, it will become possible for villagers to organise schools, dispensaries and other amenities for themselves on a much larger scale than has been envisaged so far. Profits of rural trade derived both from marketing and processing and from the supply of consumer goods and other accessories to meet the needs of rural areas, will help develop agricultural production and promote the well-being of villagers. The close linking up of producer co-operatives and consumer co-operatives will be an important factor for increasing rural incomes and employment and for raising rural levels of living.

In an economy in which there are large unutilised sources of manpower in rural areas, in a period of development, there are increasing opportunities for organising labour and construction co-operatives. It is suggested that in collaboration with other departments co-operative departments should investigate the directions in which labour co-operatives could by stages replace the existing contract system, so that each area derives the maximum possible benefit in teens of income and employment from works which are undertaken for its development. It should be an important aim in district and village planning to organise labour and construction co-operatives on sound lines and to provide them opportunities for work on reasonable terms and also to give them the necessary guidance and supervision.

Training and Organisation

The personnel requirements of programmes of co-operative development call for extensive training programmes. It is estimated that more than 25,000 persons will be required to undertake the administrative, technical and other specialised duties arising from the programme of rural credit, marketing and processing. Larger numbers will be needed if all aspects of co-operative development are taken into account. The success of co-operation rests very largely on the ability to place it on a sound business basis so that, after an initial period, co-operative organisations can perform the functions entrusted to them without causing losses to the members or placing additional burdens on the State. It is, therefore, of the utmost importance that co-operative departments and all co-operative institutions .should be manned by persons who believe in the principles of co-operation and have the practical competence and experience to translate them into action. Equally, it is essential that in all States, the people generally should be educated in the principles of co-operation and leading members of each community should be given special opportunities of training, so that they can assume fuller responsibilities in the co-operative movement.

These considerations were also stressed in the First Five Year Plan. In 1953 the Government of India and the Reserve Bank jointly constituted a Central Committee for Co-operation Training and entrusted to it the responsibility for establishing the necessary training facilities for co-operative personnel. Under the direction of the Central Committee the Co-operative College at Poona provides six-monthly courses for superior officers of co-operative departments and institutions. Five regional co-operative training centres have been established at Poona, Ranchi, Meerut, Madras and Indore for training personnel belonging to intermediate grades. Eight special centres have been established for training 4,000 block level co-operative officers needed by national extension and community project areas. For the training of subordinate staff, State Governments are establishing the necessary facilities and the Central Government shares the cost with them. Training classes for members and office bearers of co-operative organisations are to be organised by the All-India Co-operative Union and State co-operative unions or federations with subsidies provided by Government and in accordance with the programmes proposed by the Central Committee on Co-operative Training.

These aspects need to be pursued systematically and in

detail. Since so much depends on the success of co-operation, it is recommended that, in addition to special institutions set up for co-operative training. State Governments and universities should consider steps to introduce Co-operation as a subject of instruction in educational courses at various levels.

The programme of reorganisation of rural credit and marketing described above has to be carried out in close co-operation between the co-operative and agriculture departments and the national extension service. With his intimate knowledge of every family, the village level worker can be an effective liaison between the staff of the co-operative department and the village. Among the administrative tasks assumed by Government in the second five year plan, some of the most difficult ones will fall to co-operative departments in the States. It is therefore necessary that these departments should be adequately staffed and organised. Until some years ago, it was customary to select senior and experienced officials with special interest in the rural people for appointment as Registrars of Co-operative Societies. There have been departures from this practice in recent years and persons selected are sometimes moved to other posts after short intervals, so that the requisite quality and experience are not developed.

To make a success of co-operation requires on the part of officials at all levels and especially those who fill responsible positions administrative ability and experience, faith in the movement and a sense of identity with the people as well as a great deal of attention to practical detail. Much of the burden of developing co-operatives in each district will fall upon the district co-operative officer commonly known as the Assistant Registrar. This officer should make himself fully familiar with the economy of the district and with the programmes of various departments included in the district plan. He should ascertain the directions in which there are special opportunities for developing the method of co-operation and, with the help of other departments functioning in the district, he should endeavour to extend its scope on a sound and lasting basis. His success will depend to a considerable extent on the manner in which he helps to organise and strengthen the co-operative credit system in the district. He should maintain the closest liaison with the various Government departments which provide assistance to agriculturists, artisans and others and with the central co-operative bank, the State Bank of India, and other institutions.

It would be desirable, for instance, for the co-operative department in each district, in collaboration with the agriculture department and the national extension service organisation, to prepare each year a detailed plan for the provision of short-term credit. Standard scales of loans for different crops could be laid down and loan applications could be prepared and sanctioned in advance of the season so that credit for improved seeds, fertilisers etc. is made available in good time. Finally, it should be added that for organising co-operatives in directions other than credit, such as farming, consumer stores, industrial societies, labour and construction co-operatives, housing etc., district co-operative staff will need to be considerably strengthened.

Land Reforms and Co-operative Credit

There is a close connection between the success of land reform and the success of co-operation which is not always appreciated. For co-operation to succeed fully it is essential that the reorganisation of the agrarian structure should be carried out speedily so as to eliminate features which reduce the productive capacity of the community and permit exploitation. Thus, land reform programmes should do much to stimulate the growth of the co-operative movement. In the nature of things, as a result of land reform the number of small cultivators increases, those with large holdings or considerable surpluses disappear and the new owners need a great deal of credit. Also, as the national extension net work is established and the rural people are ready and willing to participate in development programmes on an increasing scale, their requirements for credit and finance greatly increase. Co-operative institutions are the medium through which many activities in the village are to be reorganised and financed. It is therefore, essential that in devising the land reform programme care should be taken to ensure that while its objectives are secured, co-operative credit institutions are not placed under handicaps which might affect their financial soundness.

The effects of land reform on co-operative credit institutions may be viewed from two ends, namely in relation to past debts and in relation to future debts. As regards past debts given on the security of land, payments due to co-operative financing institutions should be allowed a prior claim against compensation to which individual owners of land may be entitled. The liability for repaying loans should pass to individuals to whom rights in land are transferred. After allowing for the claims of co-operative financing institutions from these two sources, there may still be a possibility of co-operative institutions being put to loss, for instance, on account of decline in land values. In such an event State Governments should render the assistance needed for maintaining the financial solvency of co-operative institutions. These considerations arise specially in the case of land mortgage banks, part of whose advances to individuals were made for facilitating repayment of old debts.

As regards future operations three aspects may be mentioned. In the first place, it may be assumed that, save for exceptional reasons connected with programmes of agricultural production, co-operative institutions will advance loans only with reference to areas held under personal cultivation. Secondly, to facilitate the grant of medium-term and long-term loans to tenants who are brought into direct relationship with the State as a result of land reform, rights of transfer in favour of co-operative financing institutions should be allowed. In the third place, in respect of lands which come into the possession of co-operative financing institutions in the course of their operations, restrictions relating to ceilings on agricultural holdings or to cultivation through tenants or leasees need not be applied. Co-operatives should be free to sell the land to any one at such price as may be obtainable, subject only to the conditions that in the transferee uses the land for personal cultivation and that as a result of the purchase or transfer, the land held by him does not exceed the ceiling prescribed by law.

Third Five Year Plan: 1961-66

The Third Five Year Plan (1961-1966) stressed that "Co-operation should become, progressively, the principal basis of organization in branches of economic life, notably agriculture, minor irrigation, small industries and processing, marketing, distribution, rural electrification, housing and construction and provision of essential amenities for local communities. Even the medium and large industries and in transport an increasing range of activities can be undertaken on co-operative lines".

Co-operation and Planned Development

In a planned economy pledged to the values of socialism and democracy, co-operation should become progressively the principal basis of organisation in many branches of economic life, notably in agriculture and minor irrigation, small industry and processing, marketing, distribution, supplies, rural electrification, housing and construction, and the provision of essential amenities for local communities. Even in medium and large industries and in transport, an increasing range of activities can be undertaken on co-operative lines. The socialist pattern of society implies the creation of large numbers of decentralised units in agriculture, industry and the services. Co-operation has the merit of combining freedom and opportunity for the small man with benefits of large-scale management and organisation as well as goodwill and support from the community. Thus, a rapidly growing co-operative sector, with special emphasis on the needs of the peasant, the worker and the consumer becomes a vital factor for social stability, for expansion of employment opportunities and for rapid economic development. Along with a growing public sector and a private sector which functions with responsibility to the community as a whole, the influence of co-operation extends far beyond the particular activities organised on co-operative lines, and gives to the social structure and the national economy, balance, direction and a sense of values.

Economic development and social change are equally vital elements in the reconstruction of India's social and economic structure. Co-operation is one of the principal means for bringing about changes of a fundamental nature within the economy. As was stated in the Second Five Year Plan, in a country whose economic structure has its roots in the village, co-operation is something more than a series of activities organised on co-operative lines; basically, its purpose is to evolve a scheme of co-operative community organisation which touches upon all aspects of life. Within the rural economy, in particular, co-operation is the primary means for raising the level of productivity, extending improvements in technology and expanding employment so as to secure the basic necessities for every member of the community.

At the level of the village, co-operation implies the development of land and other resources and various services in the common interest of the village as a whole and a continuing obligation on the part of the village community towards all its members. It is, therefore, visualised that as part of a larger co-operative rural economy, the broad aim of policy should be to develop the village as the primary unit of organisation in agriculture and in many other economic and social activities which bear closely on the welfare of the rural population.

At the same time, artisans and others, according to their community of interest, will enter into co-operative associations which seek to serve their special needs. Programmes for land reform and for village and small industries, development of panchayats and the fundamental emphasis in community development on the obligations and functions of the community, all point in these directions. In due course, as the agricultural base is strengthened and efforts to diversify the occupational structure of rural areas are intensified, an increasing number of co-operative activities will call for organisation for larger areas. Once the processes of social and economic change gather force and the rural community attains higher levels of skill and productivity, co-operation has to meet larger and more complex demands. Diverse forms of co-operative organisation will continue to develop in, tune with new needs and possibilities.

Over the past year, policies for the development of co-operation have been carefully reviewed in relation especially to the programmes for the Third Five Year Plan. The conclusion reached regarding the lines along which co-operative credit and co-operative farming should be organised form the basis of programmes for the Third Plan. The Third Plan provides for specific programmes for co-operative credit and supplies, for marketing and processing, for consumer co-operatives and for industrial and other co-operatives. These are but different directions of activity, each important in itself, yet forming an integral part of a larger effort aiming at the development of a growing co-operative sector in India's economy.

For the development of co-operation, the Third Plan provides ₹ 80 crore as against the estimated expenditure of ₹ 34 crore in the Second Plan.

Co-operative Credit

In November, 1958, in its Resolution on Co-operative Policy, the National Development Council agreed that co-operatives should be organised on the basis of the village community as the primary unit, and that responsibility and initiative for social and economic development at the village level should be placed fully on the village co-operative and the village panchayat. The co-operative and the panchayat were to be regarded as the primary agencies for carrying out the community development programme which aims at the improvement of all aspects of rural life through the efforts of the people. The village agricultural plan was considered to be the foundation of the programme for co-operative development and was to be given the highest priority.

Since these decisions were reached, problems relating to the development of co-operative credit in the context of the larger needs in the Third Plan were examined by the Committee on Co-operative Credit. In September, 1960, the National Development Council considered proposals based upon the report of this Committee, and agreed that while, as a general rule, co-operatives should be organised on the basis of the village community as a primary unit, where villages were too small, the number of villages to be served by a co-operative society could be increased in the interest of viability. The aim should be to ensure viability with the inclusion of the smallest number of villages necessary, so that co-operative societies could achieve both viability and the essential characteristics of co-operation, namely, voluntary basis, close contact, social cohesion and mutual obligation. However, such extension should be subject to certain maximum limits, namely, a population of 3,000 (i.e. 600 families or about 500 cultivators' families) and a distance of not more than 3 or 4 miles from the headquarters village.

The broad test of viability should be the ability on the part of a co-operative society to meet the requisite expenses without depending upon financial assistance from Government except for a limited period. However, potential viability should always be assessed on the basis of a programme for fulfilling certain essential conditions, such as bringing into the co-operative all rural families, effective implementation of the village agricultural production plan, linking credit with production and with marketing, supervision of the use of the credit, undertaking the functions of distribution and supply, and attracting local savings to the maximum possible extent as share capital and as deposits. While a population of 3000 might ordinarily be too high for a primary village society, it was considered desirable to avoid laying down unduly rigid rules on the subject of organisation and size of co-operative societies. Within this broad framework, co-operative societies should be allowed to develop on their own. Particular care should be taken to ensure that existing societies were not interfered with merely because they did not strictly comply with the pattern of organisation now envisaged. The aim should be gradually to fit them into the new arrangements.

The pattern of organisation set out above was to be supported under appropriate conditions by State participation in share capital. The State could participate in the share capital of a primary society only if 60 percent of the members desired this, and the proposal was supported by the central bank to which the society was affiliated. The State's contribution had to be matched in equal measure by the members of the society, the maximum contribution from the State being generally placed at ₹ 5,000 and in exceptional circumstances, at ₹ 10,000. The amount to be provided by the State could be retained for a period of 5 to 8 years and retired later. As a normal rule, State participation in primary societies should be indirect, that is, through apex and central co-operative banks. Where, for special reasons, State participation in share capital is direct, nomination of directors to the managing committees of primary societies should be avoided. If such nomination is considered essential, the authority to nominate directors should be delegated to central co-operative banks.

To enable co-operative societies to admit all classes of cultivators, including marginal and sub-marginal cultivators, landless tenants, etc. as members, and provide them with adequate credit on the basis of their production requirement and repaying capacity, it was also agreed that State Governments should make an outright contribution to the funds of each society at 3 percent of the additional loans made during the year over those advanced by it in the preceding year. An outright contribution of 1 percent to bad debt reserves should be made to central co-operative banks in respect of the additional finance provided by them. In the intensive agricultural districts, where credit is sought to be made available to the full scale of production requirements, the outright grants are at a slightly higher level, being 4 percent for primary societies and 2 percent for central banks. The continuance of these outright grants is contingent on the condition that the weaker sections of the community, who have hitherto been unable to get adequate credit, should now receive the necessary assistance. The outright grants received by primary societies and central banks were to be credited by them to special bad debt reserves which would be in addition to the normal bad debt reserves created from profits. It is envisaged that at an appropriate stage, a careful assessment of the extent to which outright grants have led to the extension of credit facilities, should be undertaken.

Besides participation by the States in the share capital and outright grants for special bad debt reserves, new service co-operatives and existing co-operatives which take up approved programmes for strengthening and revitalisation, increase of membership, share capital, linking credit with marketing, etc. receive a management grant up to a maximum of ₹ 900 spread over a period of 3 to 5 years. The management grant is intended to be given only to those societies which actually undertake various service functions, namely, disbursement of credit, supply of production requisites, and arrangements for marketing of agricultural produce.

Over the period of the first two Plans, the number of primary agricultural credit societies has risen from about 1,05,000 to about 2,10,000 and their membership has gone up from 4.4 million to about 17 million. Over this period the total loans advanced by primary agricultural societies have risen from about ₹ 23 crore to about ₹ 200 crore. As the following statement will show, progress during the Second Plan was more marked than during the First Five Year Plan.

During the Second Plan, in respect of long-term credit, the amount of loans outstanding increased from about ₹ 13 crore to about ₹ 34 crore.

In formulating programmes for the expansion of co-operative credit during the Third Plan, the main consideration has been to ensure adequate support to the effort to achieve the large agricultural targets set in the Plan. The Plan envisages that the membership of primary co-operative societies will increase to about 37 million covering about 60 percent of the agricultural population.

The number of societies is expected to increase to about 2,30,000 so as to serve all the villages in the country. It is estimated that the total amount of short and medium-term credit may increase to about ₹ 530 crore and that of long-term credit (loans outstanding) to about ₹ 150 crore.

The agricultural programmes in the Third Plan lean heavily on the success of schemes for strengthening the co-operative movement. Of about 1,60,000 primary societies existing at the end of the First Plan, a large proportion were functioning in a dormant or in a poor state. In the course of the Second Plan about 42,000 societies were taken up for revitalisation. Programmes for the Third Plan provide for the revitalisation of about 52,000 primary societies. Revitalisation of the older societies which were functioning badly and the further expansion of the movement will depend largely on the extent to which primary credit societies succeed in increasing their membership, mobilising local savings, improving management and linking credit with marketing and with production. These measures are essential for strengthening the internal resources of the credit organisations, both at primary and at higher levels. In those States in which the co-operative movement has remained weak, it is important to undertake the necessary consolidation or revitalisation as a first step in implementing programmes for the Third Plan.

Short and medium-term credit provided by service co-operatives caters to the current needs of production. Credit for longer periods for increasing the productive capacity of land is equally essential. This need has to be met in the main by co-operative land mortgage banks. At the end of the Second Plan almost all the States had central land mortgage banks or special land mortgage banking department attached to the apex co-operative bank. In 1959-60 there were 407 primary land mortgage banks. To these it is proposed to add 265 new primary land mortgage banks during the Third Plan. Debentures constitute the principal source of funds for loans advanced by central land mortgage banks either directly or through their affiliated primary banks. The achievement of the target for long-term credit to the extent of ₹ 150 crore (loans outstanding) will depend to no small extent on the support which land mortgage banks receive from institutional investors and the success of rural debentures. In this field a very large measure of assistance has to come from national institutions like the Reserve Bank of India, the State Bank of India and the Life Insurance Corporation.

With a view to augmenting the resources available for long-term loans, a proposal for setting up an Agricultural Development Finance Corporation is at present being considered by the Reserve Bank of India in consultation with the Central Government. The Corporation will purchase debentures floated by central land mortgage banks in the normal course and will also provide funds for schemes for increasing agricultural production which are remunerative in character, but involve considerable investment on long periods of waiting, such as rubber, coffee, cashew nut and areca nut plantation, irrigation, contour-bunding and soil conservation and development of orchards and fruit gardens. The loans advanced by the Corporation will be channelled through the central land mortgage banks.

The Reserve Bank of India has played a very significant part in the building up of the co-operative movement during the first two Plans through its supervision over financial institutions, arrangements for training, loans to States for participation in the share capital of co-operative banks, and advances to co-operative banks, its loans outstanding having risen from about ₹ 14 crore in 1955-56 to about ₹ 85 crore in 1959-60. In keeping with the growing requirements of the economy and the agricultural objectives and credit needs in the

Third Plan, the Reserve Bank will be called upon to play an even larger role. The Bank has necessarily to relate its advances to the financial strength and administrative efficiency of the borrowing institutions arid at the same time, to take account of factors such as supervision of the utilisation of loans, and past performance in their recovery. It has also to consider the extent to which the co-operative structure in each State succeeds in mobilising deposits and in building up its own resources. Special efforts are being made by the Reserve Bank to assist the State Governments in reorganising the financial structure of the co-operative movement in States in which inadequate progress has been made during the first two Plans.

The State Bank of India has also been of considerable assistance to the co-operative movement. Following a policy of responsiveness to the financial needs of co-operative institutions, especially those engaged in marketing and processing, the State Bank has provided free remittance facilities and loans on easy terms and conditions. It has also given support to the operations of land mortgage banks by subscribing to debentures issued by them from time to time and affording interim accommodation for short periods pending the floatation of debentures. With the enlargement of operations of marketing and processing societies, on the one hand, and extension of the network of the offices of the State bank and its subsidiaries on the other, the policies and procedures which have been evolved should enable the Bank to expand its assistance to co-operatives on a much larger scale during the Third Plan.

Co-operative Marketing

Development of co-operative marketing was given a place of special importance in the scheme of integrated rural credit recommended in the Rural Credit Survey. Primary marketing societies were to be established at important markets or at other suitable centres and primary agricultural credit societies were to be affiliated to them. Marketing societies were to be assisted with personnel and. the State was to participate in their share capital. Broadly on these lines, during the Second Plan, 1,869 primary marketing societies have been assisted through the National Co-operative Development and Warehousing Board. With the addition of about 600 more primary marketing co-operatives proposed to be set up during the Third Plan period, there will be a marketing society at or near each of the 2,500 mandis in the country. Besides these marketing societies, reference may be made to sugarcane supply societies which exist in large numbers, particularly in Bihar and Uttar Pradesh cotton ginning and pressing societies which have developed most successfully in Gujarat and Maharashtra, and milk supply unions and societies which have come up in recent years in several States.

In addition to their role in the sale of agricultural produce on terms favourable to the producer, marketing societies are intended to serve as distributors of articles required by cultivators for agricultural production. They are also essential for linking up the grant of agricultural credit with marketing. Statistics concerning the activities of marketing societies are inadequate in several respects. However, it is estimated that the total volume of agricultural business conducted by marketing societies may at present be of the order of ₹ 200 crore. Their marketing operations are expected to rise to about ₹ 400 crore. Efforts will be directed towards handling by co-operatives of a steadily increasing proportion of the marketable surplus of foodgrains and commercial crops. Participation by co-operatives in the export trade will also be encouraged. Marketing societies receive finance from co-operative financing agencies and also to an increasing extent from the State Bank of India. Their principal problems are to secure sufficient finance for current operations, to improve management and to ensure continued support from their members. Price stabilisation policies will greatly facilitate the growth of co-operative marketing and the expansion of credit.

At the instance of the National Co-operative Development and Warehousing Board, the special problems of co-operative marketing in relation to jute in West Bengal, wheat in Rajasthan and paddy in Andhra Pradesh are at present being investigated.

The programme for the construction of godowns at mandi centres and rural godowns is closely linked with the programme for marketing. In the course of the Second Plan, about 1,670 godowns have been set up; about 980 additional godowns are expected to be established during the Third Plan. At the end of the Second Plan, about 4,100 rural godowns had been set up. Their number is expected to rise by about 9,200 during the Third Plan.

Co-operative Processing

Development of co-operative processing is essential not only for increasing rural incomes and facilitating credit for production but also for building up a co-operative rural economy. Where co-operative processing units have been successfully established, they have proved invaluable as instruments of development in several allied fields. Co-operative processing is, however, a recent development. Comparatively greater progress has been achieved in sugar and cotton ginning and pressing than in other processing industries. By 1960-61, 30 co-operative sugar factories out of a total of 41 were in production.

In the course of the Third Plan, depending upon factors governing the progress of the sugar industry as a whole, about 25 co-operative sugar factories may be established. The Industrial Finance Corporation has greatly contributed to the development of the co-operative sugar industry. In the Third Plan, besides continuing to assist co-operative sugar factories, the Corporation should be able to extend its support to the development of co-operative processing in other fields. An important recent development is the setting up of the National Federation of Co-operative Sugar Factories with the object of improving operational efficiency of existing factories and promoting new units.

In the course of the Second Plan, 378 co-operative processing units other than sugar factories were assisted. These included 84 cotton ginning and pressing units, 109 rice mills and hullers, 20 oil mills, 17 jute baling plants, 26 groundnut decorticators and 122 other units. Programmes drawn up for the Third Plan include the setting up of 783 co-operative processing units. These comprise 48 cotton ginning and pressing plants, 36 rice mills, 29 jute baling plants, 33 oil mills, 63 groundnut decorticators, 77 fruit-canning units, 411 rice hullers arid 86 other units.

The rapid development of the co-operative sugar industry in recent years suggests a twofold approach to the organisation of co-operative processing units in other fields. In the first place, it would now be desirable to formulate overall programmes regarding the number of new units in each branch of industry which are required in consequence of increase anticipated in the production of agricultural raw materials and in the consumption of the final product. Within this plan, the share of expansion to be assigned to the co-operative sector should be determined on broad considerations. To facilitate the working out of specific proposals, designs of plants, estimates of investment arid working costs and other technical data should be made readily available.

At the same time, as in the case of co-operative sugar factories, arrangements for financing other types of processing units should be indicated, the contribution expected from growers, State Governments, State Financial Corporations and other institutions being stated specifically in advance. Arrangements on these lines should be evolved in the near future by the Central and State Governments in consultation with the National Co-operative Development and Warehousing Board. Against this background, as an aspect of local planning and with a view to strengthening the rural economic, structure in each district in its co-operative aspects, concrete proposals should be invited.

Given the necessary conditions, there is vast scope for the development of co-operative processing not-only in relation to new units but also, progressively, by way of reorganisation on co-operative lines of units which are, at present, privately owned. This latter aspect is important on wider considerations, both because it is the aim of public policy to reorient the organisation of processing industries from a private to a co-operative basis, and because in many of these industries there is at present either excess capacity or only limited scope for adding too existing capacity. It is essential that proposals for expanding processing industries should be coordinated with programmes for the related village industries. In the organisation of large co-operative undertakings, for processing and other purposes, attention should also be given to the position of workers and employees. They should have the opportunity to participate in the management of the co-operative enterprises in which they serve.

Co-operative Farming

The role of co-operative farming in the reconstruction of the rural economy was stressed both in the First and in the Second Plan. The goal indicated in the Second Plan was that such essential steps were to be taken as would provide sound foundations for the development of co-operative farming, so that over a period of ten years or so, a substantial proportion of the agricultural lands were cultivated on co-operative lines. With the growth of population and the need to secure rapid increase in agricultural production and rural employment, it is essential to intensify efforts to develop co-operative farming throughout the country and to realise as speedily as possible the objective set in the Second Plan.

In the main, co-operative farming has to grow out of the success of the general agricultural effort through the community development movement, the progress of co-operation in credit, marketing, distribution and processing, the growth of rural industry, and the fulfilment of the objectives of land reform. The contribution of co-operative farming to rural progress will be significant in the measure in which it develops as a voluntary mass movement under genuine local leadership and as a logical growth of community development and co-operation at the village level. Given the approach of community development and the acceptance by the village community of its responsibility for the welfare of all its members, the main problems of co-operative farming are organisational, technical and educational. The problems of internal management with which many co-operative farming societies are faced need to be studied systematically and practical solutions appropriate to different regions found for them.

These problems were reviewed in general terms by the Working Group on Co-operative Farming which surveyed a number of existing co-operative farming societies and, in addition to recommendations regarding organisation and patterns of assistance, suggested a scheme of pilot projects which is intended to lead the way towards a more rapid expansion of co-operative farming. Proposals formulated with reference to the recommendations of the Working Group were considered by the National Development Council in September, 1960. The Council decided upon the broad principles guiding the organisation of co-operative farming societies and the assistance to be given to them.

For implementing the programme of co-operative farming, the Ministry of Community Development and Co-operation have constituted a National Co-operative Farming Advisory Board. Similar Boards have been set up in some of the States. The Working Group on Co-operative Farming had suggested 3,200 co-operative farming societies being set up as pilot projects, roughly 10 in each district, and these constitute the first phase in the development programme for co-operative farming. For carrying out the programme during the first year of the Third Plan, 65 pilot districts have been recently selected.

An extensive programme for orienting official and non-official workers is being carried out. Besides the pilot projects, State Governments will continue to assist co-operative fanning societies which arc formed on a voluntary basis.

In the general pattern of organisation which has been proposed for the development of co-operative farming, stress is laid on the principle that co-operative farming is a voluntary movement and there should be no question of compelling any cultivator to join a co-operative farming society. Membership in co-operative farming societies should be confined to those who are prepared to work on the farm or in ancillary activities and, ordinarily, absentee landholders should not be admitted as members. Persons who are prevented from participation in form work on account of physical disability, Government service, age, sex or because they have land in more than one village may be admitted, although they may not be participating in farm work but, taken as a group, such persons should not exceed one-fourth of the total membership.

The question of the size of co-operative farms has to be considered from two aspects, firstly, from the point of view of securing an area which will make for economic operation and. secondly, from the point of view of how best co-operative fanning should be developed so as to secure the development of the village economy as a whole on the lines visualised in the Five Year Plans. While no maximum size for a co-operative farm is proposed, for the purpose of special assistance from the Government, States may prescribe suitable minima in terms of membership and area.

Members joining a co-operative farming society are expected to pool their lands for a minimal period of five years, withdrawals during this period being permitted in exceptional circumstances. Co-operative farming societies are expected to give a reasonable return on account of land contributed by members in addition to income in lieu of work done by them. While consolidation of holdings is not a condition precedent to co-operative farming, it has been suggested, that advantage should be taken of consolidation proceedings to encourage co-operative farming. Owners of small holdings should be specially assisted to come into co-operative farming societies.

In the pilot projects as well as in other co-operative farming societies which may be selected for assistance, provision is made for medium and long-term loans to the extent of ₹ 4,000 and loan and grant for a godown-cum-cattle shed, up to ₹ 5,000 and also a management grant of ₹ 1,200 spread over a period of 3 to 5 years. In the pilot projects provision is made for State participation in share capital, especially in co-operative farming societies which are composed predominantly of landless labourers and marginal and sub-marginal farmers. Such participation is subject to a ceiling of ₹ 2,000 which should, as a rule, be matched by an equal contribution on the part of members and is intended to be retired over a period of 10 years.

Besides, a measure of preference is to be accorded to co-operative farming societies in making financial assistance available both from provisions in community development blocks and from those relating to agricultural programmes. In addition to the provision of about ₹ 6 crore for pilot projects in co-operative farming in the plans of States, an allotment of ₹ 6 crore has been set apart at the Centre for assisting the development of other co-operative farming societies. With greater progress in the development of co-operative fanning there should be no difficulty in making available such additional resources as are required for supporting the effort. As the Plan proceeds, in the light of practical experience in the pilot areas and elsewhere, it is hoped to formulate more comprehensive programmes for promoting co-operative farming.

Consumer Co-operatives

A large number of consumer stores came into existence for the distribution of controlled commodities during and after the Second World War. In 1951-52 there were 9,757 primary stores with a membership of 1.85 million and a total business exceeding ₹ 82 crore. However, in later years many of these stores were wound up. In 1959-60, there were 7,168 primary stores with a membership of about 1.4 million and a total paid up capital of ₹ 2.4 crore. Of these stores less than a third were running at profit. Programmes for the Third Plan provide tentatively for assisting 50 wholesale stores and 2,200 primary consumer stores. These targets will, however, need further consideration in the light of the recent report of the Committee on Consumer Co-operatives set up by the National Co-operative Development and Warehousing Board. The Committee suggests in each State an apex wholesale store linked with primary stores mainly in the urban areas and considers that at this stage for areas smaller than a State there may not generally be sufficient business to justify a wholesale store. The Committee has also suggested participation by the State in the share capital of the apex wholesale store and the primary stores.

There is both urgent need and considerable scope for the development of a successful consumer co-operative movement, especially in the urban areas, but so far the movement has lagged behind. For rural areas, the distribution of essential consumer goods would fall legitimately within the functions of the service co-operative, arrangements for supply of goods being made ordinarily through the marketing societies. In the rural areas, the supply of manufactured consumer foods of standard variety which are in common demand could well be a subsidiary function of primary marketing societies or such other agencies as may already exist. Conditions for the development of consumer co-operatives in the Third Plan are generally favourable and, if special efforts are made, rapid progress can be achieved. They will be of the greatest help not only in the stabilisation of retail prices but also in preventing the evils of adulteration in foodstuffs.

Industrial Co-operatives

Industrial co-operatives have had a large measure of success in the handloom industry, in coir and in certain village industries. However, their expansion as a general movement has been impeded on account of various practical difficulties. Following the Resolution of the Government of India on Industrial Co-operatives in November 1959, a series of decisions have been taken which, given the necessary climate and leadership, should facilitate the development of industrial co-operatives during the Third Plan. Industrial co-operative societies are at present following there broad patterns. In some, the members undertake production on their own account and cooperate for certain services such as supply of raw materials, etc. In others they jointly undertake production, marketing and other related activities. In the third group are societies whose members may work separately, but set up co-operative workshops for specific services. In industries like handloom and village industries, as also in several small scale industries, there is great scope for bringing the workers together into a co-operative. Over a large area in the field of small scale industries, however, there is likely to be greater opportunity for organising co-operatives for such objects as providing common facilities, initial processing of raw materials, specialised processing, joint handling of orders, and marketing.

Although the plans of States provide for several schemes for encouraging industrial co-operatives, assisting artisans etc., efforts in these directions need to be intensified further during the Third Plan. At the present stage of development, the important consideration is that effective use should be made of the available concessions and facilities for the formation of industrial co-operatives which have now been evolved so as to strengthen the existing co-operatives and to encourage the organisation of new ones on sound lines, and to concentrate on the solution of practical problems of finance and marketing. Among decisions which have been taken with the object of stimulating the growth of industrial co-operatives as a normal pattern of organisation, special reference may be made to the following.

1. Loans for working capital at a concessional rate of interest from Government and central co-operative agencies.
2. Loans to members of industrial co-operative societies for subscribing to share capital.
3. Grants for managerial staff, improved tools and equipment.
4. Subsidising for a limited period specified managerial and supervisory staffs of co-operative banks.
5. Sharing of expenditure with State Governments on additional staff appointed to look after the development of industrial co-operatives.
6. Guarantee of advances sanctioned by co-operative financing agencies to industrial co-operative societies for a limited period.

On present indications the number of industrial co-operatives in the Third Plan may increase from about 30,000 to about 40,000, their membership rising from over 2 million to about 3 million and their share capital from about ₹ 10 crore to about ₹ 20 crore.. It is desirable that in the light of recent decisions, the Central and State Governments should take steps to prepare further and more specific proposals for the development of industrial co-operatives and should ensure that they receive the necessary support from Government agencies, the All-India Boards and various financial institutions in spreading their activities.

Labour and Construction Co-operatives

The importance of organising labour co-operatives for carrying out irrigation and other projects in rural areas has been stressed frequently since the First Plan. In several States, notably in Punjab, Bombay, Andhra Pradesh and Rajasthan, efforts have been made to set up labour co-operatives, labour contract societies, etc. for taking up works involving mainly unskilled and semi-skilled labour with a view gradually to diminishing the role of contractors. In works programmes for the utilisation of rural manpower to be undertaken in the Third Plan also, labour co-operatives will be required to play a major part. While the policy of entrusting construction works to the extent possible to co-operatives and; where they exist, to voluntary organisations has been accepted, the administrative measures required to give effect to it need to be evolved in greater detail.

Labour and construction co-operatives and voluntary organisations can be entrusted with advantage with works under the following categories.

1. Earth-work of all types and simple masonry works relating to multipurpose, major and medium irrigation works and flood protection schemes, minor irrigation works and construction of roads.
2. Simple Government buildings such as hostels, administrative blocks, workshops, residential tenements, school buildings and other local development works in rural areas.
3. Supply in bulk quantities of building materials such as stones, stone blasts, shingle and sand.

To enable genuine labour co-operatives and voluntary organisations to undertake these works, certain administrative conditions have to be fulfilled, the more essential of these being the following.

1. Setting apart a certain proportion of the available construction work for co-operatives and voluntary organisations, the quantum being extended as the capacity of these organisations develops.
2. Ensuring continuous flow of work, the magnitude, types and the specific works to be awarded being indicated well in advance.
3. Giving works to co-operatives and voluntary organisations in preference to private contractors and, wherever possible, on a negotiated basis.
4. Award of works at *workable rates* on the basis of

schedules of rates, which may be increased or decreased by a percentage to be decided by the competent authority, the work order system being preferred wherever possible.

5. Avoidance of delays in payments and authorisation of "on account payments" for works completed.
6. Making technical personnel available for work with co-operatives and voluntary organisations.
7. Assistance by way of loans for working capital and purchase of equipment.

In the light of the experience which different States have already gained of the working of labour co-operatives, suitable organisational patterns should be evolved.

The aim should be to build up labour co-operative organisations and voluntary organisations as important instruments for undertaking development and providing employment through works carried out mainly on behalf of Government Departments, Panchayat Samitis and Panchayats. Once such organisations come into existence, new possibilities for enlarging their scope and extending their benefits to the community in many directions will emerge.

Housing Co-operatives

In 1959-60 there were 5,564 co-operative housing societies with a total membership of 322,000. Housing co-operatives constructed 45,000 houses in 1959-60 as compared to 44,000 in 1958-59 and 36,000 in 1957-58. Under different housing schemes which are at present being undertaken, facilities are provided for the setting up of housing co-operatives. For instance, the subsidised industrial housing scheme allows for a subsidy up to 25 percent of the cost in the case of co-operatives of industrial workers. Under the low income group housing scheme as well as other schemes which are being undertaken in a number of growing towns, co-operatives are either allotted land on favourable terms or assisted in acquisition of private lands. The village housing scheme also provides for the setting up of housing co-operatives in selected villages and for the production of bricks, doors, windows and other components.

These various provisions need to be used purposefully and as a matter of sustained policy so that, in towns and villages alike, an appreciable impact can be made on the improvement of housing and living conditions. The proposal in the Third Plan to set up a Central Housing Board and to promote the establishment of Housing Boards in the States will make it possible to channel larger funds to housing co-operatives. With the preparation of interim general plans and master plans for a large number of towns and of layout plans for selected villages as visualised in the Chapter on Housing, it will become easier to implement effectively the policy of supporting and developing housing co-operatives on a large scale during the Third Plan.

Other Non-credit Co-operatives

In addition to the various types of co-operatives discussed above, reference may be made to co-operatives engaged in the supply of sugarcane and milk and in the development of fisheries and dairying and to co-operative cold storages. Sugarcane supply societies account for a total membership of 2.34 million, milk supply societies for 2,33,000 and fisheries societies for 2,20,000. By the end of Second Plan 16 cold storages were established: 33 mw will be set up in the Third Plan. The Third Plan includes large programmes for fisheries development and dairying. These are fields of great promise for the development of co-operative activity. Transport co-operatives should also be encouraged as a means of providing new opportunities for educated unemployed persons. The principle of co-operation can be extended to a growing range of new activities in industry and services, such as, manufacture of implements, printing, supplies of raw materials, provision of common facilities etc.

In the tribal development blocks and in areas predominantly inhabited by scheduled tribes, there is considerable scope for building up co-operatives, especially for working forest areas and developing the traditional crafts. The Central Government have recently set up a committee to consider the lines along which procedures and legislation relating to co-operation should be adapted to meet the special conditions and requirements of tribal areas.

Co-operative Training and Administration

The role of trained personnel in the efficient execution of co-operative programmes was emphasised in the Rural Credit Survey, and in recent years there has been considerable development of training facilities for co-operative personnel. At the end of the Second Plan, besides the Co-operative Training College at Poona for training senior staffs of Co-operative Departments, there were 13 regional centres for intermediate and block level co-operative officers and 62 co-operative training centres for junior personnel. Special courses for land mortgage banking and marketing have also been organised at the intermediate training centres. By the end of the Second Plan, the numbers trained included 543 senior personnel, 317 block level and intermediate officers, 34,000 junior personnel and 382 in courses for land mortgage banking and 1,253 for co-operative marketing. The All-India Co-operative Union and State Co-operative Unions have organised 368 peripatetic parties for the training of office-bearers, members of managing committees and members of primary co-operatives. In these categories, about 28,500, 12,000 and 7,26,000 persons respectively were trained by the end of the Second Plan.

For the Third Plan, the programmes drawn up by the States envisage, amongst other steps, the addition of 13 schools for training junior co-operative personnel and the continuance of the scheme for the education of members of co-operative societies through peripatetic parties. The Study Team on Co-operative training, constituted by the Ministry of Community Development and Co-operation, which has recently submitted its proposals, contemplates increase in the number of centres for training intermediate personnel to 15 and in the number of centres for junior co-operative personnel to 120. These and other recommendations of the Team are at present under consideration.

Steps have been taken during the Second Plan to strengthen the State Co-operative Departments, in particular, for such functions as audit, supervision and inspection. In the Third Plan a further provision of about ₹ 5 crore has been made for strengthening the personnel of Co-operative Departments at different levels.

In planning and carrying out intensive development in rural areas, Panchayati Raj institutions and co-operative organisations have a complementary role and must cooperate closely at every step. Zila Parishads, Panchayat Samitis and Village Panchayats should promote the development of co-operatives and should endeavour to create a climate of community effort and social responsibility such as are vital for the successful functioning of co-operatives at all levels. Regulatory powers in relation to co-operative organisations may continue to remain with the Government, but some of them can be delegated progressively to federal co-operative organisations. These will help to build up the self-regulatory character of the movement and to promote local leadership.

Co-operation is a people's movement and initiative for co-operative development and responsibility for regulating the working of the movement should progressively devolve on co-operative institutions and their higher federal organisations. The building up of efficient federal organisations in all sectors of co-operative activity assumes great importance in this context. As these organisations grow in strength, more powers may be transferred to them and the departmental machinery may limit its activities to the minimum statutory duties of registration, audit, arbitration and inspection. Promotional work relating to co-operation, co-operative training, education and publicity are activities falling within the special province of co-operative unions. Co-operative unions at State and district levels should be strengthened to enable them to undertake these responsibilities, and a strong federal structure should be built from the ground.

Fourth Five Year Plan: 1969-74

Note: Regular planning process in India was disrupted when the country came under severe shocks such as hostilities with Pakistan (1965), droughts for two successive years (1965-66 and 1966-67), devaluation of the rupee (1966) and inflationary pressure.

On account of these adverse circumstances, the draft outline of the Fourth Plan prepared in 1966 had to be abandoned. Instead, three Annual Plans (1966-67, 1967-68 and 1968-69) were prepared and implemented. Proper planning process was resumed when the Fourth Five Year Plan (1969-70 to 1973-74) became operational on April 1, 1969.

The Fourth Five Year Plan (1969-1974) gave high priority to the re-organization of co-operatives to make co-operative short-term and medium-term structure viable. It also made necessary provisions to provide co-operatives with management subsidy and share capital contribution, as well as for the rehabilitation of Central Co-operative Banks. It also emphasized the need to orient policies in favour of small cultivators.

Co-operation and Community Development

The volume of co-operative credit (short and medium-term) for agricultural purposes increased from ₹ 203 crore in 1960-61 to ₹ 429 crore in 1967-68 and an estimated ₹ 490 crore in 1968-69. Long-term credit increased from ₹ 12 crore in 1960-61 to about ₹ 120 crore in 1968-69. Appreciable progress took place in the co-operatively organised processing of agricultural produce mainly in the sector of sugar factories, which now account for about a third of the total sugar production. The value of agricultural inputs distributed by co-operatives rose from about ₹ 36 crore in 1960-61 to about ₹ 250 crore in 1968-69. Of the inputs, the largest item consists of fertilisers and the value of these distributed by the co-operatives increased from about ₹ 28 crore in 1960-61 to needy ₹ 200 crore in 1968-69, representing about 60 percent of the total consumption of fertilisers in the country. The total value of agricultural produce handled by co-operative marketing and processing societies rose from ₹ 174 crore in 1960-61 to an estimated ₹ 583 crore in 1968-69. The value of retail consumer trade undertaken by co-operatives in rural areas recorded an increase from ₹ 17 crore in 1960-61 to ₹ 275 crore in 1968-69. The corresponding figures for turn-over in urban areas were ₹ 40 crore in 1960-61 and ₹ 270 crore in 1968-69.

Apart from quantitative progress, there were several organisational developments of significance during this period. One of them was the emergence of national co-operative federations. The formation of the national federations and the reorganisation of the National Co-operative Union of India at the apex, added a new dimension to the co-operative structure. Another important development was the reorganisation of the co-operative training programme. This had two main aspects. A new stress was laid on instruction in business management. In pursuance of this objective, a Central Institute was started at Bombay in 1964 to impart training in business management to key personnel engaged in consumer co-operation. This was merged in 1967 with the National Co-operative College and Research Institute, Poona thus leading to the establishment of Vaikumh Mehta National Institute of Co-operative Management. Secondly, following the recommendations of the study team on Co-operative Training (1961), a decision was taken to transfer responsibility for the management of training centres to the co-operative unions both at the national and State levels. The National Co-operative Union of India set up a special committee, called the Committee for Co-operative Training on which devolved the task of running the National Institute and the co-operative training colleges. In a number of cases, the State Governments transferred the charge of their co-operative training Centres to State Co-operative Unions.

The co-operative movement has been uneven in its development in different regions as well as in different sectors of co-operative activity. So far as co-operative credit is concerned, inadequacy of development is particularly marked, though in different degrees, in the eastern States of Assam, West Bengal, Bihar and Orissa, and in Rajasthan. The eastern region, with about 27 percent of the rural population, accounted for only about 9 percent of co-operative credit. An informal group, constituted by the Reserve Bank of India, examined the institutional arrangements for agricultural credit in 1964, and in view of the serious gaps which existed particularly in the States mentioned, recommended the establishment of agricultural credit corporations as a transitional arrangement. In pursuance of this recommendation, necessary legislation has recently been enacted by Parliament.

While, for the country as a whole, co-operative short and medium term agricultural credit nearly doubled during 1960-68, the progress towards development of a viable structure at the level of the primary credit societies and central co-operative banks has been much below expectations. Two factors have contributed to this situation. The first has been the slow progress in the programme of organising viable primary credit societies by amalgamation of the non-viable societies. The second has been the increase in overdues. At the level of (he primary credit societies, the proportion of over-dues to outstanding increased from 20 percent in 1960-61 to 32 percent in 1967-68. For central co-operative hanks, the increase was from 12.4 percent to 25 percent. Of the 344 central co-operative banks, as many as 67 accumulated overdues exceeding 50 percent of the outstandings. This has brought in its wake a new problem of rehabilitation and reorganisation of weak central co-operative banks.

One of the notable developments of the period has been the organisation of a network of consumer co-operatives in urban areas. The impetus for this development came from the national emergency in 1962. The programme was accelerated during the period following devaluation. Alongside the organisation of consumer co-operatives, arrangements were also made to facilitate flow of supplies directly from the manufacturers. In order to secure working capital accommodation, the Central Government introduced a guarantee scheme under which central or wholesale consumer co-operatives and. consumer federations are eligible for financial accommodation against a margin not exceeding 10 per cent. As a result of these measures, the volume of retail trade handled by consumer co-operatives in the urban areas has vastly increased. The expansion has not been free from adverse features. Many consumer stores are heavily dependent for their business on distribution of controlled items.

Approach to Co-operative Development

Growth with stability being the key-note of the Fourth Plan, agricultural co-operatives on the one hand and consumer co-operatives on the other will occupy a central position in the strategy of co-operative development. Growth of agriculture is largely dependent on intensive agriculture and this involves a substantial increase in credit, inputs and services. The aim will be to ensure that the services which the farmer requires are institutionalised to the greatest extent possible.

In the process of such institutionalisation, which will not be to a set pattern, the co-operative form of organisation will have ample opportunities not only to expand but also to establish itself as viable and efficient. It will be part of policy during the Fourth Plan to ensure that the opportunities before co-operatives are as large and varied as they can utilise effectively. While it will be for the co-operatives themselves to make the effort involved and reach those standards of efficiency which will enable them to compete with other forms of organisation serving similar purposes, Government for its part will endeavour to assist the co-operatives to equip themselves for the task in important aspects such as finance, organisation and trained personnel. In regard to agro-industries, preference will continue to be given to co-operatives in the matter of licensing and institutional finance.

Co-operative Credit

One of the basic weaknesses of the co-operative credit system is the non-viability of a large number of primary agricultural credit societies, During recent, years, programmes of rationalisation of the co-operative credit structure, at the primary level, have been under way. As a result, the number of primary agricultural credit societies has gone from 2,12,000 at the end of 1960-61 to 1,71,800 at the end of 1967-68. However, a number of non-viable credit co-operatives still continue to clutter up the credit system. It is estimated that as a result of reorganisation, about 1,20,000 potentially viable societies are likely to emerge and that the rest of the societies would have to be absorbed in the process of amalgamation. One of the most important tasks before the co-operative credit movement is to accelerate the pace of such reorganisation, so that the co-operative short and medium-term credit structure is placed on a viable footing. It is proposed to accord high priority in the Plan to this reorganisation. Necessary provision has been included in the State Plans for this programme for grant of management subsidy to and share capital contribution in the reorganised society.

Among the bottlenecks in the flow of adequate co-operative credit is the existence of weak district central co-operative barks in several areas. It is estimated that over one-third of the co-operative banks fall in this category. It is proposed to undertake suitable programmes directed towards rehabilitation and reorganisation of such banks. In the interim period it is proposed to devise measures whereby the primary credit societies within the jurisdiction of such banks may be financed directly by the concerned apex banks.

Slackness in recovery of loans, resulting in mounting

overdues in co-operative credit institutions is undermining the soundness of co-operative credit structure in many areas and has led to stagnation, if not recession, of co-operative credit. The feature of heavy overdues is prevalent not only in comparatively less developed States but also in relatively advanced States. This points to the deficiencies in loaning policies of co-operatives, inadequate arrangements for supervision and weaknesses of internal management of co-operatives. Recurrence of natural calamities in successive years has also accentuated the problem of overdues in many areas. Systematic efforts need to be made both by the State Governments and by the co-operative banks towards substantial reduction of overdues. The responsibility for initiating legal action against wilful defaulters rests with the primary credit societies. To meet situations where the managements of primary Credit Societies do not take prompt action, there is provision in the co-operative societies Acts of some States enabling the central co operative bank concerned to initiate action on its own against the defaulting members of primary credit societies. Incorporation of similar provisions in other Co-operative Societies Acts as recommended by the All India Rural Credit Review Committee will be helpful in dealing with the problem of overdues.

Attention will also be paid to strengthening the recovery staff in the Department and the Central Co-operative Banks. The State Plans include the necessary provision. Where failure to repay the overdues is not wilful but due to natural calamities, conversion of short-term loans into medium-term loans should be taken up expeditiously by having recourse to agricultural credit stabilisation funds maintained by co-operative banks which have been augmented by Government; as instance through a Centrally sponsored scheme and to the National Agricultural Credit stabilisation Fund maintained by the Reserve Bank. Along with the collection of past overdues, action should be taken to prevent their recurrence in future through adoption of more rational loaning policies relating to size of credit to production outlay, effective linking of credit with marketing, strict supervision over utilisation of loans and above all the education of members of co-operatives in the rights and obligations connected with their membership.

It is needless to stress the importance of bringing about a substantial increase in deposits at various levels. The urgency of this task arises from a number of considerations. Increasing the deposit resource would help to absorb overdues and keep up the Hew of credit in an uninterrupted manner. It will also facilitate increase in loanable resources for meeting the growing demand for credit in areas of intensive agriculture. Deposit mobilisation is necessary to mop up a part of the increased income in. the rural areas for productive investment. The co-operative credit structure, therefore, has to make effective measures to increase its deposits. There would also be need for State Governments to undertake necessary enabling legislation to amend the Co-operative Societies Act, so that the Deposit Insurance Scheme could be extended to the deposits of co-operative banks. Co-operative banks will be encouraged and assisted to open more branches in rural areas for facilitating the flow of credit, for rendering services more efficiently and for tapping larger resources.

The ability of the co-operative short and medium-term credit structure to expand loan operations is dependent on the viability of the structure, the progress in the rationalisation of primary credit societies, reduction in overdues, mobilisation of deposits and liberalisation of loan policies. If the programmes mentioned are effectively implemented, it should be possible for the co-operatives to aim at disbursing short and medium-term credit of the order of ₹ 750 crore in 1973-74.

One of the striking developments has been the progress of land development banks which handle long-term credit. These banks now function in all the Slates through, a network of 1,250 primary banks and branches. It is proposed to accelerate the pace of expansion of land development banking so that adequate support may be forthcoming for schemes of basic importance to agriculture throughout the country such as land reclamation, soil conservation, land shaping, and construction of surface works, tubewells and other works of minor irrigation. Organisationally and administratively land development banks are equipped to handle loan operations of over ₹ 1,000 crore. However, in the light of available resources, a loaning target of ₹ 700 crore has been fixed for the Plan. This may subsequently be reviewed in case increased resources become available. For a large number of schemes distributed in different States, constituting in each case a sizeable and integrated project and satisfying the criterion of economic viability, the Agricultural Refinance Corporation will be able to provide refinance of the order of ₹ 200 crore during the Plan period. Provision has been made for lending support to the ordinary debentures and the special debentures of land development banks.

As recommended by the All India Rural Credit Review Committee, the present lending policies and procedures of the Land Development Banks have to be reviewed in a comprehensive manner so as to bring them in line with the requirement of sound investment credit and to ensure the optimum use of scares long-term resources. In the formulation of these policies, account should be taken of the special problems of small farmers. Under intensely supervised credit programmes, they should be helped in certain lines of investment either by undertaking such operations on a group basis or by their being enabled to make the repayment over a fairly long period.

There is need for increasing coordination between the normal lending operations of the Land Development Banks with those pertaining to the Agricultural Refinance Corporation on the one hand and with the operations of the co-operative banks on the other. There should be close collaboration between the Land Development Banks and the Central Co-operative Banks. Together they should ensure that inputs for production are accessible to the long-term borrower adequately and in time. Coordination should also be ensured in regard to credit for purposes such as the sinking of wells which, depending on the repaying capacity of the borrower, may quality either for a medium-term loan or a long-term one.

Long-term co-operative credit has hitherto been disbursed to the individual borrowers either by primary land development banks or by branches of central land development banks. In the Fourth Plan, it is proposed to try out on a pilot basis, how far primary credit societies could act as agents of the central land development bank for scrutiny of applications, disbursement of credit, supervision and recovery of instalments. In each State, a limited number of societies satisfying appropriate criteria pertaining to financial strength and operational efficiency will be selected for functioning as agencies of the land development banks in their respective areas. This type of arrangement may be gradually expanded to an increasing number of societies after experience has been gained as a result of this experiment.

The bulk of the loans issued by co-operatives is in small amounts of less than ₹ 500 each Even so, farmers with relatively larger holdings are the main beneficiaries of co-operative credit. The traditional emphasis on linking of credit to security offered by a borrower in the form of land and other tangible assets, exclusion of small farmers from the membership of co-operatives, domination of co-operatives by the more affluent and powerful section of the rural community, absence of tenancy records and prevalence of the system of oral tenancies are among the major factors that have led to denial of adequate credit to small farmers. The crop loan system, recommended for adoption, aims at shifting the emphasis in loaning operations from assets nexus to production potential. The system needs to be implemented in full in all the areas.

Since 1961, Government has been giving grants to co-operative banks and societies as an inducement to them to give larger loans to small cultivators for production purposes. These amounts are credited to special bad debt reserves of co-operatives. Following a review in 1964, the basis for Government contribution to the bad debt reserve fund has been changed and is now related to additional loans given from year to year to small cultivators. So far, a sum of about ₹ 7 crore has been granted by Government for this purpose and a further sum of ₹ 5 crore is expected to be given in the Fourth Plan.

In the Fourth Plan, one of the main endeavours will be to orient the policies and procedures of credit co-operatives and land development barks in favour of small cultivators. The All India Rural Credit Review Committee has made a number of recommendations in this direction. These will be sought fu be implemented, the more important changes being in the following directions.

1. If the resources available to a particular society are inadequate to meet the requirements of all its members, it will seek to ensure that the needs of the small cultivators are adequately met on a priority basis.
2. The larger cultivators will be called upon to contribute a relatively higher proportion of their borrowings towards share capital while the smaller cultivators will invariably be extended the facility of paying their share amount in convenient instalments.
3. Stress will be laid on effective implementation of crop loan system. To ascertain whether the small farmer is receiving adequate attention, it is intended that the credit limit statements are so separated so as to identify small farmers vis-à-vis others.
4. Loaning policies of land development banks will be liberalised, e.g., liberalisation in respect of valuation of landed property offered as security, issue of joint loans for groups of small cultivators, emphasis on the operational and economic viability of the proposed investment and not merely the value of tangible security and phasing of the repaying programme in accordance with the capacity of the small cultivators.

5. Bigger cultivators who can repay loans in shorter periods will be encouraged to avail of medium term credit for investment, so that larger volume of long-term credit can be made available for small farmers from land development banks.

Co-operative Marketing

Compared to co-operative credit, 'the development of co-operative marketing of agricultural produce is of recent origin. Following the recommendations of All India Rural Credit Survey Report, an integrated programme of co-operative marketing was taken up in the Second Plan and followed up in the Third. As a result, co-operative marketing structure has been built up at various levels. On the eve of the Fourth Plan, there were nearly 3,300 primary marketing societies, of which 500 were special commodity marketing societies. The higher level of co-operative marketing structure consists of 20 apex marketing societies and three commodity marketing federations at the State level and one National Agricultural Co-operative Marketing Federation at the all India level. There are also 173 central marketing societies including 15 special commodity societies, mainly at the district level.

Consistently with the programme for increasing agricultural production, steps will be taken to strengthen the existing co-operative marketing structure, especially at the primary level. Necessary provision for this purpose has been made in the State Plans. The marketing federations at the State and national level will be strengthened to enable them to reach optimum efficiency and to provide the requisite leadership, financial support and guidance to their affiliated institutions.

At present, only marketing co-operatives in Gujarat and a few processing co-operatives in other areas have adopted the system of grading and pooling. Efforts will be made to introduce this and other improved marketing techniques in as many co-operatives as possible. As further measures to improve marketing practices of the co-operatives, the schemes initiated in the previous years for establishing grading units with equipment and suitable trained personnel and for maintenance of price fluctuation funds which enable the societies to make outright purchases of agricultural produce from small growers, will be continued.

Co-operatives will aim at handling in the last year of the Fourth Plan, 8 million tonnes of foodgrains, 36 million tonnes of sugarcane, 0.6 million tonne of groundnut, 10,000 tonnes of fruit and vegetable and 1.8 million bales of cotton. At current prices, the value of agricultural produce likely to be handled by marketing and processing co-operatives is expected to be of the order of ₹ 900 crore in 1973-74. Co-operatives are also expected to handle agricultural commodities worth ₹ 25 crore in inter-State trade and ₹ 10 crore in the export trade.

Co-operative Processing

Considerable success has been achieved in the establishment of sugar factories in the co-operative sector. This was facilitated by the licensing policy of Government and the assistance provided by the Industrial Finance Corporation. A concerted programme to develop co-operative processing of other agricultural produce was taken in hand from Second Plan onwards. It has been accelerated in recent years. By the end of 1968-69, 1596 co-operative processing units had been organised. These included 79 co-operative sugar factories, 237 cotton ginning and pressing units, 26 cotton spinning mills, 784 paddy pressing units, 188 oil mills, and 38 fruit and vegetable units. Recently the need and scope for further developing of co-operative processing in the context of increased agricultural production was examined by an expert committee. Keeping in view its recommendations and the available resources, the Fourth Plan envisages the organisation of additional 550 units.

A review made by an expert committee on planning of co-operative agricultural processing units has indicated that the tendency has been to set up processing units on the basis of stereo-typed schemes. In the Fourth Plan, it is proposed that organisation of new processing units should be preceded by proper feasibility studies, advance locational planning with reference to supply of raw material, storage and marketing of finished products and overall economics of each projects. Facilities to provide technical advice are already being developed in various apex marketing societies. Efforts will be made to strengthen this technical machinery. Attention will also be paid to the need to consolidate and maximise the operational efficiency of existing units and ensure the fuller utilisation of their installed capacity.

Co-operative Handling of Agricultural Inputs

With the development of intensive agriculture, there will be a substantial step-up in the demand for inputs such as chemical fertilisers, seeds, agricultural implements and plant protection material. It is proposed that co-operatives intensify their activities and enlarge their distribution system. The expectation is that, by 1973-74, co-operatives will be handling fertilisers worth about ₹ 650 crore, improved seeds ₹ 50 crore, pesticides ₹ 50 crore and implements ₹ 15 crore. To enable the co-operatives to handle the distribution of inputs of this order, it will be necessary for them to have access to adequate bank finance. For this purpose, a provision has been made to cover a part of the requisite margin money to be provided by the co-operatives.

Co-operatives have recently made a beginning in the production or agricultural inputs. Some marketing co-operatives in the States have organised granular fertiliser mixing units. Production and processing of improved seeds, formulations of pesticides, manufacture of small agricultural implements have also been taken up in the co-operative sphere in increasing measure.

A major venture is the establishment of the fertiliser project of the Indian Farmers Fertiliser Co-operative Ltd. with an investment of about ₹ 85 crore. This project is proposed as a complex of gas-based ammonia and urea plants at Kalol and phosphate plant at Kandia in Gujarat State. This fertiliser factory is expected to produce 3,18,500 tonnes of ammonia, 3,82,000 tonnes of urea and 6,37,000 tonnes of complex fertilisers per annum. Another factory in the co-operative sector in Maharashtra State is also proposed to be set up.

Storage

A network of co-operative godowns has been established during recent years. On the eve of the Fourth Plan, there are 15,000 rural godowns and about 4,000 mandi level or rail-head godowns. The total capacity is estimated to be of the order of 2.6 million tonnes. So far, the programme of storage has been financed entirely by Plan funds. In the Fourth Plan, it is expected that co-operatives will, for this purpose, have increasing recourse to bank finance and that the provision made in the Plan will be used essentially as margin money. On this basis, it is visualised that co-operatives will establish in the Fourth Plan an additional storage of about 2.0 million tonnes.

Consumer Co-operation

The broad institutional framework of consumer co-operatives comprises a National Federation to which 14 State federations are affiliated. The State federations, in turn, comprise 371 central or wholesale consumer co-operative societies. Linked to the central co-operatives are about 2,800 branch stores (including department stores). There are also about 14,000 primary consumer co-operatives. Apart from the consumer co-operatives organised for the general urban population, co-operatives have also been sat up for specific consumer groups such as employees in industrial undertakings and university students.

With the organisation of various central and wholesale stores, practically all districts with an urban population of 50,000 or above have been brought within the area of operation of such stores. In the Fourth Plan, therefore, stress will be laid on consolidation and strengthening of existing consumer co-operatives at different levels rather than the organisation of new institutions. On the institutional side, the weakest link in the consumer co-operative movement lies at the level of primary consumer co-operatives. While over 14,000 primary consumer co-operatives have been registered, about 3,500 of them are dormant. The rest are mostly engaged in distributing rationed and controlled foodgrains and ether commodities. One of the major tasks hereafter to be undertaken is a survey of the existing primary consumer co-operatives with a view to identifying the institutions that are viable or are potentially viable so that, on a selective basis, such primary consumer co-operatives could be further strengthened and developed.

Attention will also be paid to the reorganisation and strengthening of central wholesale consumer co-operatives with a view to building them up as large-sized multi-retail unit co-operative societies. The superstructure of the consumer co-operative movement comprising the State federations and the National Federation will have to be strengthened with a view to enabling these institutions to play an effective role in procurement of supplies, besides promotional and service functions. At the retail stage, the structure is lopsided. It comprises, on the one hand, big retail outlets in the form of department stores with a large assortment of goods and, on the other, very small retail cutlets in the form of single-roomed shops primarily dealing in rationed and controlled items. The latter category accounts for over 96 percent of the total outlets through which the consumer movement is currently operating. These stores have practically no impact on normal consumer trade. To correct this imbalance, efforts will be made to develop retail outlets of the intermediate size, diversify the range of business of consumer co-operatives and improve their operational efficiency and economic viability.

In the rural areas, retailing of consumer articles is

conceived essentially as the responsibility of primary agricultural credit societies supported by marketing co-operatives. In this field, the expansion in business has been significant. The progress, however, has been largely accounted for by distribution of foodgrains and other controlled articles. Moreover the progress has been extremely uneven and has been confined to a few States. In the Fourth Plan, efforts will be made to spread and diversify this activity with a view to enlarging the number of village and marketing co-operative involved in it. The effort will be develop an effective consumer service so that co-operatives become part of a permanent distributive set up for making available a wide range of essential consumer goods in the rural areas. With the expansion and greater diversity of operations of consumer co-operatives and marketing co-operatives there is need for evolving appropriate working relationships between them. Steps will be taken to this end.

Rural Electric Co-operatives

One of the significant developments contemplated in the Fourth Plan relates to the involvement of the co-operative form of organisation in the programme of rural electrification. Pilot rural electric co-operatives are in the process of being set up in five States. The licensing of these co-operatives is among the functions allotted to the Rural Electrification Corporation. The objectives of the co-operatives include the supply of electricity for agricultural and agro-industrial purposes and the encouragement of active participation of the people by giving them some degree of control on electricity supply.

Urban Co-operative Banks

In urban areas, the salary earners societies and the primary urban co-operative banks can make an important contribution to future development. The salary earners societies have proved highly successful in a large number of governmental departments and organisations and non-official corporations all over the country. They have proved valuable for providing consumption finance and mobilising savings. The primary co-operative banks, in the .selected urban areas in which they have come up, have been financing activities of small producers and traders and are perhaps the most suitable types of organisation for this purpose.

It is necessary for co-operative departments and the State Co-operative Banks to take active interest in the wider establishment and sound working of these co-operative organisations. It is envisaged that the operations of the urban co-operative banks will be considerably expanded especially in regard to the financing of small scale industries and small industrialists. In order to enable urban banks to discharge this responsibility, it will be necessary to strengthen their share capital base. The Reserve Bank has recently approved a scheme for giving loans to the Slate Governments for share capital participation, on a selective basis, in such of these urban banks as are engaged or interested in productive activities related to the financing of small scale industries. It is expected that the State Governments will take advantage of this scheme.

Other Types of Co-operatives

While the focus of development will be on the co-operatives conversed with agricultural credit, marketing, processing and consumer needs, other types of co-operatives will also continue to receive attention. The programme relating to dairy, poultry and fisheries co-operatives and forest labour co-operatives and industrial co-operatives has been dealt with elsewhere. In co-operative farming, priority will be given to the revitalisation of the existing weak and dormant societies. New societies will be organised only in compact areas and if they have a potential for growth. Attention will be given to the strengthening of the labour contract societies and other types of non-agricultural co-operatives.

Management, Training and Education

Placing of adequate, competent and trained staff in key positions in co-operative institutions—banking, marketing, processing, consumer stores—is crucial for their successful functioning. At present, a majority of these institutions are managed by personnel on deputation from Government, who have no continuing stake in the growth of the institutions and often lack aptitude for business. It is essential for the institutions to reduce this dependence on borrowed personnel. For attracting the right type of persons, it is necessary to have management pools in different sectors in each State to be operated by the federal organisations like the apex banks, land development bank, apex marketing federation and State federation of consumer co-operatives. In due course, such pools could become the nucleus for establishment of cadres of key management personnel in different sectors. A beginning has been made in recent years in some States. It is proposed to pursue this programme vigorously.

The programme of co-operative training and education will be increasingly linked with the co-operative activities envisaged. The Vaikunth Mehta National Institute of Co-operative Management will be further developed as an apex institute of study and research in co-operation. The co-operative training colleges for intermediate personnel and co-operative training centres for junior personnel will be adequately equipped for training the requisite personnel.

In a strategy of co-operative development, there is need for continuing to stress the role of a well-informed and enlightened membership in the promotion and working of co-operative societies. A programme essentially directed towards the education of office-bearers and members of primary agricultural credit societies through peripatetic instructors has been in operation for some lime. Of late, there has been a perceptible indication of dissatisfaction with the content and effectiveness of this programme. In some areas and even states, the programme has been curtailed or drastically modified. The programme is proposed to be revised in the light of an evaluation study recently brought out by the Programme Evaluation Organisation of the Planning Commission. It is necessary to ensure that the peripatetic instructors are liked with the co-operative training centres. Efforts will also be made to ensure that the member education programme for village co-operatives is supported and supervised by central co-operative banks, marketing societies and other functional federations.

Community Development and Panchayati Raj

The Community Development programme was started in 1952. It now covers the whole country. Its unit remains the block and its aim that of achieving rural development through people's participation and initiative. The assistance from Government, so far as resources would allow, took the shape of a budget grant for the block and a team of extension workers under a Block Development Officer. The latter was to coordinate all schemes of a developmental character within the block. In the integrated programme, divided into stages of five years each, agricultural development occupied the foremost position.

The next step was that of attempting to weld together Panchayati Raj and Community Development. This objective followed from the acceptance of the recommendations of the Study Team of the Committee on Plan Projects (Balwantrai Mehta Committee). The three-tier Panchayati Raj system, together with its modifications in different States, thus set the pattern of local development administration. At each level—village or group of villages, block or group of blocks, and district—there was to be a link between the administrative apparatus and elected representatives.

All villages are now covered by blocks. There are some 5,265 blocks, including 459 tribal development blocks. Of these 999 are in Stage I and 2,585 in Stage II. The rest have completed ten years and passed both the stages. Village

Panchayats exists in all States and most Union Territories. The other tier—Samitis at the Block level and Zila Parishads at the district level—has been constituted in all States except Madhya Pradesh, Kerala, Jammu and Kashmir, parts of Bihar and Nagaland. There is not much diversity in the functions and powers of the village panchayats and panchayat functions and powers of the Zila Parishads from State to State.

The working of the programme has thrown up a variety of experiences. The operation of the Blocks in five year stages, with tapering financial provision from stage to stage, was based on the assumption that, by the end of the initial ten-year period, there would be adequate mobilisation of resources by the local institutions and sufficient channelling of other Plan funds to make any separate provision thereafter for the Blocks unnecessary. Community Development, in other words, would then no longer be assisted and schematic but self-reliant and locally rooted. These assumptions have not proved correct. By and large the programme continues to be dependent on Government initiative and even more so on Government funds. Where funds were lacking, activities languished and the staff remained almost supernumerary.

Where, however, administrative and financial support has been forthcoming, the combined contribution of Parchayati Raj and Community Development has been significant in the formulation and implementation of local development plans. There has also been a large measure of coordination and integration of the field staff. In certain instances, the Panchayati Raj institutions have, for their part, made attempts to raise increasingly large resources through tax measures. In the majority of cases, however, local finance has continued to play very little part in local Development.

New Dimensions

With all their drawbacks, the Community Development Programme and Panchayati Raj institutions have provided a new dimension to rural development and introduced a structural change of considerable importance in the district administration. Within the limitations of resources the programme has attempted to do something which in many cases, had never before been attempted. Improvement of agriculture has remained in the forefront throughout. Investment from the available block funds on agricultural development has over the years almost equalled the provisions for all other sectors of development taken together. In many States, the block organisation has been virtually the only field agency for carrying out development programmes. There has been sizeable contribution from the local communities to the developmental effort.

Some States have recently introduced changes in the pattern of organisation. While there has to be considerable flexibility in regard to the type of organisation, contents of programme and extent of resources, the need for an integrated approach to rural development, including coordination between official and non-official agencies, remains basic. Also important is a continued emphasis on priority programmes such as agriculture and family planning. The State Plans accordingly provide ₹ 84.69 crore for programme of community development. It is necessary to ensure that these funds are supplemented to the largest extent possible by resources mobilised by the Panchayati Raj institutions. Simultaneously, there should be progressively larger devolution of programmes and resources by the States.

Pilot Study on Growth Centres

As a part of studies on area planning, a Centrally sponsored scheme of Pilot Research Project in Growth Centres is being launched. The aim of the pilot project will be to evolve a broad research methodology and pattern for identifying emerging growth centres, and to indicate how the growth potential of these centres could be promoted through comprehensive and scientific study of the overall development needs, and how these centres could be meaningfully woven into the frame of the district plan and thus help in the process of planning from below. The scheme will thus bring under close study action strategies relevant to the acceleration of integrated area development around potential growth centres. A number of projects will be set up in different areas in the States and Union Territories. A few projects would be located in institutions working on planning methodology. To facilitate integration with district planning, the growth centres will, to the extent possible, be located in districts for which detailed plans in terms of guidelines and norms provided by the Planning Commission are already being drawn up.

Integration

Panchayati Raj having been accepted as the pattern for local development administration, fuller and more active involvement of the institution is necessary in the process of economic development and social advance. The viability of these institutions would depend on the extent to which they can undertake obligations for mobilising should likewise be assisted to build up their own revenue-yielding assets. The administrative apparatus at the district, block and village level has to be integrated and, where necessary, strengthened. The integration has to comprise not only the staff of the Community Development and Panchayati Raj institutions but also normal departmental staff deal in with all development schemes of a local character. At the same time, the administrative, financial and other procedures relevant to these institutions call for a careful periodical review to ensure that they remain attuned to the responsibilities devolving on them.

Fifth Five Year Plan: 1974-79

Note: The Fifth Five Year Plan (1974-75 to 1978-79) was introduced when the country was reeling under severe economic strains such as run-away inflation caused by unprecedented increase in international oil prices in the wake of 1973 Gulf Crisis and the failure of the Government to takeover the wholesale trade in wheat. When the Janata Government assumed power at the Centre in 1977, it did not allow the Fifth Plan to run its full course of five years (1974-75 to 1978-79) and truncated it at the end of the fourth year (i.e. on March 31, 1978). The Plan was disrupted and replaced by the so-called rolling plan which proved to be a non-starter.

The Fifth Five Year Plan (1974-1979) took note of the high level of over-dues. In its recommended strategy for co-operative development, the correction of regional imbalances and reorienting the co-operatives towards the under-privileged was to receive special attention. Based on the recommendations of an Expert Group appointed by the Planning Commission in 1972, structural reform of the co-operative set-up was envisaged. The Plan recommended the formulation of Farmers' Services Co-operative Societies as had been envisaged by the National Commission on Agriculture and stressed the need for professional management of co-operatives.

Co-operation

Taking note of the desirability of strengthening the co-operative structure, provision has been sufficiently enhanced for Agricultural Stabilisation Fund, rehabilitation of weak Central Co-operative Banks and assistance to co-operative credit institutions in developing States. Thus the revised outlay for 1977-79 is almost 60 percent higher than the outlays for the first three years of the Fifth Plan. Similarly, adequate provisions have been made in the State sector to provide for strengthening of co-operative structure by organising Farmers Service Societies. Provisions have also been made for increasing the loaning programmes for minor irrigation, land development and supply of inputs.

Sixth Five Year Plan: 1980-85

Note: The political turmoil of the late 1970s witnessed two Sixth Plans. 1. The Sixth Five Year Plan (1978-79 to 1982-83) of the Janata Party Government which was abandoned when Mrs. Indira Gandhi returned to power at the Centre in early 1980. 2. The Sixth Five Year Plan (1980-81 to 1984-85) introduced by the new Government led by Mrs. Indira Gandhi. The latter ran its full course successfully. It focused on direct attack on poverty.

The Sixth Five Year Plan (1979-1985) also emphasized the importance of co-operative efforts being more systematically directed towards ameliorating the economic conditions of the rural poor. The Plan recommended steps for re-organizing Primary Agricultural Credit Societies into strong and viable multi-purpose units. It also suggested strengthening the linkages between consumer and marketing co-operatives. Consolidation of the role of Co-operative Federal Organizations, strengthening development of dairy, fishery and minor irrigation co-operatives, manpower development in small and medium co-operatives were some of the planned programmes.

Co-operation

Co-operation as an instrument of economic development of the disadvantaged, particularly in the rural areas has received considerable emphasis during the successive Plans. The founders of planning in the country saw a village Panchayat, a village co-operative and a village school, as the trinity of institutions on which a self-reliant and just economic and social order was to be built. The non-exploitative character of co-operatives, voluntary nature of their membership, the principle of one man one vote, decentralised decision making and self-imposed curbs on profits eminently qualified them as an instrument of development combining the advantages of private ownership with public good.

Review

Having begun primarily in the field of credit as a defensive mechanism against the usurious money lenders, co-operatives have through the last three decades of planning come to embrace a large gamut of activities to serve the interests of the producers and consumers. Credit, however, still continues to be the predominant activity. Taking the latest published figures, there were 1.16 lakh Primary Agricultural Credit Societies including LAMPS, FSSS etc. in 1978-79, with a membership of 5.18 crore. The number of borrowing members was around 37 percent of the total membership. The co-operatives today cover almost all the villages in the country and their working capital stood at ₹ 2,950 crore on June 30, 1979. In 1979-80, the figure of short term credit advanced is provisionally estimated at around ₹ 1,300 crore and medium and long term investment credit at ₹ 400 crore.

While all round progress has been made in the field of credit by co-operatives, a few disconcerting features deserve special notice. Firstly, the rate of growth of agricultural credit advanced by the co-operatives has lately slowed down. Notwithstanding the needs of a rapidly developing agriculture, the short term credit advanced by the co-operatives has stayed around ₹ 1,200 to ₹ 1,300 crore during the last 3 years. The position of medium and long term credit representing investment loans is distinctly worse, with a loaning of about ₹ 339 crore an 1977-78, ₹ 448 crore in 1978-79 and only ₹ 400 crore in 1979-80.

The most important reason for this stagnation in credit flow is the mounting overdues which are clogging the process of credit recycling. While the sheer volume of overdues in some states make it impractical to recover these in one instalment and demand's some practical solutions for recovery over a phased period, the tendency which has developed in some States to write off the debts can only 'be viewed with extreme concern. It sets in undesirable precedent and will hamper recovery efforts in future. Secondly, while it is satisfying to note that the share of the weaker sections of the rural community has been steadily increasing over the years and *is* at present placed at over 40 percent of the total, this share falls short of their essential production needs. Though the small and marginal farmers are apparently getting credit in larger proportion (35 percent) than the land area held by them (21 percent), considering that these farmers have to depend mainly on credit for the purchase of their inputs, unlike the larger fanners who can use their own surpluses, the flow of co-operative credit to the small and marginal farmers is still inadequate.

However, in case of tenants, share croppers, landless agricultural labourers and rural artisans, who are the poorest, and therefore the most needy, the flow of co-operative credit in terms of percentage share has continued to range only around 3 to 5 percent over the years. There have also been considerable regional disparities in credit availability. Partly due to the poor absorptive capacity and partly due to lack of coordination among concerned developmental agencies, the co-operatives have not been able to ensure an increasing flow of production loans and investment credit in most of the tribal and hill areas. Thirdly, though the co-operative's have now come to cover almost the entire country-side, the membership is only around 45 percent of the total rural families. The weakest sections of the rural community are still not adequately represented in the membership roll.

Co-operatives are playing an important role in the supply of fertilisers on credit or cash to farmers and carrying it to the remotest parts of the country. In quantitative terms, it is estimated that 23.5 lakh tonnes of NPK (₹ 900 crore worth) of chemical fertilisers would have been distributed by the network of 47,000 co-operative outlets in 1978-79. However, private retailers have been progressively eating into their share of the total sales. Stagnation in credit flow has also affected their sales which are to a large extent on credit. Consequently their share in total sales has come down to about 43 percent in 1979-80 as against 55-60 percent a few years ago.

Linking of production credit with input supply on the one hand, and marketing and processing of agricultural produce on the other, has been considered critical to the success of the production programme. Co-operative marketing infrastructure has now come to cover almost all the important secondary and terminal markets in the country, comprising 3370 primary marketing societies at the mandi-level (including 550 Special Commodity Agricultural Marketing societies), 173 Central/District Co-operative Marketing Societies, 27 State/Apex co-operative marketing federations and the National Agricultural Co-operative Marketing Federation (NAFED) and its 25 main branches.

During the last two decades, the marketing co-operatives have attained significant growth in business operations and have also diversified their activities manifold; yet their total share in the market still continues to be small, except in procurement operations (for the buffer stock) in some States, nor has their share kept pace with the rapidly growing output and volume of agricultural produce. In nominal value terms, agricultural produce marketed by the co-operatives hay risen from ₹ 1,100 crore in the terminal year of the Fourth Plan to ₹ 1,750 crore at the end of 1979-80. During 1978-79, sugarcane followed by foodgrains and cotton constituted the bulk of the value of agricultural produce marketed by the co-operative system. Bulk of the turnover is accounted for by only the five States of Punjab, Haryana, Kerala, Madhya Pradesh and Uttar Pradesh. In the marketing of horticultural and other products, the role of co-operatives is only marginal compared to the potential.

One of the constraints in the development of agricultural marketing has been the weak financial base at the primary level. They also suffer from lack of suitable personnel for such commercial operations and there is not enough linkage and business relationship among the different co-operative sectors and between producers co-operatives and consumers co-operatives. Some of these problems have wakened the ability of the co-operatives to undertake larger marketing operations on behalf of their members. In the field of agricultural processing, the most conspicuous success has been the one achieved by sugar co-operatives and co-operative milk unions in some parts of the country. Rice mills, dal mills, cotton Tinning and processing units, spinning mills, oil crushing and processing, fruits and vegetable processing units, poultry food, jute baling etc. are some of the other processing activities in the co-operative sector which are steadily expanding. In terms of impact, however, except for sugar and milk, co-operatives account for rather a small share.

Adequate and Scientific storage facilities with co-operatives are essential to their operational efficiency in the marketing of agricultural produce, agricultural inputs and consumer goods. The programme now is to ensure that all re-organised primary agricultural credit societies and marketing societies are assisted to build up owned storage of appropriate capacity within a phased period. The total sanctioned storage capacity at the end of 1979-80 in the co-operative sector comprised 67.8 lakh tonnes of which 47 lakh tonnes has been established. The completed capacity comprises 22,000 godowns at the primary societies' level with a capacity of 22 lakh tonnes and 5,040 godowns of 25 lakh tonnes capacity at the marketing societies' level. Within a period of 10 years, 1969-79, the completed storage capacity in the co-operative sector has gone up from 26 lakh tonnes to 47 lakh tonnes, though, undoubtedly the intensity of coverage has been uneven among States. Occasional scarcity of building materials, delays in acquisition of land, lack of centralised arrangement for technical supervision, cost escalation and in some cases the indifferent attitude of managements has been responsible for slow progress in construction.

With a view to meeting the growing needs of producers

especially of potato, fruits, onion, etc., a systematic programme to establish cold storage facilities at strategic places has been taken in hand. At the end of March 1980, the number of cold stores organised in the co-operative sector was 204 with licensed capacity of 4.6 lakh tonnes, accounting for approximately 15 per cent of the total cold storage capacity in the country. Of this, 125 units with a capacity of 2.14 lakh tonnes had already been installed and the rest were at various stages of installation. An assessment carried out of the cold stores indicates that these units were being utilised by the small and middle farmers also and that there had been progressive increase in the level of capacity utilisation during the last three years. Taking into consideration the need for more cold storage rapacity for a variety of perishables and the trends of potato production in certain areas, an expanded programme of cold storage capacity in the co-operative sector is being contemplated in the Sixth Plan.

Of all the major co-operative activities, consumer activity is the most recent. It has, however, made headway and come to occupy an important role in the distribution of consumer articles in rural as well as urban areas. A four tier system comprising the National federation, State federations, Central society at the district and the primary societies at the base level, has been operating in this field. As on June 30, 1979, the structure consisted of a National federation. 14 State consumer co-operative federations, 8 State co-operative marketing-cum-consumer federations, 481 Central/Wholesale consumer societies at the district level and 16,348 primary consumer co-operatives at the base level. The district level wholesale societies were also operating 3,690 branches including about 700 departmental stores. Co-operative societies have also been functioning among industrial workers, employees of railways, posts and telegraphs etc.

In the rural areas, about 1,900 primary marketing societies and over 37,000 villages/service co-operatives anti other co-operative societies were connected with the distribution of consumer articles. During 1979-80, the total retail trade handled by the urban consumer co-operatives was estimated at ₹ 800 crore. In the rural areas, the total value of consumer articles sold by the co-operatives is also estimated at ₹ 800 crore in 1979-80. One of the major problems concerning these co-operative stores both in the rural as well as in the urban areas has, however, been inadequate marketing finance, uncertainties in the procurement of supplies and lack of trained and skilled manpower.

It would thus be seen that the progress of co-operatives over the years presents a mixed picture. There has been much progress quantitatively and yet there are a number of indicators which point to serious lacunae in their development. The co-operatively weak States, particularly in the eastern region do not seem to have made up any of their lag. In fact, some of the so-called co-operatively advanced States have also slided down particularly in the field of credit due to mounting overdues. Nearly 37 percent of the total primary marketing co-operatives are not doing any business and are virtually defunct. Only five States account for more than 80 percent of the total marketing of agricultural produce done by co-operatives. Even in these States, the management studies undertaken have pointed to the scope for bringing about considerable managerial improvements. The co-operative share of total fertiliser sales which was at one time around 55 percent has come down to around 43 percent.

Sluggishness in credit development due to heavy overdues in a large number of States has eroded the overall viability of primary co-operatives and has thus affected all other fields of activity like marketing of agricultural produce, farm inputs and consumer goods. In the ultimate analysis, the most outstanding of the deficiencies, which indeed is at the root of many of the palpable shortfalls in co-operative performance, is in the area of management. In spite of considerable discussion over the years in regard to the need for proper manpower development, the co-operatives have by themselves shown a singular lack of appreciation of this problem.

Strategy for the Sixth Plan

In the light of the problems and constraints discussed above, it is proposed to specifically direct attention during the Five Year Plan to the following tasks on a priority basis.

1. A clearly conceived action programme to be drawn up for the strengthening of primary village societies so that they are able to effectively act as multi-purpose units catering to diverse needs of their members.
2. Re-examination of the existing co-operative policies and procedures with a view to ensuring that the efforts of the co-operatives are more systematically directed towards ameliorating the economic conditions of the rural poor.
3. Re-orientation and consolidation of the role of the co-operative federal organisations so that they are able through their constituent organisations to effectively support a rapidly diversifying and expanding agricultural sector, including horticulture, food processing, poultry, dairying, fishery, animal husbandry, sericulture etc., with credit, input supply, marketing and other services.
4. Development of professional manpower and appropriate professional cadres to man managerial positions.

Programmes

The primary village (multi-purpose) society is the base on which the entire co-operative structure rests. A programme of re-organisation of these societies had been undertaken a few years ago based on certain stipulated viability criteria and such a re-organisation has already been carried out in most States of the country. Nevertheless, even where this programme is said to have been completed, the basic objective of re-organisation has not yet been achieved in substance. A very large number of re-organised societies still continue without even one full time manager. Furthermore, a large number of managers so appointed have either received no training or extremely inadequate training. Stable arrangements still do not exist in many States for regular payment of salaries to managers. Financial constraint is said to be one of the reasons for this state of affairs. Nevertheless, this particular task is of such importance that it must take precedence over other schemes and projects of development on which considerable funds are presently being expended. Without a stable and properly staffed, primary society, the base of all co-operative activity will continue to remain weak. The Centrally sponsored scheme for assistance to States to contribute towards the deficit in the salary fund of managers of reorganised societies will be continued during the Sixth Plan. Besides, the share capital of these societies will be strengthened, subject to certain norms of performance, to enable them to take up diversified activities on an expanded scale.

The co-operatives have for some time been alive to their responsibility towards the rural poor. The percentage of short and medium term credit to weaker sections has moved up from 29 percent of the total co-operative credit disbursed in 1973-74 to about 40 percent presently and in long-term credit to about 38 percent. However, on further examination, it is observed that the bulk of this credit has gone to the small and marginal farmers, namely, those who have a land base. The share of tenants, agricultural labourers and rural artisans has continued to stagnate around 3 to 5 percent of the total co-operative credit during the last decade. The membership pattern of village co-operatives also reveals a similar trend. While small and marginal farmers constituted about 44 percent of the total membership in 1977-78, agricultural labourers and rural artisans constituted only around 10 percent. Without, therefore, minimising in any way the efforts which have already been made by the co-operatives and direct their benefit to the weaker sections, a much greater thrust in that direction is called for with a view particularly, to giving greater coverage to the poorest among the target group of the weaker sections.

It would be necessary for the co-operatives to mount a

systematic programme for enrolling the landless workers, members of the scheduled castes and scheduled tribes, fishermen, artisans and others among the poorest as members, so that they could get the benefit of facilities offered by the co-operatives. Mere enrolment, however, of these persons as members will not be enough. It will be necessary that each primary society systematically identifies the members who are below the poverty line and draws up a specific credit plan for them in the light of individual possibilities of development and carries it out within a reasonable time-frame. This will need to be closely coordinated with the Integrated Rural Development Programme.

A tendency has developed among co-operative federal organisations often to promote their own business at the cost of their constituents. The programmes and policies of co-operative federations at the State as well as the national level would be so oriented as to make these institutions more effective as federations of affiliated co-operatives. They would thus be called upon to enlarge not only their own business but at the same time provide leadership to their affiliated organisations and lend full support to them in their business operations. In respect of commodities, which have inter-State marketing possibilities, the State and national federations would be expected to undertake larger inter-State trade. Coordination and linkage between marketing and consumer co-operatives would be strengthened so that the latter may be able to procure farm produce directly from the farmers through the marketing co-operatives instead of resorting to procurement through private wholesalers and intermediaries. Special attention will be given to strengthening the activities of consumer co-operatives in the urban areas and to the development of consumer business of primary village co-operatives and marketing societies in rural area's to serve as a dependable adjunct to the public distribution system.

The Central sector scheme for strengthening NAFED; NCCF and other Federations and the Centrally sponsored scheme for the development of co-operative marketing, processing and storage etc. in underdeveloped States would be continued during the Sixth Plan. The capital base of National Co-operative Development Corporation, which is the principal financing and promotional organisation at the national level for the development of co-operative marketing, storage, processing, supply of farm inputs and rural consumer activity, will be further strengthened during the Sixth Plan with a view to enabling it to lend support to these activities on an expanded scale.

Irrespective of whatever objectives that may be laid down in terms of expected levels of performance and whatever programmes of assistance that may be developed, it is ultimately in the area of management and man-power development that the key to successful implementation lies. In spite of a number of committees and frequent discussions that have been devoted to this subject over the last three decades, the picture does not seem to have altered in any significant way. Neither the scheme of organisation or pools of personnel nor of formation of cadres for different sectors of co-operative activity has made much headway so far. The main resistance has come from co-operative organisations themselves, who have been averse to taking personnel required on a centralised basis either by the co-operative departments or by special cadre societies or the sectoral federations.

As most co-operative institutions by themselves are not big enough to either offer suitable salary scales or career advancement prospects to be able to attract the right kind of personnel, it appears necessary that a system be devised by which key personnel are recruited for the whole range of small and medium co-operatives in an organised manner, which should make it possible to otter adequate wages to the persons employed, provide them opportunities of career advancement within the sector as a whole and make them feel part of a larger system with potentialities of development to each according to his capacity and competence. In other words, a co-operative sector must operate as one inter-linked whole in this manner rather than as a mere collection of small scattered institutions.

Special attention will be given during the Sixth Plan to devising a suitable system in this behalf which will make available to the co-operatives, cadres of properly qualified and trained personnel to handle their diverse activities. Care will, however, have to be taken that the system contemplated is such as reconciles to the extent possible, the sensitivity and the autonomy of the individual organisations where the persons recruited will actually be employed. Along side, sector-wise surveys of co-operative activities will be undertaken on a scientific basis to identify their organisational, operational and managerial deficiencies and to work out measures for their sound growth. Another aspect of management is in regard to the commitment and quality of the elected office bearers.

The co-operatives are often criticised for being dominated by vested interests. The solutions sought so far have been in the nature of limiting the number of terms of office etc. While these measures are useful as far as they go, they still do not impinge on the basic question of commitment of an office bearer to the objectives of the society. An office bearer of a marketing society, who does not market his own produce through his marketing co-operative, is hardly likely to have any stake in the performance of that society, likewise, of a credit co-operative bank, who is himself a defaulter in payment of dues is hardly likely to pursue recovery discipline in his society. It will be necessary to take a close look at the bye-laws of various types of co-operatives and to suitably revise these, wherever necessary to ensure that such commitments are built into the bye-laws as to eliminate mere office seekers from the management of the society. In fact, dairy co-operatives of the Anand Pattern have a specific clause built into the bye-laws about the supply of milk to the co-operative for a certain minimum number of days in a year as an essential qualification for office. A similar provision needs to be built in the bye-laws of other type of co-operatives also.

Agriculture which is projected to grow at an annual compound rate of about 4 percent during the Sixth Plan period would demand substantial credit, farm inputs, and marketing and storage support. Within this overall growth rate, the rate of growth of production in dairying, animal husbandry, poultry, fishery and fruits and vegetables has been projected at a rate higher than for crops. The Integrated Rural Development Programme which would now cover the entire country would demand much larger multi-sided support from the co-operatives. Particular attention will be given to the development and strengthening of dairy co-operatives in the context of Operation Flood II, in which co-operatives constitute the organisational frame-work of the project almost wholly. The role of the fishery co-operatives has only been somewhat marginal so far, both qualitatively and quantitatively. Fishermen have been one of the poorest and the most exploited sections of the rural community. A specific programme of strengthening the co-operative structure in this field will therefore be drawn up.

Minor Irrigation Development and water management is another important area of activity in which corporations will have to be particularly encouraged. Co-operatives are also expected to play an expanded role in the public distribution system and in the supply of essential consumer articles in rural and urban areas. Considerable expansion in the storage capacity of co-operatives is envisaged during the Sixth Plan with a view to strengthening and enlarging their role in the marketing of agricultural produce, supply of farm inputs and retailing of consumer articles.

Substantial increase is proposed during the Plan in the oil seeds processing capacity, particularly for soyabean to encourage increased production and in cold storage capacity to support expanded programmes of potato, fruits and vegetables production. Programmes for setting up co-operative sugar factories and spinning mills would be suitably accelerated. The co-operative training and education programmes would also be intensified and increasingly linked to the growing and diversified needs of the various sectors of co-operative movement. Taking into consideration the demand for co-operative services and the reasonable capabilities of the co-operative system, the following targets of physical performance in important co-operative activities have been projected for the period 1980-85.

Seventh Five Year Plan: 1985-90

The Seventh Five Year Plan (1985-1990) pointed out that while there had been all round progress in credit, poor recovery of loans and high level of overdues were matters of concern. The Plan recommended amongst others development of Primary Agricultural Credit Societies as multiple viable units; realignment of policies and procedures to expand flow of credit and ensure inputs and services particularly to weaker sections; special programmes for the North Eastern Region; strengthening of consumer co-operative movement in urban as well as rural areas and promoting professional management.

Co-operation

The co-operative movement was started in India primarily as an alternative credit source to the village money lenders. However, over the successive Five Year Plans considerable expansion and diversification took place and the co-operatives now cover the entire spectrum of activities in the rural areas. According to the latest available estimates, in 1982-83 there were 94,089 primary agricultural credit societies with a membership of 63.5 million. The number of borrowing members was 22.8 million, which worked out to 36 percent of the total membership. Their working capital stood at ₹ 4,841 crore as on June 30, 1983. Further, the short-term credit advanced amounted to ₹ 1,908 crore and the medium-term and long-term investment credit amounted to ₹ 660 crore.

Review of Sixth Plan

While all round progress has been made in the field of credit by co-operatives, a few disquieting features deserve special mention. Although there has been an appreciable increase in the flow of co-operative credit, there is no perceptible improvement in the recovery of loans, and overdues have continued to be high at various levels of credit structure even though the crops have been good in some years. The ratio of overdues to demand at primary agricultural credit societies' level increased from 41.4 percent in 1980-81 to 43 percent in 1981-82 and came down only marginally to 40.9 percent in 1982-83. The overdues in the short-term credit structure assumed alarming proportion in the North Eastern States. As for the primary land development banks, the percentage of overdues was 51 in 1980-81. It came down to 41 in 1981-82 mainly due to the blocking of old loans and again increased to 43 in 1982-83. In the long-term loaning sector, the problem of mounting overdues almost crippled the land development banks in 9 States, viz. Maharashtra, Gujarat, Madhya Pradesh, Bihar, Karnataka, Assam, West Bengal, Orissa and Tamil Nadu.

The reorganisation of primary agricultural credit societies into viable units has been completed in all States except Gujarat, Maharashtra and Jammu and Kashmir. However, even in the States where the reorganisation has been completed, no substantial increase in the loaning business has been witnessed. Out of 94,089 primary agricultural credit societies in the country in 1982-83, only 66,000 societies had full time paid Secretaries. About 34,000 societies were running at loss. The Committee to Review Arrangements for Institutional Credit for Agriculture and Rural Development (CRAFICARD) had made a number of recommendations for toning up the credit structure at various levels and particularly for developing the primary agricultural credit societies into multipurpose viable units.

However, by and large, these recommendations have not been implemented by the State Governments. While the Sixth Plan target for disbursement of short-term loans for the country as a whole is likely to have been accomplished, there have great been regional disparities. The eight States of Andhra Pradesh, Gujarat, Haryana, Kerala, Madhya Pradesh, Maharashtra, Punjab and Rajasthan account for about 80 per cent of the total credit disbursed. The per hectare short-term credit disbursed varied from ₹ 4 in Assam to ₹ 718 in Kerala. The removal of regional disparities has assumed added importance with the introduction of the programme for Intensive Production of Rice in six eastern States and the consequent need for expansion of credit disbursement in these States.

A major development in the field of credit during the Sixth Plan period was the setting up of National Bank for Agriculture and Rural Development (NABARD) in July 1982. NABARD has now emerged as an apex national institution accredited with all matters concerning policy, planning and operations in the field of credit for agricultural and other economic activities in the rural areas. It is, however, necessary to introduce flexibility in policies and simplify procedures and practices.

The share of the co-operatives in total fertilizers distribution has shown a marginal increase from 46 percent in 1979-80 to 47 percent in 1984-85. The limiting factors have been the induction of public sector agencies like Agro-Industries Corporations and private trade, inadequate availability of co-operative credit due to high overdues, the high interest rate on bank credit and inadequate margins available to the co-operatives for fertilizer retailing.

The value of agricultural produce marketed by co-operatives which was of the order of ₹ 1,750 crore on the eve of the Sixth Plan is reported to have increased to ₹ 2,700 crore by the end of 1984-85. The development of agricultural co-operative marketing, however, has been very uneven among different States. The agricultural produce marketed per hectare ranged from ₹ 8 in Rajasthan to ₹ 509 in Maharashtra. The six States of Gujarat, Haryana, Karnataka, Maharashtra, Punjab and Uttar Pradesh contributed 81 percent of the overall achievement.

The Sixth Plan laid great emphasis on the development of professional manpower and appropriate cadres to man the managerial posts, and for this purpose, recommended intensification of co-operative education and training programmes and their increased linkages to the growing and diversified needs of the various sectors of the co-operative movement. 5,165 senior level personnel and 38,137 intermediate personnel received training in the Vaikunth Metha National Institute of Co-operative Management and 17 co-operative training colleges and 87 junior level co-operative training institutions. Too much dependence on Government funds has been a major constraint in the expansion of co-operative training and education programmes. Also, evaluation of the training programmes has not been given due attention.

In short, the progress made under the various co-operative programmes during the Sixth Plan period presents a mixed picture. Although quantitatively substantial progress has been made under the various programmes and the targets laid down in the Plan have been more or less achieved, a number of shortcomings have also been noticed in the implementation of these programmes. In spite of the sizeable assistance provided to the co-operatively weaker States particularly in the North Eastern Region, the co-operative movement in these States has not yet picked up. By far the most serious lacuna has been the continued existence of high levels of overdues in a large number of States which has eroded the overall viability of primary co-operatives and has also adversely affected other fields of activity like marketing of agricultural produce, supply of agricultural inputs and distribution of consumer goods.

Strategy for the Seventh Plan

Co-operative development under the Seventh Plan will embody the following main tasks.

1. Comprehensive development of primary agricultural credit societies to function as multi-purpose viable units.
2. Realignment of the policies and procedures of co-operatives to expand the flow of credit and ensure supply of inputs and services particularly to the weaker section.
3. Taking up of special co-operative programmes for

implementation in the underdeveloped States specially in the North Eastern Region.

4. Strengthening the consumer co-operative movement in the urban as well as rural areas so that it can play a pivotal role in the public distribution system.
5. Promoting professional management and strengthening of effective training facilities for improving the operational efficiency.

Credit

The primary agricultural credit societies are the sheet-anchor on which the entire co-operative structure rests. They not only supply short-term, medium-term and long-term credit but also undertake marketing of agricultural produce, supply of agricultural inputs and distribution of consumer articles. This would call for considerable strengthening of the primary agricultural credit societies, through appointment of a minimum complement of staff and provision of physical facilities. It is also essential to augment the internal resources of the co-operatives by way of deposits. In this context effective measures are required to be taken to improve their recovery performance.

The major thrust during the Seventh Plan period would be to ensure adequate flow to the weaker sections of the population and to the less developed areas. For this purpose radical changes are required in the procedures and operational formalities followed for sanction and disbursement of credit. Credit for production, investment and consumption would be provided through a single window. Steps would be taken for the integration of short-term and long-term credit in a phased manner. The existing policy of separate water tight compartmentalisation of the two credit structures would have to be given up. To give effect to the one window approach, the short-term credit structure would also provide investment credit and similarly the long-term credit structure would also provide production credit.

Special measures would be necessary for increasing the flow of credit in the States where the movement is weaker, particularly in the north eastern region. Assistance would be provided to the co-operative institutions in these States to strengthen their capital base through share-capital contribution and managerial subsidy. This would improve their borrowing capacity from the NABARD. Similarly, Scheduled Castes and Scheduled Tribes constitute the weakest sections of the society and they need special support to enable them to avail themselves of institutional credit facilities.

For improving the recovery climate and reduction of overdues, greater stress would be laid on the supervision over proper utilisation of the loans and provision of extension services. Special recovery campaigns would be undertaken and coercive methods would be used against wilful defaulters. Alongside, it would be necessary to ensure that loans would continue to be provided to the non-defaulting and new members.

A pilot scheme of mobile credit delivery system would be started for taking the co-operative banking system to the very door steps of the farmers. Under this scheme agricultural officers would be appointed to take care of primary societies/branches of commercial banks for a group of villages. These officers would be expected to go to the villagers, assess their credit requirements and sanction the loans on the spot as also provide the necessary technical guidance to the farmers. They would also be responsible for the recovery of loans.

Co-operative Marketing

The Seventh Plan would aim at strengthening the primary marketing societies and making their activities broad-based. While the co-operatives would continue to be the main institutional agency for procurement operations on behalf of the Government and commodity Corporations, they would also be developed to undertake commercial/outright business operations in important commodities not necessarily covered under the Price Support Programme. In other words, the endeavour will be to ensure that the marketing co-operatives are engaged in business throughout the year and not for limited periods just to facilitate the procurement operations. It is proposed to forge effective links between the marketing co-operatives and public sector commodity corporations such as the Food Corporation of India (FCI), Cotton Corporation of India (CCI) and Jute Corporation of India (JCI). Close coordination would also be effected among the marketing co-operatives, consumer co-operatives, Civil Supplies Corporations and the public distribution system.

Considering their pre-dominant role in the disbursement of production credit, the infrastructural facilities available with them and the coverage of interior/remote areas, there is need for increasing the share of co-operatives in the overall distribution of fertilisers and other inputs in the country and developing them as composite input distribution centres. It is envisaged that by the end of Seventh Plan period the co-operatives would undertake the retail sale of fertilisers to the extent of 8.3 million tonnes, with their share in the overall distribution of fertilisers rising from 47 percent in 1984-85 to 55 percent in 1989-90.

The non-availability of adequate credit at reasonable rates and margins has been a serious constraint in expansion of co-operative marketing activities including input distribution. To expand the role of co-operatives in the distribution of inputs, it would be necessary for the Reserve Bank of India (RBI) to provide refinance facilities to the State Co-operative Banks in respect of distribution credit provided by them to Primary Agricultural Credit Societies (PACs) for undertaking cash sales of fertilisers, seeds, pesticides and agricultural implements. Similarly, the credit policies of the RBI have to be suitably oriented to help the co-operatives in developing their business in the marketing of agricultural commodities not necessarily covered by the price support operations. The RBI should also consider providing special line of credit on concessional rate of interest, reduced margin of security and credit period in excess of 90 days in respect of marketing and procurement operations.

The co-operative distribution of fertilisers should be considered as a service activity and not as a trading activity. During the Seventh Plan all the reorganised viable primary agricultural credit societies would establish farmer service centres which would undertake the distribution of the entire range of agricultural inputs including chemical fertilisers, improved and hybrid varieties of seeds, pesticides and agricultural implements.

Co-operative Processing

The major weaknesses noticed in the working of the co-operative processing units, particularly rice mills and fruit and vegetable processing units, have been the under-utilisation of capacity and deficiencies in technical and financial management. The co-operative processing units would be required to focus their attention on removing these weaknesses in the Seventh Plan so that they emerge as useful organisation for providing better return to the producers for the raw materials supplied to them, particularly by the oilseeds growers. In this connection the National Dairy Development Board (NDDB) pattern of co-operative processing by the growers would be emulated.

Co-operative Storage

Considering the dimension of storage problems in rural areas and to meet the growing needs and challenges of the food production and distribution fronts, it is envisaged that during the Seventh Plan period an additional storage capacity of 2 million tonnes would be created in the co-operative sector. Out of about 94,000 primary agricultural credit societies, about 40,000 societies have been equipped with their own godowns. During the Seventh Plan period efforts would be made to provide the remaining societies with godown facilities.

Consumer Co-operatives

Steps would betaken to accelerate the growth of consumer co-operatives in the Seventh Plan to enable them to play effectively the pivotal role assigned to them in the distributive trade both in urban and rural areas and in the public distributive system. Under the programme of urban consumer co-operatives, it is planned to cover all the State capitals and metropolitan cities having a population of 1 lakh and above by setting up department stores of varying sizes according to local requirements. It is proposed to increase the number of department stores from 330 at the end of Sixth Plan to 430 by the end of Seventh Plan. In addition, it is proposed to assist Primary Consumers Co-operative Stores/Wholesale/Central Consumer Co-operative Stores in setting up 700 large/small-sized retail outlets so as to increase the number of such outlets from 31,960 at the end of Sixth Plan to 32,660 by the end of Seventh Plan.

Alongside, efforts would be made to streamline the programme of distribution of consumer articles in the rural areas through co-operatives. Out of 94,000 primary agricultural credit societies, 43,296 societies have so far been covered under the rural consumer co-operative programme. It is contemplated to cover all the reorganised viable primary agricultural credit societies under this programme during the Seventh Plan period. A project approach for a cluster of villages to identify the needs of primary stores/societies for infrastructure, margin money etc. will be followed.

Steps would also be taken to foster close operational coordination among the urban consumer co-operatives, village societies and agencies concerned with the production, procurement and distribution of consumer goods for effective distribution. The National/State Consumer Federations would be strengthened to ensure a regular supply line to the retail structure. It is proposed to establish regional distribution centres, to centralise the purchasing of all the consumer co-operatives working in specified regions in order to achieve better bargains in prices and to allow these institutions to concentrate on selling. Steps would also be taken to build up a cadre of key personnel to hold managerial and supervisory positions so as to improve operational efficiency in consumer co-operatives.

Co-operative Training and Education

The co-operative training and education programmes would be intensified and increasingly linked to the growing and diversified needs of the various sectors of the co-operative movement. The capacity of the Vaikunth Mehta National Institute of Co-operative Management is proposed to be increased from the present level of 5,000 to 6,000 in the Seventh Plan. Similarly, the training output of co-operative colleges located in the different States would be increased to 51,800 in the Seventh Plan against 38,000 in the Sixth Plan through effective capacity expansion of the existing 17 colleges and the setting up of three more colleges. The number of junior co-operative training centres is proposed to be raised to 150 by the end of the Seventh Plan from the existing 83 centres.

Eighth Five Year Plan: 1992-97

The opening up of the economy in 1990, and the liberalized economic policies followed by the government since then, led to increasing pressures for various governments, state and central, to bring about changes that would provide co-operatives a level playing field to compete with the private sector. The Eighth Five Year Plan (1992-1997) laid emphasis on building up the co-operative movement as a self-managed, self-regulated and self-reliant institutional set-up, by giving it more autonomy and democratizing the movement. It also spoke of enhancing the capability of co-operatives for improving economic activity and creating employment opportunities for small farmers, labourers, artisans, scheduled castes, scheduled tribes and women and emphasized development and training of co-operative functionaries in professional management.

Co-operation

Co-operatives are expected to play a major role in the distribution of inputs and services to the farmers on the one hand and in assisting marketing and processing of agricultural produce on the other. There are 76,000 fertilizer retailer outlets and 40 lakh tonnes of fertilizer nutrients were distributed during 1989-90. The National Agriculture Co-operative Marketing Federation (NAFED) has undertaken price support operations in respect of oilseeds, coarse grains, pulses, potatoes and onions. The National Agriculture Co-operative Marketing Federation-exported 3,60,220 tonnes of onions during 1989-90 which helped maintain the price line in domestic market. The NAFED also procured 6,022 tonnes of copra as price support operation.

Co-operative godown/warehousing capacity increased from 80 lakh tonnes in 1984-85 to 100 lakh tonnes by 1987-88. By 1990-91, 141 lakh tonnes of storage capacity had been created mainly in Punjab, U.P., Maharashtra, M.P., Karnataka, Andhra Pradesh and Himachal Pradesh. The NCDC was established in 1963 as an organisation to plan, operate and develop the agricultural sector through co-operatives. Sustained efforts were made in promoting co-operative storage and processing units and in strengthening the co-operatives for distribution of inputs. A storage capacity of 114.47 lakh tonnes had been completed under the-co-operative sector by 1989-90. In doing so, the Seventh Plan target for creation of additional capacity of 20 lakh tonnes had been exceeded by constructing storage capacity of 35.18 lakh tonnes. The NCDC promoted 239 cold storage units with capacity of 6.83 lakh tonnes of which 229 cold storages with 6.35 lakh tonnes capacity were installed. The capacity utilisation of the cold storages ranged between 80 and 100 percent. The NCDC has so far promoted a total of 2442 number of processing units up to 1989-90.

The NCDC is presently implementing a World Bank assisted project called NCDC-III, under which a total assistance of ₹ 575.67 crore has so far been sanctioned covering projects in the areas of storage, cotton spinning, oilseed processing, marketing of fruits and vegetables and training of project staff etc.

Agricultural Credit and Co-operation

Development of co-operatives has been envisaged as a significant strategy to build strength in the people with limited means. The co-operative movement aims at saving the rural poor, small farmers, marginal farmers, agricultural labourers and small artisans from exploitation by money lenders. Today, India has a wide network of primary agricultural credit societies (PACS) at village level. At district and state level, co-operative federations have also been set up in almost all states.

Co-operatives have, over the years, significantly diversified their activities to include credit, banking, input distribution, agro-processing, storage and warehousing. In dairying and oil processing activities, co-operative sub-sector has emerged as an important countervailing factor to the private traders, for the benefit of both producers and consumers. At present, nearly 60 percent of the handlooms accounting for 30 percent of the total textiles production in the country are in co-operative sector. Nearly 30,000 artisans and industrial co-operatives are functioning. Co-operatives have also contributed significantly in the sphere of consumer protection. Given adequate freedom of action in their management, co-operatives can emerge strong and efficient.

Growth of co-operatives sector has not been uniform in all parts of the country. The primary reasons for this situation are control of co-operatives by dominant vested- interest groups, poor management, dependence of co-operatives on higher tiers and government for financial assistance and limited range of business activities. The function of thrift has not been given due importance by co-operatives leading to resource crunch and ultimately to their inability to serve the poor. The Agricultural Credit Review Committee (ACRC) and the Committee for Implementation of Recommendation of ACRC stressed on a programme of business development planning in respect of each PACS with a view to diversifying loan operations, generation of internal resources through deposit mobilisation and enlarging package of profitable non-credit services. The Working Group on Promotion of Self-Help Groups as sub-system in Primary Agricultural co-operatives have made important recommendations relating to the improvement of functioning of co-operatives. There is a need to strengthen the resource base of PACS to enable the group members to undertake investments necessary for expanding their production levels.

Co-operative efforts of small and marginal farmers in Kerala to organise procurement of inputs, their timely distribution and marketing of products have yielded rich dividends. The model can be extended to organise the weaker sections for investment in inputs for production, processing, storage and marketing, etc. through co-operative organisation during the Eighth Five Year Plan.

The strategy for co-operative credit development in the Eighth Plan would be as follows.

1. Building up the co-operative movement as a self managed, self regulated and self reliant institutional set-up by giving more autonomy to co-operatives and by democratising the movement.
2. Enhancing the capabilities of co-operative for enabling them to play a significant role in improving the productivity of the economy and in creating employment opportunities for the people living in rural areas for service of weaker sections viz. small fanners, labourers, workers, artisans, the scheduled castes scheduled tribes and women.
3. Strengthening co-operative credit and organised structure in accordance with model laws and to make it competitive and viable.
4. Extend adequate credit support to the programmes of national priority and poverty alleviation such as the Special Rice/food-grains Production Programme, National Oilseeds Development programme. Oil-seeds Production Thrust Programme, etc. Larger flow of funds for thrust areas i.e. to dry land areas, minor irrigation, and wastelands development through non farm sector activities would be considered on priority.
5. Appropriate linking of consumer co-operatives for implementing Public Distribution System for the benefit and protection of consumers' interest will be ensured.
6. Development and training of co-operative functionaries in professional management and introduction of suitable personnel management policy would meet the demand for professional managerial personnel in the co-operatives.
7. Review of co-operatives with a view to liberalise the working of co-operative institutions and freeing them from bureaucratic control.

One of the major issues concerning the co-operative sector is the professionalisation of management. If the co-operatives have to compete in a more open economic regime, the State Governments will have to professionalise the management of co-operatives and especially the co-operative processing units, This is crucial for overall co-operative development vis-à-vis other sectors. For achieving this, it will be necessary to convince the State Governments of the need for granting functional autonomy to co-operatives.

Institutional finance is to be ensured for the thrust area activities to be undertaken in the Eighth Plan; some of the thrust areas are the following.

1. Livestock improvement, soil and water conservation measures, reclamation of water-logged, saline, fallow land, etc.
2. Minor irrigation and development of shallow tube wells, dug-wells, desilting of tanks/ponds.
3. Agro-processing of horticultural produce.
4. Promotion of high yielding plantation crops in traditional and non-traditional areas.
5. Animal husbandry and dairy development (including poultry, piggery and sericulture) and fisheries development.
6. Financial and other technical support to the non-farm sector and encouraging rural artisans and small rural enterprises.
7. Measure for smooth and efficient functioning of the agricultural and rural development banks and adequate and timely availability of finance from the national level to the Primary Land Development Banks (PLDBs).

Demand for term loans in the agricultural sector, will be met with efforts to maintain smooth and efficient functioning of the agricultural and rural development banks. The National Bank for Agriculture and Rural Development has also made a beginning to finance the non-farming sector covering artisans, agricultural labourers, cottage industries and small rural enterprises. This activity has to be intensified in the Eighth Plan so that the rural people, particularly women and youth, will be able to get gainful employment besides traditional agriculture.

The ACRC has critically examined the working of all the three credit structure and suggested that RRBs be merged with commercial banks as the committee felt that they were built-in non-viable, and proposed a National Co-operative Bank of India to replace the existing NABARD.

Co-operative Storage and Cold Storages

In order to equip the co-operative with adequate godown faculties for promoting distribution of inputs and consumer goods and also to facilitate marketing of agricultural produce, efforts would be made to provide each viable primary agricultural credit society and marketing society with a godown of its own. It is proposed to set up additional storage capacity of 21 lakh tonnes and additional 70 cold storages with 3.0 lakh tonnes of additional capacity during the Eighth Plan period.

Co-operative Processing

NCDC is assisting in the setting up of agro-industries, co-operative sugar factories, spinning units, dal and rice mills and many others. Yet, much more is left to be done. Sugarcane growers co-operatives, now account for about 60 percent of the total sugar production in the country. Co-operative processing of cotton and oilseeds has also made rapid progress. Forty-nine new co-operative sugar factories, 28 additional co-operative spinning mills and 21 integrated oilseeds processing units are proposed subject to availability of financial resources.

Agro-Processing of fruits and vegetables is a potential area for development of co-operatives of the farmers. These processing units should, ideally be part of integrated projects linking production with agro-processing and supporting by-products. The major weakness of the co-operative fruit and vegetable processing units are under utilisation of capacity and efficient technical and financial management. Efforts are to be made during the Eighth Plan for improvement of these co-operatives to secure a view to better return for the agricultural producers with higher value additions.

The recent changes introduced by the Government in several fields provide an opportunity for co-operatives to play a much larger role in several areas such as marketing of agricultural produce, creation of marketing infrastructure, establishment of agro-processing, units etc. Many schemes taken up in the past will be continued with greater vigour.

Beginning Ninth Five Year Plan (1997-2002), there has been no specific mention about co-operatives as a part of Five Year Plans.

Bibliography

Bibliography

Achanta, R.N.S.P.(1998), *The Banking (Regulation) Act,1949 Along With Banking Regulation (Companies) Rules, Reserve Bank of India Act and Allied Laws*, India Capital Bureau, Bangalore.

Ahmed, Fakhruddin Ali (1972), Co-operatives: Social Justice and Common Service, *Indian Co-operative Review*, NCUI, New Delhi, April.

Bedi, Raghubans Dev (1969), *Theory, History and Practice of Co-operation*, Loyal Book Depot, Meerut.

Chakraborty, B. (1998), Resource Management: An Appraisal of the Nadia District Central Co-operative Bank, *Co-operative Perspective*, Vaikunthlal Mehata National Institute of Cooperative Management, Pune, January-March.

Chinchankar, P.Y. and Namjoshi, M.V. (1977), *Co-operation and the Dynamics of Change*, Somaiya Publications Pvt. Ltd., New Delhi.

Dantwala, M.L. and Barmeda, J.N. (1986): 'Rural Development, Approaches and Issues' in Dantwala, M.L and others (ed.) Indian Agricultural Development Since Independence, Indian Society of Agricultural Economics.

Dharia, Mohan (1984), Co-operative Movement: Essentials, *Indian Co-operative Review*, NCUI, January.

Dubhashi, P.R. (1988), *Principles and Philosophy of Co-operation*, Vaikunth Mehata National Institute of Co-operative Management, Pune.

Dutta, Uttam and Basak, Amit (2008), Appraisal of Financial Performance of Urban Co-operative Banks: A Case Study, *The Management Accountant*, ICWAI, Vol. 3, No. 3, March.

Dutta. S.K. (1991), *Co-operative Societies and Rural Development*", Mittal Publications, New Delhi.

Dwivedi, R.C. (1981), Co-operative Movement versus Politics

(Profile of Indian Situation), *Indian Cooperative Review*, NCUI, New Delhi, January.

Elayath, K.M.N. (1984), *New Vistas on Co-operative Management*, Rainbow Publications, Coimbatore.

Ghosh, Pratyush Prasun (1992), *Public Administration and Co-operative Management: A New Dimension,* W. Newman and Company Ltd., Calcutta.

Goel, G.B and Powan, K. Kamra (1988), Co-operatives Hold the Key to Rural Development, *Kurukshetra,* February.

Government of India, Ministry of Agriculture, *Annual Reports.*

——*Economic Survey* (Various Years).

——Ministry of Law, Justice, and Company Affairs, *Constitution of India.*

——Planning Commission, Various Plan Documents.

Gujarat Urban Co-operative Banks Federation (1985), *Urban Co-operative Banking in India,* Ahmedabad.

Gulati Ashok (1998), *Indian Agriculture in an Open Economy: Will it Prosper?* in Isher Judge Ahluwalia and I.M.D. Little, 'India's Economic Reforms and Development: Essays for Manmohan Singh', Oxford University Press, New Delhi.

Gulati, Ashok (1996): *Reforms and Policies for Agriculture*, in Vijay L. Kelkar and V.V. Bhanoji Rao (eds), Development Policy Imperatives, Tata McGraw-Hill, New Delhi.

Hough, E.M (1966), *Co-operative Movement in India,* Oxford University Press, New Delhi.

Iyengar, A.S.K. (1961), *A Study in the Co-operative Movement in India,* Current Book House, Bombay.

Jain, Pramod Lata (1990), *Co-operative Credit in Rural India,* Mittal Publications, New Delhi.

Kamat, G.S. (1978), *New Dimensions of Co-operative Management*, Himalaya Publishing House, Bombay.

Kamat, *G.S. (1986),* Co-operatives and Poverty Removal, *Kurukshetra,* November-December.

Karve, D.G. (1969), *Co-operation: Principles and Substance,* Gokhale Institute of Politics and Economics, Asia

Publishing House, Bombay.

Krishna, D. (1998), Peace, Progress and Prosperity through Urban Co-operative Banks, *The Co-operator*, Volume 36. No. 5, NCUI, New Delhi.

Krishna, D. (2002), Future Strategies to Strengthen the Urban Co-operative Banks, *The Co-operator*, Volume 40, No. 5, NCUI, New Delhi.

Krishnaswami, O.R. (1968), An Overview of Principles of Co-operation, *Indian Co-operative Review,* No.1, NCUI, New Delhi.

Krishnaswami, O.R. (1978), *Fundamentals of Co-operation*, S. Chand and Company Ltd., New Delhi.

Kulandaiswamy, V. (1974), Creation of Common Cadres in Co-operatives, *Indian Co-operative Review,* NCUI, New Delhi, April.

Kulkarni, K.R. (1955), *Theory and Practice of Co-operation in India and Abroad*, The Co-operator's Book Depot, Bombay.

Laud, G.M (1980), *Co-operative Banking in India*, Sage Publications, New Delhi.

Mamoria, C.B. and Saxena, R.D. (1970), *Co-operation in India*, Oxford University Press, New Delhi.

Mathur, B.S. (1973), *Co-operation in India*, Sahitya Bhawan, Agra.

Mehta, Vaikunth L. (1975), *Towards a Co-operative Socialist Commonwealth,* The Bombay Provincial Co-operative Institute, Bombay.

Mohanan, S. and Benson, Kunjukunju (2002), Credit Through Co-operatives: Problems and Solutions, *The Co-operator*, Vol. 40, No. 1, NCUI, New Delhi.

Nanda, K.C. (1989), *Credit and Banking*, Sage Publications India Pvt. Ltd., New Delhi.

Nayak, Umesh Chandra and Roy, Ananta Kumar (1988), *Co-operation and Co-operative Management*, Kalyani Publishers, New Delhi.

Parikh, Kirit S., N.S.S. Narayana, Manoj K. Panda and A.

Ganesh Kumar (1996): *Strategies for Agricultural Liberalisation: Consequences for Growth, Welfare and Distribution*, mimeo, Indira Gandhi Institute of Development Research, Mumbai.

Patnaik, Surendra. (1999), Co-operative Banking in India, *The Co-operator*, Volume 37, No. 5, NCUI, New Delhi.

Pitre, V. (2003), Urban Co-operative Banks: Issues and Prospects, *Economic and Political Weekly*, Volume XXXVIII, No. 15, April 12.

Prabhu, P.V. (1999), Urban Co-operative Banking in India, *Urban Credit*, Volume 14, No. 3, NAFCUB, New Delhi.

Puri, S.S. (1973), Co-operatives: An Assessment of Work and Growth, *Indian Co-operative Review,* NCUI, New Delhi, April.

Puri, S.S. (1985), *Ends and Means of Co-operative Development*, National Co-operative Union of India, New Delhi.

Quaraishi, M.A. (1974), Democracy and Efficiency in Thrift and Credit Co-operatives, *Indian Co-operative Review,* NCUI, New Delhi, July.

Raikar, A.V. (2003), Growth, Profitability and Cost Efficiency of Urban Co-operative Banks in India: A Comparative Analysis, *Indian Co-operative Review*, Volume 42, No. 2, NCUI, New Delhi.

Ramesh, T. (2007), Structural Reforms in Co-operative Banking, *The Management Accountant*, ICWAI, Volume 42, No. 2, February.

Rana, J.M. (1972), *Education and Leadership for Co-operative Democracy in India*, International Co-operative Alliance, New Delhi.

Rao Hanumantha C.H. (1995), *Liberalization of Agriculture in India-Some Major Issues*, Indian Journal of Agricultural Economics, No. 3.

Rao, Hanumantha C. H. (1999), *Changing Economic Structure of the Rural Economy in Asia and the Pacific,* paper presented at the study meeting on Rural Transformation, held at Yogakarta, Indonesia, November 29 to December 3.

Rao, K. Viswanadha and V. Mohandoss (1986), Co-operative Credit: Certain Dimensions and Problems, *Indian Co-operative Review,* NCUI, New Delhi, January.

Raviprasad, S. (2004), Performance of Urban Co-operative Banks: Some Aspects, *The Co-operator,* Volume 41, No. 10, NCUI, New Delhi.

Rayudu, C.S. (1991), *Rural Credit in India,* Mittal Publications, New Delhi.

Reserve Bank of India, *Bulletin (various issues).*

——*Report on Currency and Finance* (various years).

——*Compendium of Instructions/Guidelines Issued by Reserve Bank of India for Primary Co-operative Banks,* Urban Banks Department, RBI, Mumbai, 1999.

Sangwan, S.S. (1998): *Emerging Issues of Indian Peasantry,* Yojana, October, Vol. 42, No. 10, p. 31.

Saxena, K.K. (1973), *Evolution of Co-operative Thoughts, Orient Longman*, New Delhi.

Sharma, Prem. S (1999), Co-operative Banking at Crossroads, *The Co-operator*, Volume 37, No. 6, NCUI, New Delhi.

Sheshadri, P. (1973), Latest Developments in Co-operative Legislation, *Indian Co-operative Review,* NCUI, New Delhi, April.

Singh, Katar (2002), Co-operation as an Instrument of Rural Development, *Kurukshetra*, February.

Sinha, B.K. (1968), *Co-operatives in India*, National Co-operative Union of India, New Delhi.

Siosodia, S.S. (1997), Urban Co-operative Sector: Its Importance and Needs Assessment, *The Co-operator*, Volume 33, No. 5, NCUI, New Delhi.

Sisodia, S.S. (1997), Urban Co-operative Credit and Sustainable Human Development in India, *The Co-operator*, Volume 34.No. 7, NCUI, New Delhi.

Soni, Monica (2002), NPA Management by Rural Banks: A Critical Appraisal, *Indian Journal of Accounting*, IAA,

Volume XXXIII, December.

Sreenivasulu, D. (2003), Urban Co-operative Banks: Maclagan to Madhav Rao, *The Co-operator*, Volume 40, No. 11, NCUI, New Delhi.

Srinath, A.R. (2000), Co-operative Credit in India: Problems and Suggestions, *The Co-operator*, Volume 38, No. 1, NCUI, New Delhi.

Srivastava, G.P. (1962), *Traditional Forms of Co-operation in India*, Indian Co-operative Union, New Delhi.

Stephenson, T.E. (1963), *Management in Co-operative Societies*, Heinemann Ltd., London.

Taimni, K.K. (1976), *Co-operative Organisation and Management*, W.A.F.M. Farmers Welfare Trust Society, New Delhi.

Thakur, D.S. (1973), Small Farmers and Co-operative Overdues: Views, *Indian Co-operative Review*, NCUI, New Delhi, April.

Thamarajakshi, R (1999): *Agriculture and Economic Reforms*, Economic and Political Weekly (EPW), Vol. 34, No. 33.

Thirunarayanan, R. (1996), *Co-operative Banking in India*, Mittal Publications, New Delhi.

Thirunarayanan, R. (1998), Urban Bank to the Rescue of the Needy, *The Co-operator*, Volume 35, No. 12, NCUI, New Delhi.

Tribhuvan Mahal (1996), Long-term Co-operative Financing System under New Economic Policy, *Land Bank Journal*, Volume 35, No. 1.

Tules, Robby (1995), Poverty Alleviation and Role of Credit Co-operatives, *The Co-operator*, Volume 32, No. 9, NCUI, New Delhi.

Tyagi, Lalit Kumar and Rashmi Singh (1998), Rural Credit Delivery System: Neglected Dimensions and Needed Focus, *Kurukshetra*, Volume 46, No. 9.

Tyagi, R.B. (1968), *Recent Trends in the Co-operative Movement in India*, Asia Publishing House, Bombay.

Upadhya, Vidya. V and Vasan, B. Kodag (1996), Women's

Role in Urban Co-operative Banks with Special Reference to Sri Laxmi Mahila Sahakari Bank Limited, Sangli, *Indian Co-operative Review,* Volume 34, No. 7, NCUI.

Viswanathan (1997), Future Role and Place of Co-operative Credit and Banking Sector in Asia with Particular Reference to Indian Situations, *The Co-operator,* Volume 34, No. 7, NCUI.

Vyas, V.S. (2001): *Agriculture - Second round of Economic Reforms*, Economic and Political Weekly (EPW), Vol. 36, No. 10.

Weeraman, P.E. (1973), The Co-operative Principles, *Indian Co-operative Review,* April, NCUI.

Index

Index